A Journey in Celtic Music

A Journey in Celtic Music

–Cape Breton Style

Sheldon MacInnes

Cover and book design by Ryan Astle, Goose Lane Editions
Printed in Canada by Transcontinental Printing Inc.
10 9 8 7 6 5 4 3 2

Canadian Cataloguing in Publication Data

MacInnes Sheldon, 1949-
  A Journey in Celtic Music.
  Includes bibliographical references and index.

ISBN
1. Folk music — Nova Scotia — Cape Breton Island. 2. Musicians —
Nova Scotia — Cape Breton Island. 3. MacInnes, Sheldon, 1949-
1. Title.

ML3563.7.M6M152 1997   781.62'91607169   C97-950153-9

UCCB Press
University College of Cape Breton
P.O. Box 5300
Sydney, NS
CANADA

Contents

Acknowledgements

This book is made possible because of University College of Cape Breton (UCCB) support to culture and heritage and, for that, I thank the President, Dr. Jacqueline Scott.

I am most appreciative of the UCCB Press and, in particular, the Executive Director, Penny Marshall, for her support and encouragement. Her contribution to the final stages of this publication was invaluable.

I acknowledge Dr. Robert Morgan, Director of the Beaton Institute, for his enthusiasm, interest, and endorsement of this publication. I recognize the support of the research staff in the Beaton Institute; the support staff in Extension and Community Affairs: Sherry Spracklin, Valerie Crowdis, and Anne MacLean; and also Margaret MacLeod, Carole MacLeod, and Susanne Carlin, UCCB; and Shea McInnis, Enterprise Cape Breton Corporation.

I am thankful for the information I was able to procure from several people who have been actively involved in their research with respect to the Celtic traditions of Cape Breton: John Campbell, *Cape Breton Post*; Francis MacEachern, *Am Braighe*; Frank Macdonald, *Inverness Oran*, and Sally Clouston and Brian Sutcliff, formerly of CBC Sydney and Halifax.

Furthermore, I thank several individuals who have taken the time to carefully study the music and to share their work in particular: Stan Chapman, the late Dr. Virginia Garrison, Dr. John Shaw, Dr. Liz Doherty, Kate Dunlay, and David Greenberg. Their sources were extremely beneficial in helping me to more clearly understand the music.

To all the Cape Breton musicians who have been part of my journey, I am indebted, especially Doug MacPhee, Winnie Chafe, Carl MacKenzie, Sandy MacInnis, Buddy MacMaster, and the Sons of Skye (Malcolm, Clifford, and Blanche).

Some special people in Scotland have made my link with the Old Country possible and, for that, I thank: Kenna and Norman MacDonald, Emily and Angus MacDonald, Evelyn and Jim Hunter, and special people at BBC, Allan MacDonald and Kenny MacQuarrie.

I acknowledge also faculty, staff, and administrators at UCCB who have been most supportive and encouraging at different points in this journey like Keith Brown, Denis Cassivi, Ray Ivany, Jane Lewis, Beatrice MacDonald, Charles MacDonald, Kay MacDonald, Richard MacKinnon, Terry MacLean, Ken MacLeod, Ora McManus, Celeste Sulliman-MacPherson, and David White.

Individuals in the community who have participated in my journey over many years and have been most gracious and supportive are: Jack MacNeil, Kevin MacNeil, Elizabeth A. (Betty) Matheson, Frank MacInnis, Burton MacIntyre, Fred White, Dan MacDonald, Emily Butler, Lil and Bill Young.

In addition, I recognize special contributions to this book, specifically by Hughie "The Barber" MacEachen, John Gibson, and Paul Cranford, the Archives of St. Francis Xavier University, the McConnell Library, Cyril MacInnis, John W. MacInnis, and Michael MacIsaac; and the music contributions of Sandy MacInnis, Ray Ellis, Jamie MacInnis, Stanley MacKinnon, Harry Slaunwhite, the late Malcolm Campbell, and the late Mike MacLean. A special thanks to Lindsay MacPhee and Colleen MacInnis.

I extend a special thanks to the people in the communities of Big Pond and East Bay for their support and interest in my journey. In particular, I acknowledge and thank Marlene's parents, Catherine and the late John J. MacDonald, East Bay.

I acknowledge my brothers and sisters (John, Marie, Patricia, Phillip, Jean, Bernadette, Jamie, George, Donald, and Trese) and their families for their inspiration and endorsement. I especially thank my mother, Christie, to whom I have dedicated this book. I also acknowledge my late father, Dan Joe, for his gift of music.

In closing, I especially thank Marlene, my wife, for sharing and participating in my journey, for her unconditional support, and particularly for her help in the research, the writing, and the editing of this book.

This book is dedicated to Christie MacInnis, my mother, for her love and perseverance, and to the memory of my father, Dan Joe MacInnis, a Cape Breton fiddler.

Abbass Studio

Introduction

The indigenous music from Celtic countries like Ireland and Scotland has maintained appeal worldwide. In North America, there are pockets of Celtic music which have also acquired and sustained interest at different levels — among families and in the wider community. However, there are few Celtic regions, certainly outside Scotland and Ireland, which have been more effective at "celebrating" the music than Cape Breton, Nova Scotia, Canada.

Among the many pathways to music in Cape Breton are those that are saturated in Celtic traditions. These traditions have evolved from the ancestors of immigrant Scots who settled Cape Breton in the early to mid-1800's. They are reflected in the strong sense of community and in the history, the folklore, the poetry, the language, the religion, the genealogy, and the music in rural communities like Iona, Catalone, Judique, the North Shore, and West Bay. The rich tradition in song and music, particularly, offers a myriad of old-country and home-grown creations in lyrics depicting passion, emotion, and distinctive sounds in the haunting and lively interpretations of the music by the many fine composers, musicians, and vocalists.

This book is organized to convey some insight into and reflection upon the rural roots of Cape Breton's Celtic music and to identify and describe some of the contributors who became integral to the excitement felt about the music. This excitement is not a new phenomenon but rather has been a mainstay in Cape Breton rural communities for generations.

This is a story of a musical journey in time and place — my journey — where I have engaged many artists, family, and friends as well as individuals who I have met through the many venues where the music is rendered.

If people introduced in this journey believe that this account has misrepresented or has reflected their journey in a way that is inappropriate, I take full responsibility. I also take responsibility for any errors or omissions.

To chronicle all the exciting discussions and the informative dialogue centered around this journey for the past forty years is almost impossible. In addition to my personal account, however, I have included information and data which I have documented through my research using both published and unpublished materials.

A Journey in Celtic Music — Cape Breton Style has its beginning in the community of St. Andrew's Channel which is located approximately twenty miles outside Sydney. The setting is rural. For purposes of this book, my community begins at St. Andrew's Channel and quickly moves into the community of Big Pond. I tend to refer to St. Andrew's Channel, Big Pond, Glengarry, and Ben Eoin as the Big Pond community. The period of time upon which this journey will focus will be primarily the 1950's through to the 1990's. The journey will introduce some of the people and some of the events which have been integral to my association with the music and will highlight their impact on the Celtic music of Cape Breton.

The journey will recount special performances; it will introduce legends of the music and will outline some of the efforts of many people to promote and to celebrate the music in their respective communities. The journey will highlight visits to locations as near as Glencoe Mills and Iona, Cape Breton and as far away as Codroy Valley, Newfoundland; Boston, Massachussets; Detroit, Michigan; and Barra and Stornoway, Scotland. These will be discussed in the context of my association with different concert productions in the community of Big Pond and beyond; the music of Dan Joe MacInnis, a celebrated Cape Breton fiddler; the music and travelogue of the Sons of Skye; and my work at the University College of Cape Breton.

I have learned a great deal about Celtic music as it is played in Cape Breton. This has been a journey of lessons. I reflect on how musicians and community people have influenced my knowledge and awareness of the music and its place in the community; how my family members have celebrated the music and heritage; how I have acquired a skill to produce and co-ordinate public concerts, ceilidhs, and tributes; and how I have come to value research as a mechanism of connecting the past with the present. Much of the information in this book is shared through some stories while other information is shared through the research of others. Some of the information is of a technical description; for example, a brief section depicts some of the technical aspects of Cape Breton fiddling.

It is my hope that the reader will enjoy the story as much as I have enjoyed the journey!

CHAPTER ONE

Setting the Scene

St. Andrew's Channel

The Channel is located on Highway 4, passing through East Bay en route to Big Pond and St. Peters. The house in which I lived as a young boy was built by my great grandfather, Michael Rory MacIsaac, in the mid-1870's. It was one of the few farms in St. Andrew's Channel when I arrived in 1956, at age seven, from the city of Sydney. My family settled with my grandmother, Catherine (MacIntyre) MacIsaac, who otherwise would have been alone following the death of my grandfather, Johnny Mick, and the departure of the final of their five siblings to the west coast of Canada in search of employment.

Although the total number of residents at the Channel was few, the pioneer vigour and determined temper (common traits among the earlier Highland Scottish settlers of rural Cape Breton — settlers who had arrived from Scotland to a new land in the late 1700's and early 1800's)[1] were firmly ingrained. My maternal grandparents, like their peers — the MacPhee's, the MacDougall's, and the MacIntosh's — were known for maintaining a strong sense of self-reliance. By 1956, their cohesion within the neighbouring communities was quite fragile, to say the least.

These pioneers who remained in the Channel were clinging to very brittle worldly linkages — Big Pond, immediately adjacent to the west; Ben Eoin and East Bay, to the east. They sustained the social and political links only to the extent that they prevailed among the local residents. To the south, Jonathan's Mountain separates the Channel and the Glengarry Valley. There is no passage from the Channel through Jonathan's Mountain except by walking among the thick spruce, the timber fir, and the hardwood. To the north, the brilliant Bras d'Or Lakes etched their way over to Eskasoni and Northside East Bay and on the Channel side to Big Pond and other points west.

To add to the sense of isolation, my family home was located a farm or two from the St. Mary's Parish boundary, Big Pond, and such boundaries were important in most rural communities in Cape Breton in those days. My family attended church service in Big Pond on Sunday mornings as the walk was only two miles. The walk to St. Mary's Church, East Bay, our official parish, would have been more like twelve miles, not very appealing at the time. The family was expected to believe that "God in Big Pond" could be as forgiving as "God in East Bay" as long as my family and I would accept the reality that since we were not real Big Pond parishioners, we would not be permitted to be altar servers in Big Pond.

My grandmothers are having a little chat. Mary (Campbell) MacInnis [centre] and Catherine (MacIntyre) MacIsaac [right]. A good friend and neighbour, Helen MacIsaac [far left].

Submitted by Michael MacIsaac

A bit of irony, however: it was in this rather isolated environment that I acquired my most impressionable and endearing moments with Celtic music or as it was simply called at home, Cape Breton fiddle music. But as a young boy, I was often quite perplexed by the seemingly detached demeanour among the residents of the wider communities of Big Pond and East Bay with respect to the music. With a few exceptions, the regular music sessions that emerged at home were viewed as unique to my place, and I was absolutely convinced that they would have little meaning to anyone outside my home except those wonderful musicians who were frequent visitors. Further, except for a few weekly local appearances by some of these musicians and some early morning minuets and early evening interludes, this music was not the music of mainstream radio or t.v. in any significant manner.

By the end of this journey, the reader will come to understand that my personal experience with the music would, however, not be isolated. In time, I found out that this hidden treasure of Cape Breton Island was actually integral to many homes and communities especially throughout rural Cape Breton and to some extent beyond Cape Breton.

My brother John and my sister Marie are enjoying Dan Joe's music at a mini-concert, at home (1951).

Photo by Christie MacInnis

In addition to the fiddle music in my home, there were special gatherings that had an emphasis on the Gaelic singing, in particular, in other nearby homes — for example, at Frank MacNeil's home in Big Pond. As a matter of fact, "Big Frank" was a celebrated Gaelic singer. His deep singing voice and his rich repertoire were well known in the Gaelic-speaking communities in Cape Breton. He also attracted interest from Scotland with his songs, some of which were recorded first by Annie Johnston from Barra, Scotland. Subsequently, the material became the property of the Scottish National Trust[2] and was maintained for years under the watchful eye of the noted collector and folklorist John Lorne Campbell. In 1983, Frank's daughter Margaret Gillis, now of Sydney and a close friend of my family, contacted Campbell to try and obtain a copy of the original recording. She received the following information in her reply from Campbell in a letter dated December 16, 1983.

"I enclose a copy of the recordings made by the late Annie Johnston Anna Aonghuis Chaluim from Castlebay, Isle of Barra, Scotland at the home of Frank MacNeil, Big Pond, Cape Breton, on 26th August, 1953. . .The first (tape) is headed "Mr. Joe MacNeil, Rev. Stanley MacDonald, Frank MacNeil" . . . The last (tape) is definitely put down as sung by "Mr. Frank MacNeil, Big Pond, Mrs. Bernie Gillis (Margaret), Peter S. MacNeil."[3]

The tradition of Cape Breton fiddle music at home and the wider community's link with the Gaelic heritage, especially through Frank MacNeil, lured my family's identity away from the eroding Channel and helped to foster an assimilation centered on music within the community of Big Pond.

Big Pond

Settlement in the Big Pond community began when Rory MacNeil (Ruairidh Breac) arrived from Scotland in the early 1800's.[4] By the 1950's, the community had already attracted people of Irish descent and people from other nationalities, including the French Acadian, as well as the descendents of Rory MacNeil, all of whom contributed to the growth and development of the Big Pond community. During the time period covered in this journey, the community pace in Big Pond has changed, as it has in most areas in rural Cape Breton.

During my youth, St. Mary's Church and the two earlier schools, Brack's Brook and Big Pond Centre, were the main focal points of the Big Pond community. At the time, there were approximately forty to fifty families in Big Pond, a total population of about 275-300 people.[5] Residents' occupations consisted of a mix of dairy and crop farming and some small lumbering operations. Other residents travelled to Sydney to work at the steel plant or to work in trades.

In the 1990's, however, there are fewer habitants who are native to the community and now the newer MacDonald Consolidated school has been closed. There is little or no work in the primary resource-based industries, like farming and lumbering, and most people who are employed still travel outside the community to work. Several small, independent businesses have emerged in recent times, thereby taking advantage of initiatives to lure tourists and promoting community and economic development — independent businesses like Rita's Tea Room, Big Pond Eagle Tours, Ben Eoin Crafts and Gifts, and the Big Pond Waterfront Development.

In the August 1996 edition of the *Big Pond Times*, a local publication, contributor Jack MacNeil, who is a direct descendent of Ruairidh Breac, writes with respect to the more recent emerging community of Big Pond:

> "The building of the present church in the 1890's and its location near the boundary line no doubt helped. The disappearance of the local post offices with the arrival of the rural route mail delivery; the realignment of the municipal government districts, giving common representation; the amalgamation of the two school sections and the building of a consolidated school; and the birth of community-wide organizations such as the Community Council and the Fire Department have virtually completed the unification process — but, as one would expect in Cape Breton — there is still a bit of the Brook in some of us and a bit of the Pond in others."[6]

MacNeil's article in the *Times* was written to convey a succinct background to the maturation of the Big Pond community as one knows it in the 1990's.

I was able to personally experience some of the changes outlined during the time in which I grew up in "the community" — always feeling, perhaps, somewhat peculiar. As I recall, my existence was neither a bit of the "Brook" nor any of the "Pond." The closest I came to knowing the Brook was attending Brack's Brook School for most of my elementary grades. As for the Pond, including Big Pond Centre, it seemed quite distant and remote from me; as my grandmother often said: "The Big Pond seems oceans away."

If there were moments when I felt that I might be marching to a different drummer than the Big Ponders, so to speak, I felt this was especially true, at the time, with respect to the East Bay-ers. After all, the East Bay community was progressive with recreational programs, a real little league baseball team with conventional uniforms, several clergy living within the parish, consolidated schooling with several teachers at a time, and, alas, fewer farms and less hay fields.

This was clearly not the case in St. Andrew's Channel. As youngsters, my brothers and sisters and the MacIsaac boys over at "Little Dan's" on the next farm were still cutting wood for the kitchen stove and hauling water from the nearby spring located across the highway. The Big Pond baseball team which would have been in closer proximity than the East Bay team did not originate until long after I had left the community to attend university in Antigonish.

In my early elementary grades, one teacher at a time instructed in the one-room school at Brack's Brook. My first teacher was Jack Hagen; in later years, I worked with him while cutting alder bushes for summer employment with the Department of Highways to help finance my university costs. It seems that I've always had an informal rapport with Hagen even while he taught me at Brack's Brook School.

It was a common routine to visit Hagen's home to wake him up for school. On many occasions, I walked to his home, located just across from A.A. MacNeil's store, with a classmate and called below his bedroom window: "Hey, Jack are you getting up?" The plan was simply to remind him that the class was expecting him to make his way over to the school. He usually responded by raising the upper window in his old two-storey house and by asking that we make our way back to school, make certain that the water was in for lunch, and keep the fire in the old pot belly stove burning until he arrived. These chores allowed the students to become quite adept at exploring small brooks and at wandering the back woods, as an extension to classroom learning. I believe these excursions are called nature-hikes today.

A few years back, I had a delightful moment recalling memories about Brack's Brook School; at the time, I was at the Gaelic College in St. Ann's attending a conference on community economic development. I introduced myself to Mrs. Norma Strickland who, in retirement, looked no different to me than she did when she was the Inspector of Schools, along Highway 4, while Jack Hagen was teaching; she was just as charming and professional as she always was. During that evening in St. Ann's, she recalled visiting Brack's Brook School one autumn morning, knocking at the door and being greeted by a young student. Looking up, the young student asked if he could help. Mrs. Strickland replied that she wanted to see the teacher. She explained that the boy quickly turned to the teacher who had already asked the full class to review a "Jersey Milk Bar" map of the world which had been hanging rather haphazardly from the high dusty ceiling. Hagen used the old maps effectively to teach world geography. Mrs. Strickland said she recalls the boy, with no trepidation, instantly yelling towards the back of the room, "Hey, Jack, you're wanted at the door." I explained to Mrs. Strickland at the Gaelic College that evening that I did recall the day very well — *I* was the young boy who answered the door!

When Hagen retired from teaching, Marion MacDonald, who had Inverness County roots, was appointed to teach at Brack's Brook School, where she remained until the MacDonald Consolidated School opened in 1960. The MacDonald Consolidated School was so named after Reverend Stanley MacDonald who, at the time, was the parish priest for St. Mary's, Big Pond, 1944-1966.[7] Jack MacNeil was the school's first teacher-principal and was my only teacher for all subjects, including French and Latin, and in all grades during my junior high school days. In later years, Jack MacNeil became a personal friend and he has figured significantly in my journey with Celtic music over the years.

During my youth, the Big Pond community grew and became enriched through the support and the leadership of community families boasting surnames like Sampson, MacPherson, MacIntyre, MacNeil, White, Jones, Morais, MacLellan, Murphy, MacPhee, MacLean, Carmichael, Kennedy, and the MacInnis' from the "Centre," among others. Together, the "Brook" and the "Channel," the "Rear" and the "Centre" residents began to mould a community with its own unique qualities and personality built on pride and tradition. Among the pillars of that pride and tradition is the annual Big Pond Summer Festival — an event equally as forceful in the unification process for building and maintaining community as those identified by Jack MacNeil in the *Big Pond Times*.

Notes

1. Daniel C. Harvey, "Scottish Immigration to Cape Breton," *Dalhousie Review*, Vol. 22, 1941, pp. 313-324.

2. John Lorne Campbell, Folklorist, Isle of Canna, Scotland. Letter to Margaret Gillis, Sydney, Nova Scotia, October 21, 1983.

3. John Lorne Campbell, Folklorist, Isle of Canna, Scotland. Letter to Margaret Gillis, Sydney, Nova Scotia, December 16, 1983.

4. Jack MacNeil, "The Coming of the Gaels" in the *Big Pond Times*, 3:8, November 1996. MacNeil explains that Ruaridh Breac MacNeil and his family were the first settlers around the brook (Brack's Brook) and that Ruaridh Breac received his land grant in 1809. (Jack MacNeil is a direct descendent of Ruriadh Breac).

5. See the 1961 Census.

6. Jack MacNeil, "The Coming of the Gaels."

7. Information concerning appointments to St. Mary's Parish, Big Pond is available as part of the church records. The current pastor, Reverend Bedford Doucette, made reference to information about Reverend Stanley MacDonald's appointment to Big Pond, in a conversation with me in February 1997.

CHAPTER TWO

The Big Pond Summer Festival

A.D.'s Field, Near Red Dan's

The Big Pond Summer Festival began as a community picnic which evolved in an on-off fashion over several years. In 1964, the first of the annual concerts took place near Red Dan MacNeil's in an empty farm, "partly owned by the Big Pond parish and partly owned by A.D. Morrison."[1] It was situated in close proximity to the church, a stone's throw from the "Brook." It was a cool August evening and the preparation for the concert was simply not adequate; as a matter of fact, some people might suggest that the preparation was non-existent. The first concert was not a sight to behold, despite a trip made by several community residents to Inverness that summer to visit the Broad Cove concert, the "Granddaddy" of concerts as it was described first by Jack MacNeil, who was chair of the Big Pond program from 1964 to 1992. The purpose of the visit to Broad Cove was to check the facilities and to observe the proper way to run community concerts. The Broad Cove concert had its humble beginnings August 7, 1957 as a celebration of the one-hundredth anniversary of St. Margaret's parish, Broad Cove (1857-1957).[2]

In the end, however, the Big Ponders on that memorable August evening were somewhat like the "keystone cops" of rural Cape Breton and were not prepared for the unexpected, like rain. In fact, in retrospect, I wonder if the audience and the performers were also unexpected. There was little or no attention given to the program configuration. The event emerged more as an opportunity for the community to gather in an open field despite the rain and to talk about the events of the day — like Hector's new truck, Joe Johnny's new car, Duncan Martin's new belt for the saw mill as well as the political affairs of the day. Community residents appeared quite excited about the traffic moving towards the community. The visitors from the Sydney area, in turn, were being greeted by lengthy conversations with long lost cousins — in fact, many people were just that: long lost cousins!

Some major infrastructure was lacking in Big Pond that evening — an adequate power system for platform lights and for the public address system, which consisted of a single microphone, maybe two, rented the day before from MacKnight's music store for $10.00 (no tax); sufficient and authoritative parking attendants to provide some sense of orderly parking on the muddy and wet field; and a formal program rather than a "put them on the stage as they appear" approach. If individuals had a fiddle case in the back window of their cars, someone rushed them forward and pointed them to the stage (what stage?), and hoped that they were introduced to someone working around the performance area. There were some performers who actually were charged admission at the gate and who gladly made the donation. Organizationally, the 1964 concert was not very efficient but the music was grand and how could it not be? Among the artists, there were no less than twenty-one great Cape Breton fiddlers participating; solo performances first, then the grand finale.

Such were my memories from the first outdoor Big Pond Concert. That fiasco, crudely lacking in experience and organization, however, changed. As co-founders of the Big Pond Concert, local residents Jack MacNeil and Dan Joe MacInnis, together with members of the wider community, were determined not to let that happen again. During the few days following that first Concert, Jack was already thinking about the next one.

Jack realized that the successful concerts in other rural communities, which were sponsored at that time by local parishes, were usually centered around the appeal of resident performers within those communities. Dan Joe, a well-known Cape Breton fiddler by the late 1950's, attracted local performers to the emerging Big Pond effort, especially the Cape Breton fiddlers.

A Look Back: Some Highlights

By 1967, I had become actively involved in one or more aspects of planning and organizing the concert program.[3] The community had already matured at hosting the outdoor gatherings, especially the concert which, by this time, had been relocated to MacIntyre's Farm in Big Pond Centre. A standing concert committee had been established representing the parish council — Louis Sampson, Michael MacInnis, Hector Morais, Johnny Murphy, Jack MacNeil, and Dan Joe MacInnis. The year 1967 was, of course, Canada's Centennial year and a series of celebrations were planned to attract people to the community to raise money for the parish council. Perhaps the seeds for the Big Pond Festival as one knows it today were planted during those celebrations.

The Centennial celebrations actually began in earnest on Canada Day. The residents of the community had gathered for a flag ceremony. Two of the senior members of the community participated in a special detail as was reported later that week in the local newspaper:

> The Canadian flag was unfurled by Mrs. Frank MacNeil (Mary Ann) while "O Canada" was sung. Mr. A.D. Morrison unfurled the Centennial flag while the Centennial Hymn was being sung.[4]

Members of the MacIntyre family gather at the site of the annual Big Pond Concert, MacIntyre's Farm. [Standing left to right] Eddy MacIntyre, Ann Digout (Eddy's sister), Ann MacIntyre (Eddy's wife), and Kelvin Digout [seated].

Photo by Sheldon MacLeod

Later that summer, activities were planned for the week of August 6-12 and consisted of a Reverend Father Stanley MacDonald Day; the opening of the 4-H museum; a multicultural concert; a milling frolic and dance; a youth day chaired by summer residents Reverend Al Maroun and hockey star Al MacNeil; a horse and buggy ride; a display of Jack Hagen's art work; and the dedication of a cairn in memory of the early settlers. As well, the 1967 celebrations included the now well-entrenched Big Pond Concert, a program designed, first and foremost, to reflect the community's values and traditions.

In addition to the music, the songs, and the dancing that were in the spotlight of each Big Pond Concert, beginning in 1979, the "Reverend Father Stanley MacDonald" award was presented to a student from the Big Pond community who had demonstrated academic excellence in school. The awards program for academic excellence was later expanded to include the "Cecilia Sampson," the "Reverend John Hector MacGregor," and the "Francis MacNeil" awards named, like the Reverend Stanley MacDonald award, after individuals deemed special to the Big Pond community.

In 1983, the concert program recognized many individuals for various reasons. One such recognition was given to Reverend John Angus Rankin of Glendale for his support of the Big Pond program, including the Gaelic Church service which had become an integral aspect of the celebrations by 1980 and also for his work with the Cape Breton Fiddlers' Association. Over the years, media representatives were honoured, including Brian Sutcliff of CBC Radio's *Island Echoes* and *Talent Cape Breton* fame. In 1989, a member of the MacIntyre family was presented with a special plaque to show appreciation to the family and especially Eileen and Alex Eddy, for their continuing generosity to the community in allowing the concert to be presented each year on their property, MacIntyre's Farm. Christie MacInnis also received a special plaque in 1989 to show appreciation for her support and work at the concert over the years.

Other activities which reflected community interests became a part of the legacy of the annual concert weekend, as well. The horseshoe tournaments in the late 1970's and early 1980's were introduced with special appearances by the legendary world champion of tournaments, Elmer Holm. Many of the concerts, as a matter of routine, included a skydivers' act. In 1979, the Cape Breton Development Corporation (DEVCO) organized a fashion show of wool garments to complement the tour of the Woolen Mill at the Cash residence in the nearby community of Irish Cove. At the time, DEVCO was encouraging local investment in sheep farming, island-wide.[5] By the 1980's, a nature display became a feature of the concert program depicting professionally-mounted specimens of indigenous wildlife like the fox, otter, lynx cat, and American bald eagle. This nature display theme continued for several years as an interesting attraction promoting local environmental awareness. These were some of the value-added events which made a significant contribution to extending the concert activities beyond the stage at MacIntyre's Farm.

The centre stage, however, always highlighted excellent musicians like the Cape Breton fiddlers, vocalists like The Men of the Deeps, and dance troupes like the Mabou Dancers. In 1975, the performance by the exciting Ukrainian dancers reintroduced a multicultural presence and gave the concert an opportunity to feature a dance troupe that was recognized as world-class performers following their successful performances and competitions across Canada. Dance enthusiasts from the Big Pond community have also participated in the Big Pond Concert — highland dancers Allison MacPherson, Erin Mansfield, Michelle and Melissa White; and stepdancers Joanne Donovan, Bernadette (MacInnis) MacNeil, and Trese (MacInnis) MacNeil. Eight-hand reel dancers from Big Pond have included Lloyd and Christie White, Melvin White, Donnie (Brother) and Marie MacNeil and Christie MacInnis.

Homespun talent from Big Pond, including vocalists Rita MacNeil and Blanche Sophocleous, and fiddlers Mike MacLean, Cliff Morais, and Dan Joe MacInnis, was always featured at the annual concert. Later, Blanche Sophocleous, Cliff Morais, Malcolm MacPhee, and I formed the Sons of Skye. The Sons of Skye performed in the Big Pond Concert for ten consecutive years, beginning in 1974.

Other musicians native to the community or having roots in the community often performed, as well — like Deanie Munroe Beaton (a prize piper from Loch Lomond — close enough to Big Pond), Jamie MacInnis (piper), and George MacInnis (piano). Seeing and hearing the MacNeil Family from Michigan, especially Bobby MacNeil, whose roots go back to Glengarry, was always a treat. In later years, the treat included Bobby's sons, also from Michigan and exceptionally fine exponents of the Celtic music tradition — Jimmy (fiddle), Stephen (pipes), and Tommy (piano).

Some of the above-mentioned artists have, collectively, been featured on more than thirty commercial recordings in addition to many non-commercial recordings with CBC and BBC radio and television. These achievements augment Rita MacNeil's extraordinary success in the music industry, nationally and internationally, which continues today.

Occasionally, entertainers from off island were invited to perform at the Big Pond Concert. Vocalists Dick Nolan from Newfoundland and Owen McBride from Ireland via Toronto were guests in 1973 along with Scotland's Na-hoganaich, gold medal winners at the 1972 National Mod in Scotland. Scotland's Capercaillie band appeared in 1985, followed later by the world-travelled group, Ossian, also of Scotland. In 1975, vocalist and recording star Angele Arsenault from Prince Edward Island and fiddler Jeremie LeBreton from New Brunswick were special guests. Other guests over the past thirty years of the Big Pond Concert included: Newfoundland's Harry Hibbs; great solo Highland pipers like Dr. Angus MacDonald of Glenuig, Scotland and Jake Watson from Ontario; Gaelic singer and scholar Margaret Bennett, whose roots are in Skye and Lewis; and Scottish Gaelic singer Gillen Anderson, who also played Clarsach. Cape Breton Gaelic singers often included Laughie Gillis, Reverend Allan MacMillan, Neil MacPhee, Beth MacNeil, Kay MacDonald, Jim Watson and from the Rear Glengarry, some entertaining descendants of Peter S. MacNeil.

The special emphasis at the Big Pond Concert, however, was always on the Cape Breton fiddlers: Joe MacLean and Paddy LeBlanc who were among the early Cape Breton recording artists; radio and t.v. personalities Jerry Holland, Dave MacIsaac, Carl MacKenzie, and Winnie Chafe; Inverness County legends Donald Angus Beaton, Donald MacLellan, Theresa MacLellan, and Hugh Allan "Buddy" MacMaster; and aspiring and spirited fiddlers Howie MacDonald, Rodney MacDonald, John Morris Rankin, Brenda Stubbert, Joe Peter MacLean, and Kinnon Beaton. Their sound was Cape Breton, and their music at the Big Pond Concert often included the compositions of renowned Cape Breton composers like Dan Hughie MacEachern and Dan R. MacDonald. Doug MacPhee and Marie MacLellan, the sought-after accompanists by the fiddlers, were always a feature at Big Pond. All of these musicians played a role in the development of the Big Pond Concert.

Popular Cape Breton artists who have performed included John Allan Cameron, The Rankin Family of Mabou, The Barra MacNeils from Sydney Mines, and a very young Ashley MacIsaac of Creignish, all appearing in Big Pond before they had received their regional or national music awards. First Nation Cape Bretoners making regular appearances have included the Poulette Brothers, Wilfred Prosper, and Lee Cremo from the community of Eskasoni.

Why would so many great entertainers want to return to perform at the Big Pond Concert? In most cases, the honorarium paid to the performer could at best be described as break-even for the artist, money to at least ensure that their travel and out-of-pocket expenses were recovered. Moreover, it was always the policy that the artists who lived in the Big Pond community or who had roots in the community would donate their talent to this community endeavour. Clearly, the illusive financial gain was not the appeal for the artists. Conceivably, though, the appeal to the artists was the quality of organization and production, which became the community's strong point as a result of many years of experience. This provided some comfort to the artists as well as to the audience. It was imperative, for example, that the technical facilities like the sound system be operated professionally to ensure quality production. The Big Pond Concert had become a place where the local artist could shine in a live performance.

As well, the concert was usually viewed by the participating artist as an important venue at which to appear to help foster their respective careers. The concert gave an opportunity to the artists to meet new musicians on the scene and to mingle with old acquaintances. Fiddlers visiting "from away" were always popular and helped to foster the sense of comradery among the artists. Consequently, the Big Pond Concert usually attracted a large and enthusiastic audience who openly displayed their joy, interest, and appreciation upon hearing the music of these great entertainers. The event always created a festive atmosphere which encouraged performers and the general audience to find time to mingle and to exchange pleasantries. These were all contributing factors to attracting quality performers to Big Pond. In many instances, the Big Pond Concert became the main venue for introducing many of the more popular Celtic musicians from across the island to an audience within or in close proximity to the industrial area.

Signs of Success

Beginning in 1979, the Big Pond program had confined itself to a weekend festival of several presentations, and its ace, the fifteenth annual concert to be exact, was the spotlight in Cape Breton County's Centennial and Nova Scotia's first International Gathering of the Clans, which probably resulted in the concert's largest audience ever. It was estimated that as many as seven thousand people attended the Big Pond Concert that year. The Cape Breton Tourist Association and the Nova Scotia Department of Tourism realized that this type of event — showcasing local and regional talent and heritage — had potential for attracting visitors to the province, thereby supporting the growing tourist industry. In an open letter to festival organizers in Nova Scotia, dated July 11, 1980, a provincial Co-ordinator of Major Attractions and Events, described how the province viewed these types of activities:

> The role of festivals and events and their strengths as drawing cards
> for tourism is proven. For the past three years the "fun" of the festival
> and event has been increasingly utilized as a "lure" to visitors.[6]

Over time, the community of Big Pond, like the communities of Broad Cove in Inverness County and Iona in Victoria County, established popular outdoor entertainment venues for the summer. The residents of these small rural communities came to know the ropes and the tricks of the trade for organizing their respective concerts and had a pool of local, quality, performing artists to showcase; and the provincial marketing sectors knew it! As a matter of fact, in 1991, the Nova Scotia Department of Tourism recognized the community of Big Pond and its concert efforts by awarding the Big Pond Festival with the Festivals' Award from the Tourism Industry Association of Nova Scotia (TIANS). The minister responsible at the time, the Honourable Terrence R.B. Donahoe, wrote in a letter dated April 5, 1991:

> Your (the Big Pond community) efforts have greatly enhanced
> tourism in Nova Scotia, contributing to the development of the
> tourism industry for the economic and social benefit of all Nova
> Scotians. Activities such as yours make our beautiful province a
> better place in which to live and work, and provide tourists with an
> enjoyable experience.[7]

The Festival Award in 1991, however, was a rather sharp contrast to the
lack of attention by the provincial and federal tourist promoters in 1986,
when the Big Pond Concert was not selected as an event to participate in a
"$500,000 promotion of Scottish culture to attract foreign tourists to Nova
Scotia," as reported in the April 22nd edition of the *Chronicle Herald*. The
article, prepared by staff reporter Wilkie Taylor and titled "Scottish Culture
Focus of New Tourism Campaign," states that "while most of the funds will
be used outside Canada to promote tourism, about $100,000 will be used to
improve the eleven festivals involved in the promotion package."[8] The program was part of a major campaign to promote the 1987 International
Gathering of the Clans.

On behalf of the committee for the Big Pond program, I contacted provincial representatives through written correspondence and expressed
disappointment that so many festivals from mainland Nova Scotia, including
Halifax, were identified to take part in the special promotion while Big Pond,
which, at this time, had over twenty years of history and success promoting the
music of the Highland Scot, was excluded from the promotional program.

In a letter dated May 20, 1986 addressed to me, Nova Scotia's Minister
of Tourism, the Honourable Jack MacIsaac, stated that:

> Where we have people in this department who are currently working
> with this project, I would like to suggest that you meet with them as
> soon as possible in order to determine how we might best be of
> assistance to the Big Pond Scottish concert.[9]

As a result of this exchange, an adjustment was made in the promotion
package, which facilitated some special assistance to Big Pond. I received a note
of personal satisfaction, in a letter dated May 1, 1986, from Don Blackwood,
Executive Director, Cape Breton Tourist Association, in which he imparts:

> Your suggestions to the minister are very worthwhile and I personally
> will remind the Department of Tourism of those suggestions, in an
> effort to see your wishes realized.[10]

Despite my successful efforts to acquire assistance from the 1986 special tourist promotion program, the CTV television special, *Where the Heart is Highland,* which was broadcasted in the fall of 1987 and which resulted from the filming of select concerts that summer, did not include the Big Pond program. The production concentrated, for the most part, on the popular Scottish culture of mainland Nova Scotia, kilts and pipe bands!

Often, in the efforts of many people involved in the local rural concert productions, time and energy were consumed in trying to convince the authorities in funding agencies and the media in Halifax, in Ottawa, and in Sydney that the concert scene in rural Cape Breton is worthy of recognition and support.[11] After all, the rural festivals are more than a musical production; they often reflect a community's lifestyle and values.

There were many years of success and growth for the Big Pond Festival; however, the business side was not realizing its full potential, in the opinion of some observers. This was not a lucrative enterprise for the performers or for the community, for that matter. Yet, there was certainly a tremendous amount of work involved for everyone and, understandably, some people believed that the community was not getting a return for its labour and general input, despite the fact that the gross receipts showed a significant increase every three to five years, beginning in the late 1960's through to the 1990's. There was no question — the annual event would be a mainstay; but, to what extent the community could expand activities was a matter for continual debate and discussion.

After almost a quarter century, the production costs associated with the annual Big Pond Concert were offset almost exclusively by the revenues generated from the gate. Some small businesses throughout Cape Breton Island made contributions over the years, and those dollars helped to offset advertising costs. All other costs, including talent, utilities, technical, telephone, decorations, equipment rental, and additional seating, were offset by the revenues generated from the gate.

Ideas to improve the concert's capacity to generate revenues were constantly explored. For example, representatives from New Dawn Enterprises, an agency with a good track record in community development, made a presentation to the concert committee in 1990, suggesting that the festival be incorporated as a society. The society could then apply for certain types of grants, otherwise not available to the community, and engage government, for example, to form special partnerships. This might result in spin-off activities like studies and related projects. Clearly, efforts would have to be taken to help communities like Big Pond, with limited infrastructure and depleted human resources, to become even more entrepreneurial, creative, and imaginative in the business transactions concerning festival capital and operating costs.

In addition, a review of the level of government funding available to other festival attractions in the industrial area, in particular, suggested that perhaps Big Pond was not getting its fair share of support grants from agencies like the Nova Scotia Department of Tourism and the federal agency Enterprise Cape Breton Corporation (ECBC), which was actively promoting events like the Big Pond Concert as a major tourist attraction, on the one hand, but was seemingly reluctant to provide financial assistance. This concern peaked in 1989 when the community decided that a special week-long celebration was in order, the Big Pond Homecoming, to highlight the 25th annual Big Pond Concert. The occasion became an opportunity for the community to review its place among funding agencies that have a mandate to support cultural programs like the Big Pond Concert.

Included in my responsibilities for the homecoming celebrations were fundraising and promotion. I was asked to develop a significant advertising campaign for the homecoming which would reach regional and national proportions, using written and electronic mediums. This would only be possible if significant external dollars became available. Initially, my efforts in trying to make a case for assistance at the provincial level were met with deaf ears. I was beginning to have déjà vu as I was reminded of my efforts with respect to the 1986 federal-provincial promotion program. In the June 1989 minutes of the planning committee for the Big Pond Festival, it was stated that:

> Our requests for assistance from the Nova Scotia Government and Enterprise Cape Breton have not received as positive a response as we would like — or so it seems at the moment. We shall wait for developments.[12]

The issue became a matter of public debate as revealed in Ron Stang's article in the *Cape Breton Post*, June 5, 1989, "Culture Department Should Review Priorities for Funding Cape Breton Events." The article indicates, in part," . . . when it comes to funding music festivals, the Department of Tourism and Culture may have its priorities just slightly skewed." Stang outlined the funding available to three festivals within the industrial area, which had received over $50,000, while grassroots music festivals in rural communities like Big Pond received little or no support.[13] The issue was discussed on local radio and regional television; consequently, the media response did catch the attention of the Department of Tourism and Culture.

In the end, the Minister of Tourism for the Province of Nova Scotia, the

Honourable Roland Thornhill, intervened and instructed his department to provide financial assistance to the Big Pond Homecoming program; the community continued to receive support from provincial sources in subsequent years. In addition, ECBC became more sympathetic towards the rural festival initiatives in Cape Breton, including the Big Pond Festival.

In 1995, for example, I had the opportunity to conduct a major research study on behalf of ECBC and to write the final report outlining the strengths and weaknesses of festivals in rural Cape Breton.[14] The study included select festival programs depicting Celtic music of Cape Breton — festivals like Broad Cove, Iona, Glendale and Mabou, as well as Big Pond — which, in my opinion, were the very pulse if not the heart for nurturing and promoting Celtic music in Cape Breton. The data presented in the study provides an opportunity to festival operators to discuss their needs at their respective sites and indicates ways that the various festivals might work together to reach common goals and objectives. In response to the study and to the interest expressed among the municipalities of greater Cape Breton, UCCB's Extension and Community Affairs Department designed a training program through the services of Robert Sampson, Consultant, Training and Development Services.

The Homecoming

As for the homecoming program itself, serious discussion concerning the possibility of a celebration began at the February 18th, 1988 concert committee meeting. By August, following the 1988 concert, a tentative program was introduced. The event was officially promoted as the Big Pond Homecoming and the week-long activities were planned, with the following objectives: showcase the community to the wider public; invite ex-patriots to return home; celebrate; and raise money to support community-wide efforts.

The star of the celebration was singer/songwriter Rita MacNeil who had become an international celebrity by that time. The community was now prepared to work with Rita so that she could appear in her first solo outdoor concert in Big Pond. The preparation for her program alone was demanding and comprised a scope not encountered by the community before. The preparation for Rita's solo concert in 1989 was far greater and more significant than the preparation for the 1975 annual Big Pond Concert in which Rita appeared, shortly after her return home from Toronto to try and make a full-time "go" at the music.

In addition to Rita MacNeil's solo concert as part of the homecoming celebrations during the week of July 16, 1989, Dennis Ryan of Ryan's Fancy fame performed at the local firehall; the children participated in a series of activities: there were family reunions, a eucharistic service, community dances, fireworks, historical displays, nature displays, sport programs, and an evening of pastoral airs in the community church. The pastoral airs program introduced in Big Pond that year became a model for other rural communities to bridge cultural and music values with the spiritual values of the respective communities. An additional highlight was the school reunion, including the Centre, the Brook, and the MacDonald Consolidated.

The 25th annual Big Pond Concert itself was the special high point for the 1989 homecoming. There was little doubt in the community that the task to deliver an exceptional concert was a challenge but there was no doubt in the minds of the residents of the community that "they" could deliver! In a letter to the wider community during the fall of 1988, the chair of the homecoming program, Jack MacNeil, observed that:

> This committee has been working hard for some time now, and have come up with a basic program that they hope meets with everyone's approval. It is an ambitious program certainly, but Big Ponders have always demonstrated that they can handle challenges, and no doubt community spirit and pride will carry the day once again.[15]

The concert committee provided the leadership for planning; sub-committees for the entire celebration were established — including fundraising and promotion, grounds, parking and traffic control, gates, canteens, souvenirs, sound, food service, stage, signage and tickets sales; other sub-committees were established to prepare for the church reunion, the school reunion, the children's festivities, the sports day, the community dances and the displays; an additional committee was established to prepare the July 16th kick-off.

As the months toward the final countdown advanced, committee members worked arduously to complete tasks. Getting ready for a major spruce-up was a community-wide priority. Painting was underway, flowers were planted, and a general clean-up was in process. The early summer in Big Pond was a buzz as families prepared for sons and daughters to return from various parts of Canada and the United States to celebrate the homecoming. A community spirit began to jell. Support was available from neighbouring communities wanting to help and to participate in the celebrations. For example, the East Bay and Johnstown choirs were integral to the special church celebrations; small businesses from across the island provided financial support; and for the first time, major partnerships were established with the Province of Nova Scotia and the Enterprise Cape Breton Corporation. Air Nova partnered with the activities to offer a special homecoming contest to fly a native Big Ponder, who was living anywhere in Canada, home for the celebration. The contest was won by Donald Jones who was living in Toronto at the time.

Furthermore, the regional and the national media promoted the event: CTV recorded the Rita concert for national broadcast at a later date as a *Rita MacNeil Homecoming*;[16] CBC television from the Quebec region recorded the *Pastoral Airs* program for the Quebec audience;[17] CBC Radio Halifax recorded a segment of the celebrations for broadcast in Atlantic Canada at a later date; and local newspaper and radio reporters circulated throughout the community on a daily basis to report the activities of the day to Cape Breton.

The Homecoming kick-off day proved to be among the highlights and set the tone for the balance of the week's activities. The day-long celebration began with a Sunday morning church service which was attended by many people from the community including members of the First Nation's community of Eskasoni, who made their way across the Bras d'Or Lakes by canoe to attend church just as they did in an earlier time. The service was followed by a tree-planting ceremony with Rita doing the honours, immediately followed by a proclamation which took place at the cairn constructed in 1967 during the centennial celebrations. Later that morning, a large flock of homing pigeons was released. This was followed by a community photo of all present, the strawberry festival at the firehall, the pastoral airs at the church later that evening, and then the fireworks on the shore as a finale to the day. In all, it was a splendid opening kick-off!

The next highlight was the Rita concert on July 22, the event that attracted a national audience. The program, a collaborative effort between Brooks Diamond, Rita's manager, and the Big Pond community, went off without a major hitch and lay the foundation for future Rita MacNeil concerts in Big Pond. Rita, clearly enjoying the evening which embodied a clear sky and a warm summer breeze, was the homecoming star. It was a most appropriate time for Rita to introduce her new song, at that time, "We'll Reach the Stars Tonight," and that is exactly how the residents felt following Rita's performance. The week had moved as planned; the weather had cooperated fully allowing all outdoor events to go as scheduled.

The 25th Annual Concert

For me personally, the climax to the 1989 Big Pond Homecoming program was the 25th annual concert, a finale to a great week. Throughout the activities, I often reflected on the first concert near Red Dan's and all its shortcomings. With a private chuckle, I recalled how I had enjoyed my many years as a member of the planning committee for the annual concert — the meetings after the weekly church service, the many cups of tea which were served, the stories and the debates concerning program detail (budgets, entertainers, the allocation of the bull-work in collecting extra chairs and repairing benches, and the general spruce-up campaign). The meetings and discussions were always in search of consensus. I reflected on the many people I met, especially the musicians who I would call friends for life. This celebration of twenty-five years was a moment in time for me to savour for many years to come, and I believe the many other Big Ponders who were involved in the concert preparations shared the same sense of pride and personal satisfaction.

The morning of the 25th annual concert began like the mornings of the many previous concerts. I left my home early to prepare and to get ready for the concert. The morning was bright and clear as I drove along Highway 4. I went directly to Jack MacNeil's house with the final copy of the concert program. Jack was in the backyard quietly reflecting while he enjoyed the peace and quiet of his garden in the early morning.

Jack carefully observed the small flock of barn swallows hovering overhead and the finches flittering about the Virginia Creeper wrapped around John Duncan's old barn. He surveyed the flowers and the wild shrubs encroaching the grass and the wide variety of trees surrounding the farmhouse, trees which he planted over the years to commemorate significant events in the lives of people close to him. Periodically, Jack gazed at the majestic eagle soaring with calm and serenity in the deep sky, a reminder to him to keep the day in a composed and serene perspective, like the eagle, while riding the turbulence of a day that would, consequently, manifest fruition.

Meanwhile the hustle and the bustle in the community were evident as the local traffic made its way along the road transporting odds and ends to the concert site — extra water containers, a piece of decoration for the stage, some utilities for the canteen, and an extension cord for backstage. These were part of the last-minute chores which had to be achieved in the early-morning preparation for the concert day. Unlike the first concert in 1964, Big Pond was ready on this day; the pride and the tradition would shine and glitter for everyone to see and to enjoy.

Jack is a tall person who, while seated, can cross his legs and still allow the toes on the foot extending from the top leg to touch the floor — dangling and tapping to a quiet tune rolling around in his head. Always gracious and polite, he speaks with a soft tone.

While teaching school in the community for over thirty years, Jack disciplined by gaining respect from the students and from the parents as well. In the eyes of the parents, Jack was never wrong in his interpretation of the day's events, and the students knew it. Although retired from teaching, he continues to provide quality leadership in the community, in education, and in citizenship.

Back to my arrival at Jack's, I turned the car engine off and I gathered my notes and the large bristol board displaying the full program of performers. Taking a lawn chair which had been leaning against the old dairy shed, I sat next to Jack to review the program. Jack always began this annual summit by asking a set of routine questions: "Do you have a good spot on the program for Dan Joe MacInnis and Theresa MacLellan?" Jack remained loyal to Dan Joe, always recalling Dan Joe's role in the early concerts. He remained loyal to Theresa also because of her role not only at the annual concert but also in the community dances dating back to the early 1970's. Besides, both Dan Joe and Theresa were popular among the local fiddlers and the audiences who supported the different concert programs in Cape Breton.

Dan Joe, co-founder of the Big Pond Concert, performs at the 25th Annual Concert. [Left to right] George MacInnis (Dan Joe's son), piano; Dan Joe, fiddle; and Malcolm MacPhee (Dan Joe's son-in-law), guitar.

Photo by Sheldon MacLeod

Glancing over the program detail, Jack then inquired whether the individuals listed in the first five or six acts had been notified of their position on the program so that they would arrive backstage early and whether the individuals listed in the last five acts were advised of their position on the program so that they would not rush to the concert grounds as they may not get on stage until late in the day. In all, the program consisted of no less then thirty-five acts comprising over one hundred performers — each artist requiring special attention; this was always demanding and intense as the concert day progressed.

I recall fiddler Ashley MacIsaac's first appearance, in 1988, at the Big Pond Concert. Ashley was a young thirteen year old filled with energy, which he expressed that day through his dance and his music. A decision had been made for him to perform late in the day, at around 6:00 p.m., but Ashley had not been advised of this detail. As a result, Ashley arrived on the scene in the very early afternoon and anxiously waited for the concert to begin, usually by 2:00 p.m. sharp, so that he could render his performance. The rationale to have this young, budding star appear late was simple — he had also been asked to play at the community dance (imagine — at the age of thirteen) which was to follow the concert. So, programming Ashley to appear at the concert just a few hours before the dance seemed reasonable, at the time. Patiently, Ashley lingered for about five hours listening and watching and waiting for his turn. When the time came, he played a set of haunting pipe marches followed by lively old-time strathspeys and reels, and his perform-ance was so appreciated by the audience that he was given an encore. His violin performance was followed by an exciting exhibition of some nifty stepdancing in the traditional style.

Ashley MacIsaac is a gifted musician, and his love of the music and the excitement that day at his first Big Pond Concert kept the young entertainer on location until the program organizers were ready to introduce him. De-spite the fact that the detail to contact Ashley and to advise that he take his time leaving Creignish to travel to Big Pond on that occasion was overlooked, he, like so many other great performers over the years, accepted the wait in a most professional manner. It is not likely that the Big Ponders would get away with keeping Ashley on hold today!

Every minute detail from decor to fencing to budgets to performers was important to Jack and his vision of the annual concert. In the Spring, 1989 edition of *Forerunner*, Anne Marie Campbell writes the following observation after her interview with Jack concerning the history of the Big Pond Concert:

> But he's all serious when he speaks about the committee's com-mitment to providing a showcase for Cape Breton's Celtic culture and maintaining an atmosphere where exponents of that culture can flourish.[18]

The program always allowed for one or two unexpected acts. The surprise element was always a feature at the Big Pond Concert — in fact Rita's role for many years was just that — the surprise! The strategy to allow and to even encourage this to happen without having to bump performers already listed was to simply leave a blank space after every nine or ten acts on the written program, which was always posted. Therefore, if necessary, an act could be inserted without tramping on toes. The challenge was to present a balanced program and to be fair to the entertainers who had travelled many miles and especially to those entertainers who had been so loyal over the years, while at the same time maintaining a sense of professionalism for the benefit of the entertainers as well as the audience.

Once the performers located their spot on the program, they relaxed and enjoyed conversations about the music and about the day in general with the other artists, renewing old acquaintances and friendships. The aspiring youth sharing stories about their last gig and the old-time county rivals sharing tunes from old collections and local composers all made for some of the interesting chat in the sometimes cluttered and clamorous room known simply as backstage.

The planning of the program was organized in the absence of formal agreements and contracts. Simple invitations were issued, usually by way of a letter and in some cases a telephone call or a chance meeting. An honour system and keeping one's word were the core of presenting the annual program. Maintaining a professional rapport with the performers and presenting a balanced program were always Jack's responsibilites during my tenure with the Big Pond program.

On the day of the 25th annual concert, July 23, 1989, the usual quality list of great entertainers was scheduled to perform — vocalists, dancers, and pipers. As well, the traditional Cape Breton fiddlers were challenged by a new wave of visiting fiddlers like Allister Fraser from Scotland and David Greenberg from New York who had made his way to Big Pond via Toronto. Greenberg, who began studying music at the age of four, is an accomplished violinist.

> Although classically trained, he (Greenberg) learned by ear at first, enabling him to learn different styles — the Western Art Music of the 17th and the 18th-century Europe. He performs Baroque music with the Tafelmusik Baroque Orchestra, an ensemble of 10-20 members, all of whom perform on original instruments (or copies) and in the original style of the Baroque Era.[19]

This might sound like a rather uncharacteristic background for a guest fiddler at the Big Pond Concert but David Greenberg was able to enthrall the audience that day in Big Pond in 1989. Greenberg and fiddler Donald MacLellan, an Inverness County native, together shook the moss and the weeds in MacIntyre's field when they played in unison a spirited rendition of traditional strathspeys and reels to the extent that the crowd of several thousand people were not satisfied until Greenberg and MacLellan returned for an encore despite the lengthy list of backstage performers waiting for their turn to play to an already excited audience.

I was first introduced to Greenberg's amazing music by way of a telephone call from George MacInnis, when he was studying in Toronto in 1987. George had explained in a conversation that he had met David Greenberg at a music session in Toronto and said that David's version of high-bass selections was very close to the master herself, Cape Breton fiddler Mary "Hughie" MacDonald. Well, in my world of Cape Breton music, it was not possible that a young man born in New York could dare attempt to imitate the likes of Mary MacDonald or any other great Cape Breton fiddler of the day. But I was in for a surprise!

During the following summer of 1988, I was able to hear Greenberg in person at my mother's home. Kate Dunlay, a highly respected musician, also attended the music session; she acquired her interest concerning Cape Breton music from earlier visits to Cape Breton. And I *was* surprised! George was right! Since that evening's session, Greenberg has made several visits to Cape Breton and is widely accepted as one of the finest traditional Cape Breton fiddlers of his day.

> The music that is closest to David's heart is the Scottish music of Cape Breton. He heard his first strathspey a short two years ago January, but the classical training and the ability to learn by ear have sped his progress. Although he draws inspiration from every Cape Breton musician he hears, he has been the most influenced by the playing of Mary "Hughie" MacDonald, Doug MacPhee, Buddy MacMaster, Carl MacKenzie, Joe Cormier, Jerry Holland, Margaret Chisholm MacDonald, Donald MacLellan, and of course Winston "Scotty" Fitzgerald.[20]

Today, David Greenberg is enjoying the success derived from his 1996 recording, *Puirt a Baroque/Bach Meets Cape Breton*, which offers a nice blend of classical and Cape Breton traditional music.[21]

In addition to the Greenberg-MacLellan performance at the Big Pond Concert that day, Cape Breton's stepdancer, Joe Rankin from Mabou, dazzled the audience to the extent that he, too, was called upon to give an encore, the first I have ever seen for a Cape Breton stepdancer.

The magic had more than emerged that day — it continued to everyone's delight for over five hours as the celebration of the music, song, and dance of Cape Breton Island was unfolding exactly as it should. What a day!

As in the past, the 1989 concert appealed to the Cape Breton residents especially and also to the returning Cape Bretoners who were home for the summer. The concert setting, nestled in the natural beauty of a farm at the foot of a splendid hill overlooking the beautiful Bras d'Or Lakes, delighted all patrons. Its beauty coupled with the music appealed immensely to a travelling public from many parts of Canada and the United States. For some people, the setting reflected a romantic vision of community character and community tradition but for most people, the day simply generated fun and entertainment.

In the end, however, the Big Pond residents and those individuals of an earlier era who worked tirelessly on the development of the festival over the long haul were perhaps the real stars of the day: people like Louis Sampson, Duncan "Mick" MacPherson, Duncan M.A. MacPherson, Hector Morais, and Michael MacInnis who were among the early pioneers involved in planning the detail with Dan Joe MacInnis and Jack MacNeil. Their vision was to build a concert with which Big Ponders could be proud to associate in years to come.

Many other people from the wider community volunteered their time and support, including Duncan Martin MacNeil who took charge of the electrical operations following the first concert and made certain the flaws of that time would not be repeated. Joe Donovan and Alf MacLellan provided security at the lower gate and stage area for many years, and Joe MacInnis and Frank Sampson managed the main gate detail. Carpenters like Leonard MacLellan, Gerald Thomas, and Benny Martin MacNeil helped construct and maintain the centre stage. Donnie "Brother" MacNeil mobilized every facet of the grounds crew in an effective and efficient manner despite whatever shortcomings might have been inherent in equipment and other resources. Marty MacInnis took charge of the annual hay cutting. The parking attendants included John William MacInnis, Malcolm MacPhee, Cyril MacPherson, Melvin White and Eddy MacIntyre. Ticket sellers like Christie MacInnis went the extra mile to promote sales in the interest of seeing the community realize a return for their effort. Ann Thomas, Ann Marie Donovan, Ann MacPherson, Darlene MacInnis, and Marie MacPhee were among those who for many years established a quality canteen service. Others involved in a variety of ways, preparing those famous lunch trays for the artists, for example, included Sis MacLellan, Margie MacLellan, Claire Morais, Catherine MacNeil, Bertha MacPherson, Hilda MacPherson, and Kay MacInnis. Anthony and Barbara MacInnis did their usual fine job with stage decorations.

These people were only some of the volunteers who made personal sacrifices to put the show on; their efforts were all nurtured under the leadership of Jack MacNeil who presided as chair for the Big Pond Concert for over twenty-five years. Jack retired from the festival's planning committee in March, 1992. The annual Big Pond Festival continues to be a going concern in Big Pond, and its future rests in the hands of a new generation of shakers and movers.

I recall standing in the open field on the day of the 25th annual concert with my friend and fellow committee member Fred White, a workhorse on the committee for many years, and heard him say aloud words to this effect:

You and I will not live long enough to see an event like this repeated. We will not be able to capture, in the same way, again, the spirit of the day — indeed the spirit of the week of the 1989 Big Pond Homecoming.

Later that same day just as dusk was settling in, I stood with Jack MacNeil for a photo near the back of the stage area. I believe that Jack, too, may have shared those same sentiments that were expressed by Fred White. He provided quality leadership for one of Nova Scotia's prominent community attractions. On many occasions, over the twenty-five years, there were moments of disappointment and frustration, but Jack's efforts to maintain harmony and a strong professional image prevailed, culminating in the celebration of the 25th annual concert, a most memorable occasion!

The twenty-five year history of the Big Pond Concert was one of immense spirit and pride as Jack MacNeil had described in his letter several months earlier, and that volunteer spirit and that community pride carried the day just as Jack MacNeil had expected. The efforts put forth by the community realized some monetary gain to assist with infrastructure needs in the church, the local hall, and the firehall as well as in a variety of recreational programs.

Jack MacNeil [far right], Chair of the Big Pond Summer Festival 1964-92; [standing with, left to right] Fred White, Sheldon MacInnes, and Brooks Diamond.

Photo by Sheldon MacLeod

By 1992, because of the success and the expertise acquired through the history of the concert, in particular, and the summer festival program, in general, the community was called upon to respond to a greater need, one focused on the devastation felt by a community on the mainland as a result of a tragic and fatal incident. Big Pond's response to the May, 1992 Westray Mine explosion at Plymouth, Nova Scotia was initiated in a least likely location, Yonge Street in downtown Toronto.

The Benefit Concert

In June 1992, Balmur Limited, a talent agency located in Toronto, issued a press release concerning the Big Pond Festival. At the time, a principal in the company was Leonard Rambeau, official agent for international entertainers Anne Murray and George Fox. Rambeau issued a statement to the Canadian media which read in part:

> The Big Pond Summer Festival itself is recognized as one of Nova Scotia's most popular summer attractions. The festival has become a showcase of music, song, and dance reflective of the local Cape Breton heritage. The various festival activities demonstrate the depth and breadth of the many Cape Breton artists who have gained popularity across the region.[22]

Leonard Rambeau's statement continued with detail announcing a benefit concert featuring another of his celebrity clients and star performer, Rita MacNeil. The concert, he stated, would take place in Rita's home community, Big Pond.

> The concert is expected to attract a large audience who will want to be with Rita as she performs "Working Man" for the first time in public since the mining disaster which shook the small rural community of Plymouth, Nova Scotia. The disaster caught the attention of the world while rescue attempts were made to try to free the trapped men. An outpouring of support from across the country followed. The Big Pond community council will join Rita to further contribute financially to the cause and also to make the evening a most memorable occasion.[23]

The event was Big Pond's way to show support and recognition of the efforts by many people across Canada and the Atlantic region in particular, to rally behind the community of Plymouth which had been devastated by the crushing and fatal explosion at the Westray Mine, which killed twenty-six men.[24] What more could be done in the short term except to contribute to a fund to help the victims' families? Who more appropriate for the Big Ponders to showcase in an effort to raise those dollars than Rita MacNeil? Initially, Rambeau wondered whether the community could deliver. He felt he had a great deal at stake as this was his first public event with his new client, Rita MacNeil.

Rambeau had been in the entertainment world for several decades and had become accustomed to the glitz and the bright lights of large productions with Anne Murray across Canada and the United States and Europe. The question certainly was not whether Rita could perform well or whether the event would attract a large audience, but rather could the Big Ponders deliver the production with dignity and professionalism on what was being introduced as a most sombre occasion. Could Rambeau be satisfied that one of his clients would be provided with the necessary technical and human support required to make the event successful? Or should he take the Rita MacNeil concert to some other location where he would be certain that the required resources would be guaranteed?

There was little doubt in Rita's mind, however, that the community could deliver. As expected by the local residents and by the people in the wider community who had attended earlier Rita concerts in Big Pond, the community rose to the occasion once again and hosted a national, indeed an international, audience.

During that July evening at MacIntyre's farm in Big Pond, many people sang along with Rita in a controlled joy as Rita's music evoked empathetic and compassionate feelings of sadness and sorrow, especially by the many people from Plymouth who travelled to Big Pond for the concert. Families of the deceased miners who had met their untimely deaths as a result of the explosion were hunched together in the area at the front of the stage — holding, hugging, and clutching so as to help one another make their way through Rita's signature song, "The Working Man," written to commemorate the hardships of the working miner. Rita's performance was emotional and stirring.

Over thirty years of organizational experience by the Big Pond Concert planners emerged on that occasion to help make the event most memorable. The proceeds realized from the "Rita MacNeil Working Man Benefit Concert" were presented to the University College of Cape Breton to establish a $20,000 scholarship for families of miners anywhere in Nova Scotia wanting to enter post-secondary studies, a Big Pond community and Rita MacNeil legacy in the spirit of giving.

In a letter addressed to me immediately following the concert, Leonard Rambeau wrote:

> As you know, it was my first experience with the Big Pond Festival and it was a most pleasant and enjoyable one. I really appreciated your enthusiasm and professionalism . . .[25]

In 1995, only three years after Rita's "Working Man Concert," I felt deep sadness when I learned of Leonard Rambeau's death, following his lengthy illness with cancer. My time with Leonard Rambeau of Smelt Brook, Victoria County, Cape Breton, while preparing for the 1992 Rita MacNeil concert, was perhaps only a brief moment in his incredible journey in music. It will always be treasured as a special and endearing time for me personally. Leonard's personal enthusiasm and professionalism set a standard in the music scene and in the entertainment industry in Canada.

1. Laurel Munroe, "Tradition Continues," *Cape Breton Post*, July 12, 1997, p. 7A.

2. Rev. J.H. MacEachern, "The Broad Cove Concerts 1957-1981," in *St. Margaret's Church 1857-1982*, on the occasion of the 125th anniversary of St. Margaret's Church, Broad Cove, Inverness County, Nova Scotia.

3. The segment, "A Look Back: Some Highlights" will identify specific program detail, dates, activities, and names of performers which are contained in the minutes and brochures of the Big Pond Concert, 1967-1992.

4. "Canada Day is Observed," *Cape Breton Post*, July 8, 1967, p.3.

5. "Cape Breton Development 8th Annual Report," year-ending, March 31, 1975, pp. 25-26.

6. Brien E. Fraser, Co-ordinator, Major Attractions and Events, Nova Scotia Department of Tourism. Letter to Big Pond Concert Committee, Cape Breton, N.S., July 11, 1980.

7. Terence Donahoe, R.B., Q.C., Minister, Nova Scotia Department of Tourism and Culture. Letter to Sheldon MacInnes, Big Pond Summer Festival, Cape Breton, N.S., April 5, 1991.

8. Wilkie Taylor, "Scottish Culture Focus of New Tourism Campaign," *Chronicle-Herald*, April 22, 1986, p. 16.

9. Jack MacIsaac, Minister, Nova Scotia Dept. of Culture & Tourism. Letter to Sheldon MacInnes, Big Pond Concert, Cape Breton, N.S., May 20, 1986.

10. Don Blackwood, Executive Director, Cape Breton Tourist Association. Letter to Sheldon MacInnes, Big Pond Concert, Cape Breton, N.S., May 1, 1986.

11. John Campbell, "Tourism Minister Listens," *Cape Breton Post*, October 19, 1989, p. 15.

12. Minutes of Big Pond Concert, June 1989.

13. Ron Stang, "Culture Department Should Review Priorities for Funding Cape Breton Festivals," *Cape Breton Post*, June 5, 1989, p. 9.

14. Sheldon MacInnes, "Rural Cape Breton Festivals — A Research Project with Recommendations," research report submitted to Enterprise Cape Breton, Sydney, Nova Scotia, January 1996.

15. Jack MacNeil, Chair, Big Pond Homecoming. Letter to residents of Big Pond community re the homecoming plans, Fall 1988.

16. Rita MacNeil television show, *The Rita MacNeil Homecoming*, was filmed in Big Pond, was produced for television by CTV Toronto, and was later broadcasted on national television.

17. CBC Quebec filmed the program, *Big Pond*, for broadcast in Quebec. The

production focused on the spiritual, cultural, community links, and the pastoral airs presented at St. Mary's Church on July 16. The musicians included: B. MacNeil, J. MacNeil, G. MacInnis, D.J. MacInnis, A. Fraser B. McGogne, and D. Campbell. The t.v. special was narrated by B. Harding and was produced by R. LeClerc, Quebec.

18. Anne Marie Campbell, "Big Pond Homecoming," *Forerunner 3: Cape Breton's Community Magazine*, 2:1, Spring 1989.

19. David Greenberg, written document called "Dialogue with David Greenberg," April, 1989.

20. Ibid.

21. David Greenberg is featured on the 1996 recording *Puirt a Baroque - Bach Meets Cape Breton*, Marquie ERA 181.

22. Press Release by Balmur Ltd. on Rita's special Big Pond Concert, June 29, 1992.

23. Ibid.

24. "Westray: Day to Day Story Since Deadly Explosion," *Cape Breton Post*, May 16, 1992, p. 7.

25. Leonard Rambeau, President, Balmur Limited. Letter to Sheldon MacInnes, Big Pond Summer Festival, Cape Breton, N.S., June 27, 1992.

CHAPTER THREE

Dan Joe MacInnis — A Cape Breton Fiddler

The Final Recording

It would be difficult for me to take the reader on *A Journey in Celtic Music — Cape Breton Style* without crossing paths with Dan Joe MacInnis. There is a great deal I can share about the man and his music and, equally, so much I cannot share about him because as he would say, "it was no one's business but my own."

His life was one of music and whatever insight and understanding I may have acquired about the music, I attribute to Dan Joe and our mutual association with the Cape Breton fiddlers, in particular. Perhaps my relationship with Dan Joe was no different than the typical relationship between some fathers and sons. There were times of profound differences and irreconcilable actions, occasions of understanding as well as misunderstanding, and still other times of praise and support. In the bigger picture of life, however, there was nothing that quite linked Dan Joe and me like the music. Whether the point or issue was one on which we might agree, or otherwise, there was definitely a mutual respect for each other's personal assessment and critique of the music, the tunes, the players, their techniques, their interpretation, and their music arrangements. We both viewed Celtic music as a serious intervention in our respective personal lives. Therefore, I feel it is imperative that I provide some background about the Cape Breton fiddler, Dan Joe MacInnis, as part of my journey.

While introducing Dan Joe and his music to the reader, it is important that I not describe his role in the music tradition larger in his death than was in his life. However, I think it is important to recognize his participation in the Cape Breton music tradition. In my discussion of Dan Joe, I reiterate what George Riddell wrote in an article he had prepared following the death of the Scottish violinist James Skinner in 1927:

> ... but the present writer desires it to be understood that he has no wish to indulge in extreme statements, or to give expression to opinions which are not in some degree susceptible to proof.[1]

One evening during the first holiday season following Dan Joe's death, December 23, 1991 to be exact, I was walking along Charlotte Street in Sydney and pondering over that last-minute gift. The evening was crisp and there was a chill in the air; the sight of many busy shoppers conjured in my mind a storybook setting. Bells were ringing in the background, likely from one of the local churches, while the store fronts were suited in a decorative display to help paint the festive spirit. People were mingling as they made their way in and out of shops, walking and talking, and sharing greetings and best wishes for the holiday season.

Off to the side of this busy street was a new and obscure store I had not noticed before. It had been clearly established as a short-term rental space to take advantage of the seasonal shopping spirit. When I entered the shop, I could smell the fragrance of perfumed candles and the aroma of some freshly-ground coffee. There was even free hot apple cider that was located near the entrance, surely to entice people to enter this store. As well, appropriate seasonal music could be heard. I first noticed the long rectangular table displaying an array of homemade crafts in many shapes and sizes. But in the far corner and on the floor near one end of the table was a modest stack of long-play recordings in the old vinyl format. These were now considered almost obsolete with the current use of the new CD recording. After a careful inspection, one particular recording proved to be special for me personally — *Celtic Music of Cape Breton — Volume 1*.[2] I was familiar with the recording because I had been involved with its production through my work at UCCB.

The recording was issued by the UCCB Press. In 1984, primarily through the efforts of Tim Belliveau who, at the time, was Director of Public Relations and responsible for the project. The recording featured fiddler Donald MacLellan with his son Ronnie at piano; fiddler Dave MacIsaac with John Morris Rankin on piano; and fiddler Dan Joe with his son George on piano.

Like many Cape Breton fiddlers, Dan Joe had engaged in the art of commercially recording his music. He had witnessed the technology applied to the recording process change over the years. In the late 1950's, Dan Joe recorded on the old 78 rpm format, Celtic label. Beginning in 1962, his interest in the recording activity was sustained with the arrival of the 33 1/3 rpm or LP. By 1964, Dan Joe had recorded three long-play solo recordings for Celtic and Banff labels, which were owned by Rodeo Records. In later years, he recorded on the British label, Topic. For the moment, however, I want to reflect on the LP I found among the trinkets and garments in the Christmas store on that December evening in 1991.

There was a moment of personal reflection and a touch of emotion as I glanced at the recording and reviewed the liner notes pertaining to Dan Joe which had been prepared by Ian MacKinnon of the popular Celtic group, Rawlins Cross. Ian's notes had made particular reference to Dan Joe's early efforts to learn to play the fiddle but also, as if to come full circle, to Dan Joe's vast repertoire of music which was evident even in this one recording. The tunes recorded were from several of the many music collections he had acquired over the years, *Skinner's, Robertson's, MacGlashen, O'Hern* and the *Atholl.* These were among the many collections of music Dan Joe and other Cape Breton fiddlers had accumulated over their lifetime. These collections were a valuable source for tunes which the fiddlers would often render for their own enjoyment and for others' enjoyment as well. Dan Joe believed that learning and playing the great tunes from the many Celtic regions, worldwide, including those from Cape Breton, were essential to his efforts in acquiring and maintaining the Cape Breton fiddling tradition.

To Be Or Not To Be a "Teacher"

Dan Joe's approach to acquiring the music, his efforts to participate in the tradition, his technique for learning to play the fiddle, and the processes in which he engaged for acquiring and expanding his repertoire may have some application to many of the Cape Breton fiddlers I came to know through Dan Joe from the 1950's to the 1990's, a community of fiddlers which some Cape Bretoners continue to celebrate and a community of fiddlers whose zest for the music is integral to my inspiration for recalling this journey.

Dan Joe's need to reflect differently on his playing technique became a "necessary evil" for him in 1974. Because he was regarded as an accomplished fiddler among many of his contemporaries, I invited Dan Joe and his close friend, fiddler Sandy MacInnis, to prepare a Cape Breton fiddle instruction program which would be offered through UCCB's Continuing Education Department in response to the emerging interest in the community to learn to play the fiddle Cape Breton style.[3] Later, Francis MacDonald, also a noted fiddler, joined the team to teach in the program.

In my efforts to assist Dan Joe in preparing for the UCCB program, I was given the opportunity to consider his music with a different focus or perspective. Matters like the definition of and the origin of the music have been discussed among people in the wider circle of music for decades; but in the 1970's, particularly, the mission to help aspiring musicians in Cape Breton and beyond with the art of learning to play the fiddle began to flourish. The old-fashioned way of learning the music, in the home and among community and family mentors, was not as readily available to some people. Thus, the need for some fiddlers like Dan Joe to think of ways to transmit their skills to others in a classroom setting emerged.

> Stan Chapman — arguably the teacher who has made the greatest contribution to the younger generation of fiddlers since the 1970's — is convinced that while the transmission process may effectively have moved from the kitchen to the classroom, a solid home environment, while perhaps no longer a prerequisite, is certainly an important element.[4]

The early efforts in the community to teach Cape Breton fiddling, in a formal setting, most likely began with the initiative by Frank MacInnis of Creignish[5] and Reverend Colonel MacLeod, parish priest in Inverness County.[6] Reverend MacLeod had asked John MacDougall, an Inverness County fiddler, to set up a program to teach a group of young people from the Inverness area. MacDougall's initial reaction was typical of others, like Dan Joe, who were subsequently engaged to teach in their respective communities as well:

> I didn't know if I could put across to others what I knew. I knew what to do, but to put it across to others was another thing. I took a chance and started, and in a little better than a year, I had six of them — four girls and two boys — playing at the Scottish Concert at Broad Cove in July, 1972.[7]

Preparing a teaching guide for a learning process, which was integral to the oral tradition, became a challenge for Dan Joe as well. He pondered how he might teach students in a group setting to execute certain techniques in bowing, in embellishment, and in tempo, for example. Without training in the theory and mechanics of the music, the process became frustrating for Dan Joe. Furthermore, how would he teach students to render the music with feeling and passion? Teaching would not be an easy task for Dan Joe because his experience in learning the music was a lifetime of observation of those musicians who he viewed to be exceptional exponents of the music. He learned to listen and to watch carefully and then on his own to try this and to try that to see what happened.

Although Dan Joe participated in the UCCB program, he maintained that the music had to be "in the blood" or, otherwise, one could not learn the Cape Breton style. After only a semester or two, he decided that teaching was not his "cup of tea." He concluded that the process was not a teachable process. Unlike his playing career, his teaching career was short-lived; yet, if anyone wanted to listen and to watch and to talk with him in some brief moments at a concert or a session and have him clarify whatever he was doing with the music, he always responded in as helpful a way as possible.

As the music became more accessible to a wider audience, including academic researchers and/or musicians from different musical experiences, new and innovative interpretations on the unique style and character of the Cape Breton music emerged. The interest to learn to play the fiddle was increasing among many people from outside and inside the tradition. Among the local fiddlers who established quality methods for teaching the Cape Breton fiddle style were Stan Chapman who began teaching in Antigonish in 1975 and Winnie Chafe who began teaching at UCCB in the early 1980's. Later, other local fiddlers who established fiddle programs "include Kyle MacNeil, Neil Beaton, Dougie MacDonald, Carl MacKenzie, and Allie Bennett."[8]

The observations and insights acquired from outsiders, through close contact and study of local fiddlers like Dan Joe, give some insight to help better understand the music and, thus, more effectively transmit the music to future generations. In the early 1980's, a study on the traditional learning process. For example, among the Cape Breton fiddlers was undertaken by American-born Dr. Virginia Garrison.[9] Later, the research of other musicologists with background training and skills like Kate Dunlay[10] and David Greenberg[11] and more recently, Liz Doherty,[12] analytically describe some of the finer but often complex features of the music in a manner which might facilitate the transmission of technique in new directions. But not everyone who has nurtured the music and the tradition share the same enthusiasm for this type of analysis of the music.

Mary Campbell, daughter of the celebrated Cape Breton fiddler Dan J. Campbell, of Glenora Falls, Inverness County reacts with passion and with a deep concern to any suggestion that the music can be transformed from outside the tradition to some analytical process in the interest of preservation. In a July, 1996 edition of the *Inverness Oran*, she writes:

Gaelic music and song goes by assonance [the rhythm of accented notes of like sound] as opposed to the rhythm of controlled movement found in written notation or classical methodical interpretation. Assonance produces the cadence and swing required for lilt and dancing rhythm.

. . . our Campbell music is based on a very traditional art form requiring emotional self-expression and generations of learned musical skills acquired by the proper grammatical interpretation and theory of written notation plus oral transmission.[13]

Mary's article appears to suggest that there is only one way to learn the music. The traditional learning process available to the Campbells was a special gift and a wonderful experience enabling the Campbells to acquire and render the music with passion and feeling or, as Mary states, with "self-expression." That same tradition has been carried on by so many of the legends of the great Cape Breton fiddlers like Dan J. Campbell's sons, John and Donald. Despite any inclination that fiddlers like Dan Joe MacInnis may have had to encourage a process to follow the traditional learning pattern, the tide to do differently will likely prevail and a continuing effort to analyze the music will continue.

Learning New Tunes

Despite Dan Joe's views and frustration with respect to teaching the music, a focus on his music provides some understanding of the respect, tenacity, and commitment he and others had to the music. It is likely that Dan Joe would be the first to suggest that others are much more worthy of such a focus.

In the article, "A Tribute to Dan Joe MacInnis," following his death in August 1991, Frances MacEachern described Dan Joe's passion for the "written" music:

His insatiable appetite for music also made him an avid collector of violin books and eventually he was to own one of the most enviable collections including: *The Atholl, The Oswald Collection, The Beauties of Neil Gow, The Glen Collection, The Duncan Collection, The Alexander MacGlashen*, and an original of Simon Fraser's first book (1816).[14]

Dan Joe's commitment to extrapolating the music from the various music collections gave him the ability to group the tunes effectively, a process which was very much a part of the Cape Breton fiddling tradition. Dan Joe selected the appropriate strathspeys to follow a particular march; then he selected the most effective reels to follow the strathspeys. Some of his contemporaries, along with the new young and aspiring fiddlers, would often try to emulate the manner in which Dan Joe rendered the tunes and arranged the selections from among his vast repertoire.

MacEachern alludes to this in her article with particular reference to Dan Joe's ability to recall the music he had taken great strides to learn. She quotes Dan Joe's close friend and fellow fiddler, Big Pond native Mike MacLean, as he comments on Dan Joe's ability to remember the tunes:

> I tried to copy Dan Joe's style although I just didn't have the tunes. Dan Joe learned them fast and could remember them.[15]

MacEachern also quotes well-known music authority and performer Doug MacPhee about the passion that local fiddlers like Dan Joe, Bill Lamey, and Dan R. MacDonald had for the old Scottish book collections. Doug explained:

> They had contacts in the old country who would seek out these collections, sometimes searching abandoned farm houses where rare books would be left behind. These books which no longer found any use in Scotland, were passed around, studied and copied by hand by the eager musicians in Cape Breton. Dougie said Dan Joe copied by hand 171 tunes from *The Alexander Walker Collection* which he had borrowed from Dan R. MacDonald.[16]

MacEachern also went on to write about Dan Joe's commitment to playing tunes correctly and the respect he received from some of the great local composers. She quotes Inverness County native fiddler, Sandy MacInnis:

> . . . he was a correct player. He was, in turn, respected for his knowledge and perfection in fiddling. Fiddlers Dan R. MacDonald and Dan Hughie (MacEachern) would be sure to send copies of their new compositions to him (Dan Joe) to ensure the correct tune gets picked up by the non-readers.[17]

John Campbell's article, "Fiddle Festival at Gaelic College Celebrates our Musical Heritage," features an interview with Dan Joe and other fiddlers in which he highlights Dan Joe's comments about his interest in the local Celtic music collections:

> He plays tunes from most of the local composers, noting Dan R. MacDonald's compositions are hard to beat. He collected and plays the compositions of Gordon MacQuarrie, Dan Hughie MacEachern and the Beaton family, the late Donald Angus Beaton and sons Kinnon and Joey.[18]

As if feeding on one another for the music, fiddlers like Dan Joe would often share their music. Copies of new tunes were given backstage at the different venues as well as through the mail. Dan Joe had established a great friendship over the years with composer Dan Hughie MacEachern. They shared music regularly.

> Dan Hughie recalls that when Dan R. was overseas (1941) he would send him music from Scotland. Dan Joe MacInnis, John Donald Cameron, and Joe MacLean also contributed to Dan Hughie's musical repertoire when they had occasion to spend time together.[19]

I continued to read the information about the tunes on the sleeve of *Cape Breton Celtic Music — Volume 1* on that December evening and noted, in particular, the selection called "Michael Deleski's March," which had been composed by Malcolm Campbell of Sydney for his grandson, who had the same name. This beautiful 2/4 (two-four) march captured the typical tune construction that had a special appeal for Dan Joe. Malcolm Campbell had always enjoyed a close relationship with Dan Joe, one which was usually centred around the music. As a matter of fact, Malcolm played the fiddle himself as did his uncle Peter. Malcolm and Peter encouraged Dan Joe to learn the fiddle or violin, which Dan Joe called the instrument as a young boy growing up on Alexandra Street in Sydney. Dan Joe often referred to Peter Campbell's version of "Christie Campbell" as "just tremendous."

Perhaps the one Cape Breton fiddler, though, whose music most influenced and indeed inspired Dan Joe's music was the legendary Bill Lamey of River Denys, Inverness County, to the extent that, in Dan Joe's formative years, he would often position a photo of Bill in front of himself whenever he was trying to master new tunes. Bill Lamey lived in Sydney before moving to Boston in the early 1950's and, while in Sydney, he spent considerable time with Dan Joe and Joe MacLean, another noted Cape Breton fiddler. Joe had

Lower Washabuck roots and lived in Sydney. Together, they met as often as possible and shared music from their respective collections. Bill Lamey actually taught Dan Joe to read music.

The respective styles acquired by Dan Joe and Bill Lamey were similar, and they often played the same tunes from the music collections. In addition to the usual tunes from collections they gathered featuring the fiddle and violin compositions, both fiddlers had a particular interest in rendering the old pipe tunes, especially the marches from the different music books. Like his collection of violin music, Dan Joe took great pleasure in collecting pipe music as well. *The Ross Collection, The Glenallan Collection, Pipe Major Donald Ross Collection, The Glendauruel Collection*, the *Edcath*, the *Logan, The Robertson Collection*, and popular collections like the *Seaforth* were among his music books.

In the Cape Breton tradition, the use of the written music is helpful in expanding one's repertoire and in learning the basic melody. Subsequently, embellishments are added to the tune to better it. On the other hand, the written music for many individuals is limited to learning to play Cape Breton style. In other words, within the tradition, the written music will be followed as a valuable and essential source for most individuals once a certain mastery in playing is achieved. For many fine Cape Breton fiddlers, however, the written music is not considered a necessity at any time. Some great fiddlers have acquired an ability to play well, exclusively by ear. The mix of fiddlers who enjoy learning the music from the books and those who play by ear only adds a dynamic feature to the fiddling tradition of Cape Breton.

In 1985, the late Dr. Virginia Garrison documented the learning to play process of several Cape Breton fiddlers. In her field work, she spent considerable time observing several local fiddlers. She found that:

> Almost 80% of the fiddlers interviewed reported that as a beginning fiddler they were totally dependent on their aural skills — their ear — for learning. . . . Although most Cape Breton fiddlers appear to have learned by ear, it should be noted that 16 of the 23 fiddlers interviewed did learn to play by note (read music) at a later time.[20]

In the case of Dan Joe, he played the instrument for several years before learning to read.

My most vivid recollections of Dan Joe as a student of the music was while he was learning new tunes, as he was already an accomplished fiddler when I was in my youth. He always sat while he practiced his music and frantically thumped one foot to the rhythm of his jigs and reels, over the course of several hours in the early evenings and especially during weekend mornings. His ambition was to succeed in memorizing as much of the music as possible from his vast collections.

I recall sitting at the kitchen table with Dan Joe while I was still a young boy and watching and listening as he selected tune after tune from his different collections. Often, different family members were called upon, like myself, to hold books in an upright position so that he could more easily sight-read the music. The book pages had to be turned at the precise moment, thus allowing him to play the tunes and to maintain a continuous flow.

Dan Joe proceeded to play so that he could advance each tune from the pages of the different books without an interlude, allowing him to advance the group, the marches, the strathspeys, and the reels, with minimum interruption. While putting the music to memory, this process could carry over for a couple of evenings until he recalled each tune to a point where he no longer required the written music in front of him. When that was accomplished, he focused on the integration of his personal flavour or unique sound and interpretation of the music.

I could hear the stops and starts and those frequent moments when he would repeat certain aspects of a tune as he applied his bowing techniques and nurtured his own musical style. Often, in excitement, when he felt he had mastered a particular tune, he called for members of the family to sit for a few minutes while he played his mini-concert. The satisfaction he felt in his accomplishment was evident.

Often, some listeners in the general public assume that the local Cape Breton fiddler is musically illiterate since the fiddler never follows written music in a public performance. In fact, many of the fiddlers read very well; this is reflected not only in the manner in which they render the music with accuracy and precision but also in the many wonderful compositions which have been written by so many fiddlers over the decades. Their remarkable ability to recall the many tunes without the aid of the written music in the public setting is an exciting trait of the Cape Breton fiddlers, thereby contributing to the sense of spontaneity and vibrancy in the music.

Personal Style

The manner in which Dan Joe used the bow and held the fiddle was developed during a very early learning stage and it became second nature to him. His objective while learning was simply to be comfortable, which he considered a prerequisite to learning to play the fiddle. Then, he proceeded to the real challenge, trying to emulate those distinctive sounds he heard in the music of his mentors, for example Peter Campbell's version of strathspeys like "Christie Campbell." Dan Joe developed a keen ear for the range of sounds in the music and then worked diligently at recreating those sounds.

For Dan Joe, the unique sound in his music was determined, in part, by the way in which he would, to use his own expression, work the bow, a bow style he acquired at an early age through observation and applied through trial and error. This allowed him to generate the sounds which he believed were unique to the music of the Cape Breton fiddler, sounds that have been nurtured by the individual fiddlers and passed on through several generations.

For Dan Joe, the art of bowing included highlighting rapid cuts and accenting grace notes, that is the use of additional subtle fingering between notes. Kate Dunlay and David Greenberg in their 1996 publication, *Traditional Celtic Music of Cape Breton*, describe Dan Joe's execution of placing rapid cuts in his music. They point out that the technique is integral to the Cape Breton style of playing and is frequently heard in strathspeys like the "Devil in the Kitchen" which is often played by many fiddlers and which was recorded by Dan Joe on his 1962 LP, *The Cape Breton Fiddle of Dan Joe MacInnis*. However, they make particular reference to Dan Joe's use of cuts in the reel, "The Grey Old Lady of Raasay," which he also recorded in 1962 (listed on Dan Joe's album as "Old Lady of Rothesay.").

> They are fast and clean, in order to fit the timing . . . Four-note cuts seem to simulate pipe burls more closely, and they also aid in keeping the direction of the bow consistent when two sets of cuts in a row are called for (as in the "Devil in the Kitchen").[21]

Dunlay and Greenberg remind the readers that "few fiddlers make use of the cuts in the reels."[22]

As I think about the use of cuts and the tune, "Devil in the Kitchen,"[23] I remember that Dan Joe often asked me, a young person at the time, to give a little step on Jessie and John P. MacNeil's veranda in Gillis Point, near Iona, or in Kate MacDougall's kitchen in Ben Eoin. He always began his group of tunes with the "Devil in the Kitchen" strathspey!

Dan Joe's bowing technique suited the manner in which he grasped the bow, usually high on the frog. He applied pressure to the bow with the thumb and forefinger for certain aspects of a particular tune, and he introduced minimum pressure on the bow at other points in the tune, often engaging the full flat of the bow as well as the edge of the bow, especially to execute the cuts.

Dan Joe strived to use as much of the bow as possible but usually applied the upper half of the bow more frequently and often used the upper quarter of the bow for prolonged moments at select points in his music. What he described as his Achilles' heel! Through his bowing technique, he controlled the accent he wanted to interject in his music. His objective was to embellish the music to suit his style and interpretation, but he always continued to play the melody, the core of the tune as he called it, just as he had learned it from the written music.

Generally, most of the discussion concerning the subtle features and characteristics of the music has been described by the community of people who perpetuate the music and the wider traditions of the songs, dance, and music, and so it was with Dan Joe. He remarked that some fiddlers had a great bow hand and snappy wrist action, which is the way he would describe a young Kyle MacNeil, for example. Some fiddlers had great timing through an effective use of the bow, especially in the jigs and reels for dancing which is the way he described Buddy MacMaster and Sandy MacInnis. Other fiddlers were noted for their terrific bow for the old strathspeys, which was the way he would make reference to Alex Francis MacKay.

Like many others fiddlers, Dan Joe referred to Angus Chisholm as simply Chisholm and to Winston Fitzgerald as simply Scotty and often described these artists as classic performers who rendered even the most difficult bowing techniques in certain tunes in an almost effortless fashion. He often complimented the bowing of Theresa MacLellan and Paddy LeBlanc and Joe MacLean while they played the pipe marches, especially. Fiddlers like Donald Angus Beaton had the Gaelic in the music, and Dan Joe always referred to Donald Angus's spiccato. He said other fiddlers had a great lift and drive in the bow, like Carl MacKenzie; and that Winnie Chafe's slow pastoral airs were moving and touching and rendered as such because of the manner in which she used the full bow.

These were vernacular or familiar labels which, in the opinion certainly of Dan Joe and perhaps of many other fiddlers within the tradition, best depict the manner in which the fiddlers may be assessed. Outside the tradition, however, these labels may not add a great deal to effectively describe the music of the Cape Breton fiddler. Dan Joe's observations might suggest that what has emerged within the tradition, evidently, is not so much an analysis of what is happening but rather an illustration of how it is happening.

The renowned James Hunter, who studied at the Royal Scottish Academy of Music in Scotland and at Trinity College in Ireland, researched traditional music over a lifetime. In his publication, *The Fiddle Music of Scotland*, Hunter writes the following about the traditional fiddlers of Scotland:

There are many other subtle tricks of technique employed by the traditional fiddler, most of which are difficult, if not impossible, to communicate on paper. Where and when to use them — and the various bowing techniques — in order to obtain the maximum musical effect, can only be learnt from direct contact with a good exponent. For there are many things one can pick up just by listening, there are certain things — particularly in bowing — which can only be assimilated through the eye.[24]

For the most part, as Hunter suggests, the manner in which one might render a distinctive sound through select bowing techniques, for example, is not always illustrated in the written music itself. Following an interview with Ashley MacIsaac, journalist Bruce Headlam offered a simplistic interpretation of Cape Breton bowing when he wrote in the September, 1995 edition of *Saturday Night*:

> . . . what virtuosity does exist in Cape Breton is found in the bowing hand. A good bowing arm is really just a matter of physics. The centre of percussion on the violin bow — that is the part of the bow that provides the most jump and precision — is about three-quarters of the length of the bow shaft from the grip, about where you find the sweet spot on a baseball bat . . . Violinists are often most comfortable playing with short, rapid strokes in that part of the bow . . .[25]

Headlam might see the bowing as simply a matter of physics and a Cape Breton thing, but it may not be that simple. Dr. John Shaw, a noted folklorist and researcher who has studied the Gaelic traditions of Cape Breton including the fiddle traditions for many years, describes the bowing of the traditional fiddler, in part, in the following:

> . . . the bow is usually held with the ball of the thumb touching the stick underneath and the index and the middle fingers resting on the grip above. The remaining two fingers often rest lightly on the stick to guide the bow. However, many players tend to raise and partially curl these two fingers. The middle section of the bow is the one most frequently used . . . [26]

While discussing the origins of the bowing techniques, Shaw dwells heavily on the generations of isolation of the Cape Breton fiddlers; thus, the Cape

Breton fiddlers were not tainted by outside influences. He gives little credence to the idea of an Irish influence in his account. For example Dr. Liz Doherty, however, of the Music Department at the University College of Cork, Ireland, who has done extensive research on the Cape Breton fiddle tradition, comments on the bowing style of the Cape Breton fiddler as having parallels with the Donegal style of bowing in Ireland. The two views may simply be representative of two distinctively different time periods. Shaw's position appears more centered on the idea that the immigrant Irish to America and to Cape Breton in the 1800's had little influence, whereas Doherty's view seems to acknowledge a much earlier period when the music and techniques in the fiddle tradition of Ireland and Scotland may have had the opportunity to assimilate.

Doherty explains that the use of the single-stroke bowing and the preference for the bowed cut or treble are characteristic of the fiddlers in Donegal and Cape Breton. In her publication, *The Music of Cape Breton — An Irish Perspective*, Doherty explores the historical opportunity for sharing and transmitting similar techniques when she describes the early social and cultural ties of the Irish in the highlands and the islands of Scotland.[27] Kenneth MacKinnon, in *The Lion's Tongue*, describes the shared culture between the Scots and the Irish as far back as the Middle Ages.

> Within the Lordship and within the great Gaelic houses of the Highlands an integrated Gaelic way-of-life continued throughout the Middle Ages. It is true that a common language and a common culture continued to be shared by Gaelic Scotland and Gaelic Ireland, and there was little to prevent the free coming and going of people across the narrow seas which joined rather than separated the Gaelic Lordship of the Isles with the then most Gaelic of all provinces of Ireland, Ulster. There were native learned orders of bardic poets, seannachaidhs or historians, clerics and ecclesiastics, latimers, judges, musicians, harpists, scribes, medical men and the like. Their reputation might be as great in Ireland as it was in Scotland and they may have been as travelled in one country as the other.[28]

In his publication, *Scotland from 1603 to the Present*, Scottish historian George S. Pryde describes the presence of the Irish among the Highlanders as being so prevalent that, by 1709, the Gaelic Highlander was scornfully called Irish by the Lowlanders.[29] (This view of the Highlander was convenient among the Lowlanders at the time because of the efforts to promote

Gaelic as a foreign language and, thus, Gaelic would not be worthy of inclusion in initiatives that supported Scottish Education, for example.)

Further to his bowing, Dan Joe, while seated, held the fiddle in a seemingly awkward manner. The back end of the fiddle rested against his lower chest, for the most part, while the front end rested firmly on the upper wrist of his fingering hand. Ironically, in a concert performance, he usually stood (something he would never do while practicing) while holding the fiddle firmly perched under his chin and on an angle which allowed him to access the finger board so that he could render those techniques peculiar to his style of playing. Personally, I was never convinced that the concert position was the most effective manner for Dan Joe to play his music.

I recall Dan Joe's admiring reaction and positive comments towards Bobby MacNeil's performances. Dan Joe was very impressed as Bobby, the versatile and exciting violinist who renders the classical music and the Cape Breton style of music with ease, executed quick hand and wrist movements along the fingering board as he effectively moves from the first position to the third position and back again, in the blink of an eye and without missing a beat. Listen! and Watch! were Dan Joe's words when he had the opportunity to hear and to see Bobby MacNeil perform.

There is an on-going, friendly debate concerning the proper way to hold the fiddle. Cape Breton fiddler Sandy MacIntyre, who now teaches fiddling at the Gaelic College in St. Ann's, comments on this:

> . . . the violin rests on the fingering hand, while the purfling edge of the upper body of the violin rests on the wrist. When playing first position on the finger board, this poses absolutely no problem. However, when playing in higher positions on the finger board, the wrist becomes arched and takes on the more classical appearance. Many of the younger Cape Breton fiddlers today are receiving classical training or are holding the violin and the bow in a more classical manner. Contrary to the recommendations of many Cape Breton fiddling colleagues, I personally feel new fiddlers should be taught to hold their fiddles in the classical manner.[30]

The efforts by some researchers and by some students of the Cape Breton music to change the manner in which the playing techniques are described may, in the opinion of some individuals, effectively aid in transmitting the music and diverse sounds of the Cape Breton fiddler.

The Gaelic Flavour

Dan Joe, like many Cape Breton fiddlers, was determined to refine his style and to play the music as he felt it best suited his abilities and skills as a musician. The sound, the tone, and the accent emanating from Dan Joe's fiddle were his mark or signature on a tune or group of tunes. His style was one which he believed would lend itself favourably towards rendering his preference for the Gaelic airs and the pastoral airs, as he called them. It is likely that Dan Joe's interest in the Gaelic flavour was in part influenced by his mother's love for the Gaelic songs and his association with the wider Gaelic communities of Woodbine and Grand Mira.

Dan Joe's family genealogy is deeply rooted in Margaree and in Woodbine. Like his paternal and maternal grandparents, Dan Joe's mother and father were native Gaelic speakers. Mary "Danny Peter" especially enjoyed singing the old Gaelic songs written by bards like Dan Alex Macdonald ("Oran Do Cheap Breatuinn"), Jonathan MacKinnon ("Eilean Gorm"), and Malcolm Gillis ("Nighean Donn A Chuil Reidh"). In his music, Dan Joe often tried to emulate the Gaelic lilt. Such were his efforts in the Gaelic Air, "Lord Lovet's Lament," recorded on the *Celtic Music of Cape Breton — Volume 1*. Not speaking the Gaelic language himself did not seem to be a barrier for Dan Joe as he played the fiddle in the Gaelic tradition.

It is common knowledge that some music lovers explain that the very heart of the Cape Breton traditional music is the Gaelic language itself. Many of the active and sometimes determined proponents of the language agree that the very existence of the vibrant music culture is because of its strong link with the Gaelic language. This view concerning the fiddlers' music has evoked some very interesting debate and discussion in select communities of rural Cape Breton and beyond, where some individuals also hold fast to an opinion which places less of an emphasis on the link between the music of the Cape Breton fiddler and the Gaelic language.

Until the 1950's and early 1960's, the conversation about the music would largely have been in Gaelic, which at that time was the medium for conversation in rural communities.[31] Therefore, it is not surprising to learn that much of the commentary on the nature of the music has been by linguists whose perspective on the music, understandably, has been concerned almost exclusively with the role of the Gaelic language.

Again, John Shaw, who might be prepared to further reflect on the possibility of the Irish influence with respect to technique is not likely, however, prepared to relinquish his stand on the importance of the Gaelic language and song especially in the Cape Breton style fiddling, and he is not short on company with equal authority on that issue. In 1978, Shaw and two associates, Rosemary (Hutchinson) MacCormack and Tony Engle, produced one of the more authentic compilations of the traditional music of Cape Breton, in my opinion. The recording offers an excellent mix of instrumentals and Gaelic vocals which are representative of several regions which effectively depict Gaelic music and the Gaelic songs of Cape Breton. Shaw writes in his notes:

> The fortunes of Scottish fiddling in Nova Scotia have always been tied to those of the Gaelic language — most of the players recorded here (the recording) speak the Gaelic as a first langauge and the rest are no more than one generation removed.[32]

Even the analysis of the technical aspects of the fiddle music by musicologists makes some provision for the Gaelic language in the music of the Cape Breton fiddler. Greenberg and Dunlay make a brief reference to the role of Gaelic in the Cape Breton fiddle music:

> The Scottish Gaelic language itself played an important role in both the vocal and instrumental music of Cape Breton. Singers, pipers, and fiddlers all exchanged tunes, and there were words (known as puirt a beul or mouth music) for many of the fiddle tunes. . . . Some authorities believe that, without the Gaelic language, the old fiddle style with its characteristic Gaelic-inspired rhythms and inflections will disappear in time.[33]

Again, Dr. Liz Doherty of the University College of Cork, in her extensive research, makes allowance for the Gaelic in the music when she writes:

> The process of transferring melodies from vocal source to violin, the musician, with his or her knowledge of the Gaelic words, would try to reproduce them as closely as possible. Subsequently, through this process, certain inflections of the language were absorbed into the fiddle style, particularly in the form of grace notes, or certain accents of the bow. This has given rise to the expression "he's got the Gaelic on his music."[34]

Alexander MacDonald, however, whose roots are in Mabou, describes himself as a "hobby fiddler with an intense interest in the subject and roots deep in Cape Breton fiddle country."[35] Alexander has researched the topic of

Cape Breton fiddling for "over forty years and maintains that he has not found any evidence that language, English or Gaelic, has influenced the fiddle music."[36] Rather, he believes that the music of the Cape Breton fiddler has four basic distinguishing elements intrinsic in the music: the music structure itself, the instruments used to play the music, the techniques used by the players, and the influence of the composers. Alexander summarizes, in part, his view:

> There are hundreds of permutations and combinations of fiddling techniques which players may adopt. It is the fiddler's selection of these, coupled with tune structure, which make the style different or unique as a group.[37]

While studying at St. Francis Xavier University, Jackie Dunn, an accomplished Cape Breton fiddler and grand-niece to the prolific composer, the late Dan Hughie MacEachern, prepared her senior thesis on the Gaelic language and its possible influence on Cape Breton fiddling.[38] Jackie is not so quick to dismiss the role of the Gaelic langauge in the music and offers a very good technical analysis of the music overall in dealing with her quest as to whether the Cape Breton fiddle music is linked directly to, and indeed dependent upon, the Gaelic language.

When discussing the Scottish airs, Jackie explains that when she collected her field data, not one person she interviewed could verbalize the meaning of the Gaelic sound.[39] In her attempt to explain unique features of the Cape Breton fiddler's style by way of comparison, Jackie comments on obvious detail like the use of the rapid cuts by the Cape Breton fiddler which highlight, in part, the music's variance from the Old Country's fiddlers, for example. (Old Country fiddlers often are characterized by many people in the Cape Breton tradition as having a non-Gaelic flavour.)

Jackie's impressive study illustrates (through the use of specific tunes often played by the Cape Breton fiddlers) that the different musical scales in the Celtic music tradition have, at the very least, an association with the music of the Cape Breton fiddler. Scales like pentatomic which is used in Gaelic vocals, heptatonic which is used with the Celtic harp, and the "hexatonic scale often used in fiddle tunes and in Gaelic songs, lie between the pentatomic and heptatonic scales . . ."[40] (A brief analysis of scale application in traditional Gaelic singing is also located in the introductory notes by S.R. Cowell and J.P. Hughes in the 1955 recording of the North Shore Gaelic singers issued by Ethnic Folkways, New York.)[41]

Jackie further illustrates the use of clichés and ornamentation describing the rhythmic and melodic clichés used in the pipe and fiddle tunes as illustrated in the use of the ". . . repeated sequential passages on major triad. This pattern, sometimes identified as 'double tonic' is also in vocal music" (presumably Gaelic vocals). [42] Jackie is successful at pointing out that there may be some direct influence between the language through the traditional Gaelic songs, for example, and the Cape Breton fiddle music. Jackie Dunn's conclusion, however, suggests that one may not need to speak the Gaelic to play Cape Breton style. Most fiddlers would likely agree with Jackie Dunn concerning the Cape Breton fiddling when she points out (as Hunter did for the Scottish fiddlers) that only when the "outsider appreciates that there is more to producing the proper sound than what is noted on the printed page, will he/she be successful in his/her attempts (to copy)."[43]

As for Dan Joe's view on the issue of Gaelic in the music, I recall his positive reaction when I shared with him an article I had come across in the August 22nd, 1986 edition of *The West Highland Free Press*, which outlined several statements by the Gold Medal piper, Alan MacDonald, a native Gaelic speaker from Glenuig, concerning the place of the language in his piping.

> The language is part of the culture, so is the Gaelic song. It is that idiom rather than the language that produces the style. It doesn't matter if you speak Swahili, it's not going to make you play the pipes better.[44]

Dan Joe savoured Alan's comments concerning the role of the language in the music. There was no question for Dan Joe: he believed that without actually speaking the language, he could still effectively reproduce what he understood to be the Gaelic sound in his music. In fact, I know that he never doubted that thought for a moment but he recognized his proximity to the Gaidhealtachd and how that was reflected in his music.

Dan Joe enjoyed the music of the MacDonald pipers from Glenuig. He took special delight in any opportunity to hear good piping, whether it was from Scotland (the Old Country) or from Cape Breton. Although he was not overly familiar with Alan MacDonald's piping, he knew Alan's brother, Angus, also a gold medalist who spent several years in Cape Breton; Angus was one of the finest pipers Dan Joe said he had ever heard.

It has been often said that Dan Joe played his music with heart, and that may very well be the Gaelic in his music. Many people who knew his music often described it in that manner. There was feeling in his music, and he would take great delight in the person who would tell him that this was so. David Greenberg certainly had fiddlers like Dan Joe in mind when he said:

It's the feeling that is put into the music. There must be thousands of tunes in the Cape Breton repertoire, and each one is different in feeling. Some are just for fun tunes, and others have a potent emotional quality to them. It's beautiful to be part of the sharing of these emotions.[45]

The House Session

Dan Joe always enjoyed the great outdoors. He was an avid woodsman in all seasons; he enjoyed the country, the gardens, and the backwoods. He often explored the old, abandoned farms in areas like Woodbine, Glengarry, the Sterling, and out the Glen Morrison. He frequently hunted deer in the hidden orchards and fished for trout and smelts in the local brooks and streams. But more than anything, Dan Joe wanted to play the fiddle and to simply make music.

He enjoyed performing in concerts and at the lively square dances in small community halls throughout rural Cape Breton, but as he grew older and became less involved in public performances, he frequently played at different church settings where the mood might be sombre, for example, at a funeral service for a fellow fiddler, a personal friend, or a relative.

The setting most challenging to Dan Joe's ability to not only recall the many tunes he had acquired over the years but also to render the feeling, the heart, and the passion he felt for his music was the old fashion house session — in the company of other fiddlers, in particular, and quality musicians, in general. The session, as I know it, may be one of the more unique features of the Cape Breton Celtic music scene.

As I continue this Celtic music journey, the reader will come to know some of the musicians who were close friends of Dan Joe: musicians who befriended the MacInnis family, musicians who bestowed many wonderful musical memories, and musicians who helped make the often challenging moments of a large extended family and the difficult features of rural living somewhat more accepting. These musicians who travelled from their respective communities throughout Cape Breton to visit my home came during all seasons. Often, I reflect on how fortuitous my brothers and sisters and I were to have these people want to visit and share their music at these house sessions. As the amenities were few, what was the appeal?

During my youth, the old homestead lacked central heating and running water for many years. The food served during the sessions was homemade and simple. The dram was circulated discreetly around the room in the right proportion and at the right time, not too early and not too late, almost as some ritual artistry or token reward for a splendid performance. There was certainly nothing elaborate about the setting or the food or the dram. My mother, Christie, would often say about those times: "we were as poor as church rats."

For the visiting musicians, however, it was their opportunity to have a good session of music with Dan Joe, in addition to the wonderful music the visiting musicians also offered. The idea of gathering together and celebrating and sharing the music was the genuine appeal. As the gift of music was very much a part of the ritual of the visiting musicians, in retrospect, I understand Dan Joe's music was his gift to these people. Music gatherings were commonplace in Cape Breton communities, towns and villages, rural and urban settings; not all music gatherings were the same. Some gatherings were simply parties; other gatherings were contrived ceilidhs, although a mainstay themselves and integral to maintaining the tradition; the sessions were different. Some sessions were even awesome for young and impressionable minds.

At good sessions, for example, the music is often discussed in a serious demeanour as well as being played. This is an important element in the process of sharing new compositions and in offering a spontaneous critique on local works like those by Dan R. and Dan Hughie among a trusted and informed gathering. Often, book collections like the *Harp and Claymore* or *The Petrie*, that offer inspiring and exciting tunes, might take the spotlight for a few moments. Early in a session, for example, there might be an interest in reviewing a fiddler's interpretation of a certain melody from a favourite composer like Skinner or Marshall. The music of these composers is usually discussed as if these icons just live over the mountain or up the road when, in fact, they lived in Scotland decades ago and in some cases, centuries. Bits of a new tune discovered among the old gems might be whistled briefly or jigged just sufficiently to give an impression about how the melody might sound. It appeared that these musicians could not wait to take their instruments from the case or have them tuned before sharing these brief musical interludes — which, as I remember at the sessions out home, were as intimate to the setting as the kettle boiling on the back of the wood stove and the smell of the burning, sizzling spruce from the same stove.

The more serious business of the session, however, starts with one fiddler playing several selections, followed by a second fiddler, followed by a third fiddler. Hence, the magic number, three fiddlers! As preeminence, the sessions offer an opportunity for the artist to perform from his or her repertoire a lasting musical impression. The fiddler with depth and intensity can play a gruelling session for several hours to an attentive and informed group of listeners.

At a session, the listeners want more than just the mechanics of a performance. They want heart; they want feeling; and they want passion. This is only possible when the listener becomes an integral aspect of the performer's delivery during the session; quality and attentive listening are essential to getting the best out of select fiddlers. Once the initial performance is completed by a particular fiddler, the next fiddler will quickly take centre stage, will perform with equal endurance, and will incrementally add to the already powerful presence of emotions evoked by the airs, the marches, the jigs, the reels, and the strathspeys — ah, especially the strathspeys that are so unique to the music of the Cape Breton fiddler!

Fiddler Dave MacIsaac always enjoys a good session. [Left to right] Margaret MacPhee, piano; Dave, fiddle; Cliff Morais, guitar; and Al Bennett, guitar.

Photo by Cyril MacInnis

In the tiny peasant-like room at home, where I enjoyed so many great sessions, I recall how the solo performances lasted for three or four hours while those present huddled around the piano, the only necessary back-up instrument expected at a good session. The momentum was occasionally distracted, only momentarily at the right juncture, for a hot cup of tea, or for a slight nip of the dram, or for a good stepdancer — an exciting dimension at a session. The stepdancer, though, had to know when to take to the floor and not to intrude in the midst of the enchanting strathspeys.

The dancer's appearance too early on the floor could pre-empt a performance of lively strathspeys; therefore, adherence to an unwritten protocol is usually expected. For the dancer to hold back was usually a challenge to one's will-power and self-discipline, but often necessary if the setting is to support the fiddler who is anxious to render a slash of great strathspeys requiring total diligence and absolute concentration. Dan Joe often commented that the dancers should wait until they are called upon before invading the flow of music. After the exhausting and often strenuous solo performances, including those tunes for the dancers, the fiddlers paused briefly and made adjustments for the high point — the group performance!

All the fiddlers took a moment to check their tuning and added a slight bit of rosin to the bow and, from my recollections at the sessions out home, invariably turned to Dan Joe and asked that he take the lead for the first group or two. This seemingly spontaneous play in unison made a good session great! Together, each fiddler became fixed on his or her own playing but always perking to the delight of the listeners as the fiddlers progressed from one tune to the next. Dan Joe would give a slight nod or sudden stare or slightly lean his fiddle forward whenever he was ready to introduce the next tune for the fiddlers to perform — first, the attention of the fiddlers; second, the attention of the piano player.

Without a pause from the music or break from the rhythm, the fiddlers would interject the already-captivating mood with yet another delightful tune emanating from their passion for the music. The tunes that were so carefully embodied and then released, at the right moment and in the right place, as if liberated from the depth of the human soul, elicited a wide range of emotions. The fiddlers were sharing what they seemingly understood to be their right of passage, to make music for those people who listened and enjoyed. All that mattered now were those tunes which poured forth — more marches, more strathspeys, and more reels! The usually small audience listened and watched and reaffirmed each other with a wink or a smile or a slight nod of the head recognizing that these great performers were in the mood. Out home, a winter session embraced the heat of the warm morning stove in the adjacent room as a slight intrusion, and the summer session snatched the warm breeze as a sparse distraction.

Over the course of an evening at a typical session at Dan Joe and Christie's, the many selections rendered included some of the old standbys — marches like "John MacDonald of Glencoe," "John MacColl's Favourite," "Kitchener's Army," "Tom Dey," "Trip to Mabou Ridge," "Leaving Glenurquhart," "Donald MacLean's Farewell to Oban;" strathspeys like "Alex Beaton's," "Calum Breugach," "Dusty Meadow," "Sandy Cameron," "Maggie Cameron," "Duke of Gordon's Birthday," and "Welcome to Your Feet Again;" and reels like "The Bird's Nest," "Farmer's Daughter," "Pigeon on the Gate," "Angus Campbell," "The King's Reel," and "The Old King's Reel." These old favourites added immeasurably to the evening's music; and just when one might think that nothing could top the initial group performance, the fiddlers would pause again and tune-up to high base, introducing melodies like "Johnny Cope" in the old setting and strathspeys like "Cairstiona Chaimbeul" followed by a slew of traditional reels.

Such were some of the essentials for a great session — fine hospitality, fine tunes, well-seasoned fiddlers, and an attentive listening audience. So, it was with pride and delight, I read the liner notes on the album, *"And his sound is Cape Breton"* of one of Cape Breton's great session fiddlers, Carl MacKenzie:

> When you listen to this record, imagine you are in Cape Breton spending the evening at a session, perhaps at the MacInnis's residence in Big Pond. Everyone is happy, full of life, and really feeling the music. Carl (MacKenzie) is playing airs, jigs, hornpipes, strathspeys and reels responding to the enthusiasm of those present. His sound is lively, flowing and full of feeling.[46]

Special Friends: Special Legends

The fiddlers who participated in these sessions were like family and when injury, difficulty, or even worse, death, inflicted a member of this fraternity, it evoked deep feelings of loss for everyone.

Such was the case one particular evening in February, 1974. Upon opening the door of my Halifax apartment, I was surprised to see my good friend, Lloyd White, a native Big Ponder who lived at the time with his family in Dartmouth. Immediately, I sensed that something happened to a member of my family and that Lloyd was the bearer of bad news. As Lloyd entered my apartment, I recall he engaged me in some small talk for a few moments. He then explained that he had bad news from home. He said that Paddy "Scotty" LeBlanc, a close family friend, had died that day as a result of a fatal heart attack. Paddy lived in Sydney and operated a small barber shop on Charlotte Street. Lloyd explained that he had received a call from my mother earlier that day and, knowing that I was without a telephone, he visited me to convey the sad news.

This moment evoked a series of memorable flashes about Paddy and his love of the fiddle music of Cape Breton. He was a noted fiddler who enjoyed the company of many fine fiddlers of his day. I recalled, in particular, his visit to Halifax in 1972, at my request, to perform at a public concert I had arranged. However, my thoughts about Paddy that cold February winter evening centred around the many music sessions in which he participated at my home while I was still a young boy. I recalled his many fine performances at these sessions which explained for me why he was clearly one of the essential fiddlers in the community for house sessions. He played with such enthusiasm and respect for the music. His French Acadian background, which was so evident in his accent, gave him a wit and charm which made him a very likeable and personable individual. He loved to play, but equally so, he loved to listen to a good fiddler.

Paddy listened in awe to the many Cape Breton fiddlers of Scottish ancestry or "the big guys" as he would refer to them. As a native to East Margaree, he likely was influenced by some of the best fiddlers, including Angus Chisholm and Angus Allan Gillis. Paddy often said that he couldn't seem to make those cuts or handle the bow the way he wanted and always made reference to those fiddlers he felt had particularly fine techniques and an ability to execute cuts. But Paddy's cuts were clear and crisp, and his bowing allowed him to render a great mastery of even the most difficult tunes; this was evident to me when I listened to him play in person and is reaffirmed on the homemade and commercial recordings of Paddy which are still available and enjoyed today.

Among the fine attributes of Paddy was his command of written music. His admiration for Dan R. MacDonald's compositions, especially, was a feature of his music, and Dan R.'s admiration for Paddy is evident in the fact that Dan R. composed a tune for Paddy — a gesture of friendship on Dan R.'s part.[47] The 1996 recording by Natalie MacMaster, *No Boundaries*, includes "Memories of Paddy LeBlanc," which was composed by Mabou's Donald Angus Beaton.[48] It was always a treat to have Paddy with Dan Joe and other fiddlers at home engage in a discussion about the music. The serious commentary about the music, the composers, and the players was informative and quite stimulating. Even as a young boy, I could ascertain the pride and fellowship among these artists for their music and comradeship.

Paddy also took great delight in playing the difficult tunes of the Old Country's Scottish fiddlers like Skinner and Gow, a trademark he had certainly acquired through Dan R. Like so many of the great fiddlers of his day, he exercised discipline and scholarly effort to extrapolate good tunes from the many fine collections of music available from the local fiddlers. Paddy LeBlanc had a powerful presence in his music and played with a hardy volume. He enjoyed an opportunity to perform as a soloist but seemed also to relish the opportunity to perform with two or three other fiddlers in unison.

I recall Paddy teaming with Dan Joe and Mike MacLean at my home and always encouraging Dan Joe to take the lead while he and MacLean rendered harmonic tones, especially in the slow airs and marches. Paddy often complemented group play at sessions with many fiddlers like the great team of John Archie MacIsaac and Duncan MacQuarrie.

Paddy took delight in the fellowship he acquired with the many fine fiddlers in his day. Like so many of his contemporaries, he nurtured a special respect for Duncan who was loved and revered by those people who were fortunate to have the opportunity to enjoy the man's company and music. Duncan's ability to play the fiddle exceptionally well resulted in a distinctive blend of music which definitely placed him among Paddy's big guys.

Unlike Paddy, Duncan played in the Mabou Coal Mines' tradition, which he acquired growing up in his native Glenora Falls, Inverness County where he was born in 1884. Duncan's quiet and gentle ways seemed to appropriately complement the view held by many that he was, in my most youthful days, the grandfather of the Cape Breton fiddlers. Duncan's visits, along with Paddy's visits, to my home left a musical indentation during these special occasions which will always linger passionately in my fond memories of excellent traditional music sessions in Cape Breton.

Duncan MacQuarrie died at the age of 94 in February of 1979, almost exactly five years following Paddy's death. In the March 24th 1979 edition of Scotland's *Oban Times*, Doug MacPhee was quoted as saying, " . . . when Duncan played, his foot hardly moved; he barely moved himself, and the music just came from him with ease, no labouring. He had exquisite timing, a beautiful bow arm; he played sweet music." The article further stated that "with Duncan's passing, Cape Breton loses another strong link with the music and language of Gaelic Scotland; a link which he (Duncan), with his every action, had striven so long to maintain."[49] Doug inscribed in the liner note of his second solo album, which he recorded shortly after Duncan's death:

> . . . Duncan MacQuarrie, a Cape Breton violinist in the Old Tradition, and a very special gentleman who I was honoured to have as a close friend. A gentle, unassuming man with a delightful wit, who enjoyed the affection and respect of a wide circle of friends. As a token of my affection for Duncan and my appreciation of his good influence on me, I humbly dedicate this album *Cape Breton Piano — Volume 2* to his memory."[50]

Both Duncan and Paddy, like Doug MacPhee himself, were seen as great sports, always ready to perform when called upon and willing to share a good story to get an evening's entertainment started. Such were my thoughts as I prepared to pack my small suitcase and make the long drive to Cape Breton that February evening so that I, too, could join my family in paying my final respect to Paddy. The drive was certainly no inconvenience as I recalled Paddy's efforts over my lifetime to share his music with those people who wanted

to listen at a good house session or with an audience at a benefit concert organized by a charitable group to raise money for a worthy cause.

Perhaps the most frequent visitor to our house sessions was Big Pond
native, Michael MacLean, a long-time friend of the family until his death in
1996. There was no question in MacLean's mind whether he was from the
Brook, the Pond, or the Centre; MacLean, as he was known in the community, was a true Big Ponder. He was a gifted fiddler, a fine piper, and a
charismatic storyteller.

Although he was one of my favourite players at local dances, my greatest
pleasure with MacLean was in the house session where his music and stories
delighted the listeners, always evoking moments of joy and laughter with
innocent humour about the oldtimers who he admired and cherished and
always held in such high esteem. He often roused moments of yearning and
nostalgia about the old times, which he came to know firsthand, through
story and song, acquired from his association with A.D. Morrison, Neil R.
MacIsaac, Fred Hudson, and his long-time friend Joe Neil MacNeil, all exceptional characters of form and wit from the wider Big Pond community.
Like these characters, MacLean lived a lifestyle that placed little emphasis on
worldly and material possessions.

MacLean's affection for the Gaelic was not unlike the affection attributed the early bards of the Celtic traditions. MacLean's scholarly account of
the literature, the music, and the language provided him with a remarkable
ability to understand and to comment on the Celtic music and the Gaelic
language customs. His version of these traditions, according to current
scholars, was often described as exemplary of those nurtured and cultivated
traditions that developed over five and six generations of immigrant Scots
to Cape Breton.[51]

After MacLean's sudden death in May, 1996, at age sixty-two, John
William MacInnis, who was perhaps one of MacLean's closest friends, published in his weekly column in the *Cape Breton Post*:

> Nothing gave MacLean more intense pleasure and joy than to
> speak the lines of a noble Gaelic song aloud or to render sweet tunes
> of beauty and age on the fiddle. He loved the language and he
> honoured in his lifetime the masters of the tradition. MacLean
> himself was an extraordinary Cape Breton bard.[52]

As for the sessions at my home with my family, it seemed like Paddy,
Duncan, and MacLean were always there, whether there was a cool summer
breeze making its way from the Bras d'Or Lakes through the tiny window

near the piano in the small dining room (where so many great fiddlers had gathered over the years); or whether there were frozen, snow-covered lakes right across to Eskasoni during a cold winter evening. The musicians always made the evening enjoyable, and that same joy was felt in the company of other people who often frequented additional sessions out home, musicians like Mike MacDougall, Eddy Irwin, Reverend Angus Morris, Carl Mac-Kenzie, Doug MacPhee, and Dr. Angus MacDonald. In more recent years, wonderful fiddlers like Howie MacDonald, Jimmie MacNeil, and Dave MacIsaac attended these house sessions, always delighting the entire MacInnis household with their music.

The Parish Hall

In addition to the intimate house sessions of music, there were the local parish hall square dances at which Dan Joe performed in Big Pond. On Saturday evenings throughout July and August, from the late 1950's and to the mid-1960's, Dan Joe announced on his weekly CJCB radio program, *MacDonald Tobacco*, the detail concerning his dance circuit. At the top of the list were the Big Pond dances, although his circuit included Sydney, Grand Mira, Eskasoni, and Bucklaw. Although I was still too young to frequent the dances regularly, certain moments are indelibly etched in my mind, especially the dances in the Big Pond parish hall.

My recollection of early dances in Big Pond take me back to performances by the stalwart Winston "Scotty" Fitzgerald. I sometimes stood at the back of the hall or sat at the foot of the stage as I was too small or too shy or both to join the square sets. I watched this artist electrify the dancers on the floor. He performed like a machine with seemingly every inch of his body moving to the music resinating from his bow and fiddle. Winston performed while firmly seated on an old wooden chair which he placed near the piano on the dimly lit stage. The scene depicted a long-standing ritual and deep-rooted tradition, moulding the image of a living legend. Winston's ability to concentrate upon some mysterious speck or mark or object at the back of the hall allowed the artist to become fully involved in his music without distraction. Winston's ability to sustain a crazed-like or fixation tactic while performing was a special gift which perhaps contributed to his powerful musicianship and to his status as a public idol.

In retrospect, I realize that I was admiring an individual who may very well have been responsible for introducing an approach to the music that was different from some of the more traditional styles. Arguably, in Winston's case, his style of presentation may have altered the more traditional format to some degree given his interest in playing the music in a wide range of settings and variations. His regular work in the recording studios producing records and programs for radio and television helped set a dynamic and invigorating pace to the music. As well, Winston's dance followers were enjoying his crisp sound and his lively tempo as they attended his frequent and gruelling dance performances, island-wide. Cape Breton native, Alfred Leblanc, in his article, "The Reel Thing," which was written primarily about young Ashley MacIsaac in the December, 1994 edition of *Equinox* states:

> Winston "Scotty" Fitzgerald, whose Cape Breton fiddle credentials are impeccable, had a lot of people in Inverness County talking when he first came on the scene from White Point, Victoria County. He added guitar (including base and drums) to the conventional fiddle-piano combination and played a lot cleaner, more precise style, with crisper grace notes and livelier and faster rhythms.[53]

D*an Joe MacInnis is joined by some excellent musicians and friends. [Left to right] Winston "Scotty" Fitzgerald; Ron Gonella, Scotland; Doug MacPhee; and Dan Joe.*

Photo by Cyril MacInnis

Dan Joe's dance music became the first music for my own square dancing enjoyment and likely the first music for many other people in Cape Breton where he played his dance circuit. The visiting fiddlers to the Big Pond dance hall were among my fondest memories of Dan Joe's dances. In addition to being at the many house sessions at our home, Dan Hughie MacEachern and Dan R. MacDonald often visited the hall over the years. In retrospect, I realize their interest was to hear Dan Joe play their latest composition of a jig or a reel in a dance setting.

The occasion of a visiting fiddler at one of Dan Joe's dances, which stands out most for me, was when the pride and joy of Judique, Inverness County, Buddy MacMaster, had been invited by Dan Joe to perform at a Big Pond dance. Buddy MacMaster is the fiddler I had come to worship as I listened to his music on CJFX Radio in Antigonish. Up until the time that Buddy played at his first Big Pond dance, I had not heard Buddy MacMaster in person.

The evening was in early fall 1961, and Buddy and Dan Joe were going to perform at the hall to help raise money for some special community project. Buddy MacMaster entered the old hall in the early evening and mingled gracefully with the large crowd. Young and robust, he made his way to the front of the hall to the stage area and quickly proceeded to prepare for the dance. He was to be the spotlight of the dance for the duration of the evening. As the dancing progressed the excitement generated. At the end of the dance, I recall Dan Joe offering Buddy a sum of money which had been agreed upon for his performance. Buddy very quietly asked Dan Joe to give the money back to the community.

After the dance, I learned that Buddy and Dan Joe were off to Sydney for a house session of music which had been arranged to keep Buddy going while he was in the area. At the time, it was rare for Buddy to give a public performance in the Sydney area, and some people wanted to make the most of his visit. An additional treat for me was when, the next day, Buddy, after the all-night session in Sydney, made his way back to my home in Big Pond for breakfast and a few tunes before returning to Judique.

A few years ago, Buddy and I had a delightful chuckle recalling that first Big Pond performance, a most memorable moment on my journey of Celtic music. Some thirty five years later, I recall my excitement at meeting Buddy and hearing his music live for the first time.

Stepdancing

At the Big Pond parish hall and at many other dance halls in Cape Breton, I came to know some wonderful Cape Breton dancers. Among the highlights were the dances in Mabou where I came to fully appreciate the dancing by the people from that community and surrounding areas who precipitated the ever so popular and legendary Mabou dancers, Inverness County dancers like Raymond and Sarahbelle Beaton, Jeanette and A.J. Beaton, Mary Janet MacDonald, Harvey MacKinnon, Harvey Beaton, Jackie MacEachern, Joe Rankin, Donald Roddie MacDonald, Benedict MacDonald, and Rodney MacDonald.

These great dancers and in some cases awesome and inspiring dancers continued the tradition and dazzled the dance floors of Inverness County with their nifty footwork as they danced to jigs, reels, and lively strathspeys. Whether they danced to the music of fiddlers like Donald Angus Beaton, Cameron Chisholm, or Buddy MacMaster, these dancers permeated the dance hall floors with high-level synergy as they advanced the unique Mabou steps which have evolved as an integral aspect of the square dance styles of Inverness County. They have nurtured the ever so popular and dynamic free-style dance, simply called stepdancing.

Over the years, as I watched these great dancers, I concluded that the art of stepdancing is alive and well in Inverness County. It is commonly understood, also, that the art of dancing has an impact on Cape Breton's cultural history and tradition, island identity, social cohesion, and economy. Furthermore, it certainly attracts outside attention to Cape Breton from people who are interested in folklore and history and from the general travelling public. Discussions about stepdance, including its origins, have some relevance in my journey. Is it an Irish dance or a Scottish dance?

From an Irish dance perspective, Colin Quigley, well-known researcher of traditional dance and music, offers some interesting information in his publication, *Close to the Floor*.[54] Quigley's publication describes, in detail, the formal structuring of steps commonly used by stepdancers. He describes the notion that the steps are presented in intricate detail and that the steps move in rhythm to select music, including jigs and reels. He describes the body posture of the dancer with the emphasis on movement from the knees down, while the upper portion of the body is more relaxed and subtle so as not to be a distraction from the footwork. The dancer's main objective is to gain equal co-ordination of both legs and feet, a basic requirement of a good Cape Breton stepdancer.

In addition, Quigley explains that the art of good stepdancing requires a great deal of individual style, some regional variety in steps, and light and near-silent footwork. Quigley learned that styles may differ in body stance, arm use, or in characteristic ways of using the feet. Quigley goes on to describe how traditional stepdancers aspire to the music played. Much of his description seems to depict two great Cape Breton stepdancers rather nicely: Harvey Beaton and Willie Fraser. Quigley's research actually outlines the link between a Newfoundland stepdance and an Irish stepdance in technique and in the terminology applied to both dance and music. In Cape Breton, similar research was conducted by Barbara LeBlanc, a native Cape Bretoner, culminating in her 1986 report on *Dance in Inverness County*. She cites examples of conversations with members of the Cape Breton Irish community who say that stepdance in Cape Breton is an Irish dance.[55]

The more familiar research about Cape Breton stepdancing illustrates documented discussions among elders in several Cape Breton communities, elders not far removed from the generation of Scots who immigrated from Scotland, and gives some credence to the notion that the stepdance originated in Scotland. A review of literature by scholars like Frank Rhodes,[56] J.P. Flett,[57] and George Emerson,[58] who have taken the time to research the origins of different traditional dance forms, also gives some legitimacy to this view. Furthermore, the historical facts disclosed in the publication, *A History of Inverness County*, convey stories and recollections about the art of stepdancing and its link with Scotland through the early dance masters like Alan MacMillan and Lauchlin MacDougall.[59]

These researchers exhibit a preoccupation with the idea that the stepdance, as it is known in Cape Breton, has its origins in the Highlands of Scotland, like the Gaelic language and the Scottish violin music of Cape Breton. Therefore, it should not come as any surprise that dance enthusiasts also want to be part of this linkage with the Old Country despite the fact that some of the traditional qualities of the Cape Breton music, song, and dance are no longer found in Scotland today.

Furthermore, efforts are ongoing to help rekindle the Scots' lost dance as Cape Breton stepdancers make visits to Scotland to teach, including Harvey Beaton and Mary Janet MacDonald. In 1996, one of Cape Breton's most celebrated and gifted stepdance bards, Willie Fraser of Deepdale, Inverness County, was invited by Hamish Moore of Scotland to visit South Uist to offer workshops on the Cape Breton form of stepdance. As reported in a July edition of the *Inverness Oran*, Willie Fraser attended the workshops in the company of, among others, fiddlers Joe Peter MacLean and Reverend Angus Morris. Willie, whose reputation in Cape Breton is impeccable as a Gaelic singer and storyteller as well as a stepdancer, may discuss the origins of the dance, but apart from whatever his conclusion may be on that issue, he certainly knows what Cape Breton stepdancing is and describes it, in part:

> There is one style of stepdancing, lift the feet as little as possible. There are no quivers and no tap-dancing. If the feet are high, then you are going to lose a note, and those notes come awfully fast.[60]

In addition to his father, Willie learned some steps from Mossie MacKinnon of Cape North who he described as a very, very good stepdancer. When one considers the presence of the Irish in the Cape North community in the 1800's and in the early 1900's, this in itself might have interesting implications for the possible links between Cape Breton stepdance and the Irish stepdance.[61]

My personal journey in the art of stepdancing was initially confined to those moments at Jessie and John P. MacNeil's in Iona and at Kate MacDougall's in Ben Eoin, which I mentioned earlier with reference to Dan Joe's recording of the "Devil In the Kitchen." It is never my intention while participating at the various square dances in Inverness County to even try to match the dancing intricates of the Mabou gang, but I always enjoy trying. In a rather quiet and humorous manner, my trying efforts seem fine with the dancing masters provided I continue to know my place among the past and present bards of this great Cape Breton tradition. For me personally, my participation in the dance tradition reaches a pinnacle in the community of Glencoe, especially throughout the 1970's and the 1980's.

> The star performer at Glencoe is Buddy MacMaster, well known violinist from Judique. His music makes you want to dance — in fact his music is what dancing is all about.
>
> This seemingly ageless musician wraps his arms around the violin and cradles the instrument for the evening. With his heart and soul, he plays gracefully as his bow swings in an almost effortless fashion. In harmony with the dancers, he pours forth a rhythmic sound that keeps the feet moving all evening and beyond midnight.
>
> The sets form on a continuous basis: first figures, second figures and ah, the highlight, the third figures. The footwork or "free-style steps" among all the participants move in various formation and invariably depict styles representative of particular communities: the Judique steps, the Mabou steps and so on.[62]

The Visits: Far and Near

Recalling that visit to the Christmas store one December evening when I reviewed the liner notes on the LP, *Celtic Music of Cape Breton — Volume 1*, Dan Joe's personal attitude towards Christmas loomed. As I left the crowded store and continued on my way to complete my shopping, I remembered the enthusiasm Dan Joe always felt for the holiday season. For Dan Joe, this enthusiasm had little to do with the giving and/or receiving of material gifts, but rather had more to do with a time that always provided additional opportunities for the special music sessions which made the hoopla of the holiday season worthwhile!

The Boxing Day tradition was always a session at Doug MacPhee's in New Waterford. Many of the fine fiddlers of the day gathered for the lengthy and sometimes gruelling, yet delightful, evening of music. In my younger years, I was not permitted to make the long journey to New Waterford on the sometimes hazardous winter highways; the descriptions the next day about the session were always a delight to hear, however! Also, the Boxing Day visit to New Waterford would likely lead to yet an additional session to be held within the next couple of days, and it would likely be that the subsequent session would be arranged for our house and that would make my Christmas as well!

Dan Joe's musical travel took him throughout many Cape Breton communities and beyond. A fitting description for Dan Joe might well be the wandering Cape Breton fiddler. He often visited communities like Grand Mira, Membertou, Loch Lomond, East Bay, Eskasoni, Baddeck, Broad Cove, St. Ann's, Iona, and Glendale. In 1965, while enjoying a busy playing schedule in Cape Breton at concerts, dances, and numerous house sessions, Dan Joe received, what he considered to be, a special invitation to perform in the Codroy Valley in Newfoundland. As he was not aware of the historical link between the people of the Codroy Valley, Newfoundland and the people of Inverness County, Cape Breton, he was simply not prepared for the response he received while performing at the Chignic Lodge that weekend in June.

I recall the personal satisfaction he said he felt from the visit to Newfoundland. He described the oldtimers as having tears in their eyes as he played the slow airs. He described their knowledge of the music and their awareness of his success with his recordings and, in particular, of the weekly program on which he performed live over CJCB Radio, Sydney. The program was received in Newfoundland and was popular in the Codroy.

Dan Joe also took personal delight in the manner in which the residents of Codroy Valley had followed his successful first-place effort in a popularity contest in the early 1960's conducted on CJCB television, Sydney. The idea of having the fiddlers compete was banished from the Cape Breton fiddlers' tradition by the early 1950's. To have their music judged and scored was not acceptable to the local fiddlers, but to have a popularity contest seemed like a good compromise; Dan Joe and many other popular Cape Breton fiddlers of the day participated.

The knowledge and the interest of the Codroy Valley settlers in the Gaelic and Celtic music tradition are justified. Historian A.A. Johnston explains this to some extent:

In, or before, the year 1844, many Scottish and Irish families began to migrate from Cape Breton to the west coast of Newfoundland, attracted by reports of the soil there and the ease with which grants of land could be obtained. In Cape Breton, suitable and available land had now become scarce, and so, by the late 1840's many of the people settled in the Codroy Valley bore names such as MacNeil, MacIsaac, MacLean, Murphy, Farrell, and Ryan.[63]

When one reads Margaret Bennett's *The Last Stronghold*, the close link between Cape Breton's Celtic music and the people of the Codroy Valley is clear. Bennett traces the Celtic music of the Codroy Valley as having strong links with Cape Breton and 17th and 18th-century Scotland:

> . . . a visit to the Codroy Valley would seem like stepping into another musical world. Distinctively Scottish, with the inclusion of the strathspeys (unknown elsewhere in Newfoundland) among the many reels and jigs, the choice of melody speaks volumes about the people who play so skilfully. Many of the tunes were brought over from Scotland in the mid-1800's and along with them are Gaelic airs and waltzes picked up "across in Cape Breton" or via the Sydney radio station (CJCB). Favourites include strathspeys such as "Calum Crubach" or "Tom Dey" played in a melody with such tunes as "Muileann Dudh" or "Lord MacDonald's Reel." [64]

Bennett lived in Newfoundland while doing her research but was born in Scotland where she grew up in the Isles of Skye and Lewis among Gaelic-speaking families. Her research on the Codroy Valley focused, in particular, on the McArthur family explaining the pride and tradition of Frank McArthur's stepdancing and Allan McArthur's piping. Both of these gentlemen figured in Dan Joe's visit to Newfoundland as was reported in the 1965, July 3rd edition of Newfoundland's *The Western Star*.

> Dan Joe MacInnis, one of Cape Breton's prominent fiddlers and recorders, with his accompanist Mrs. Margaret MacPhee were performers at the Chignic Lodge Sunday afternoon when A.L. Gillis the proprietor, threw the building open to the public. People ranging from babes in arms to ages of 90 came to enjoy the afternoon of old-time fiddling.

As Dan Joe swung into his quick tempo, Codroy Valley's popular step-dancer, Frank McArthur, took to the floor. He was quickly followed by others . . . White-haired Allan McArthur aged 82, put the final touch on the whole thing as he played his pipes to the very appreciative audience.[65]

That passion for the Celtic music was still present among the people when I visited the Codroy Valley in March 1975, as a member of the Cape Breton folk group, the Sons of Skye.

In 1973, Dan Joe visited the community of South Uist, Scotland, from whence the MacInnis' family had migrated (according to Dan Joe who acquired the information from Johnny Hughie MacInnes — spelled with an "es") in 1842 to settle in Woodbine, Cape Breton County. Dan Joe made the journey over to the Old Country with friends of the Cape Breton Gaelic Society, which organized the tour. He was accompanied by his good friend, Paddy LeBlanc. Reverend John Hugh MacEachern, who was on the tour, noted in his journal some of the detail about that tour of October 3-18, 1973. A highlight of the visits described was the visit to Stornoway on October 14.

A bus tour was arranged for the afternoon and many took advantage of this opportunity. On Monday evening a Civic Reception with the Mayor or Provost and a Cabinet Minister, and many others received our group. All our ladies were in evening gowns and our men were in their best (attire). Present were outstanding talent and we were told in advance not to have dinner.

Trays of treats of all kinds awaited our group and a delicious dinner was served. A presentation of the Nova Scotia flag to the Provost was made by Donald MacEachern (Chief of the Cape Breton Gaelic Society) assisted by Malcolm Campbell.

(later) . . . arriving at different places of interest the Cape Breton group, due to advance publicity, engaged adulation perhaps never experienced by any other (visiting) groups. The days together created a spirit of great friendship among the ninety-six. Everyone shared in some way for the good of all concerned. . .the violin music by Dan Joe MacInnis and Paddy LeBlanc (Gili Ban) prompted a dance . . . John Campbell, in a pensive mood, meditating all artistry for the *Highlander* (A newspaper published weekly in Sydney) had travelled many miles to talk with relatives of two hundred years separation . . . John Alex MacPherson renewing old

acquaintances made with the BBC six years ago (1967) . . . Helen
Howatt took great care that everyone kept talking (in) Gaelic . . .
(and) Cyril MacInnis kept a close eye on all proceedings.[66]

Besides Dan Joe, Paddy LeBlanc, and Reverend MacEachern, the tour
included Dan Joe's mother, my grandmother, Mary "Danny Peter" MacInnis,
Sydney; and her friends Tic and Emily Butler, Sydney; Josie MacNeil, Big
Pond; Archie Neil Chisholm, Margaree; Sister Florence MacLellan, Big
Pond/Sydney; Archie Rankin, Mabou; and more. This was an important
event in bridging the Gaels in the two Celtic regions.

John Campbell of Sydney, who was also part of the tour, recalls the performance Dan Joe and Paddy LeBlanc gave with the Strathspey and Reel
Society in Glasgow, one of the highlights of the tour for Dan Joe. The program was aired by BBC Radio, Scotland as well. Campbell went on to explain
that Dan Joe also performed with Anne Lorne Gillis, one of Scotland's traditional Gaelic singers. Each was delighted with the other's repertoire, Anne
Lorne for her lyrics of the many Gaelic airs and Dan Joe for the many melodies
he was able to render on the fiddle. Perhaps the entire occasion was a magic
moment for the people of the two Celtic regions separated by miles of water
and generations of time but closely knit in music and song.

The Legacy in a Tune

Personally, I feel that Dan Joe, like many of his contemporaries singled out
in the "Friends and Legends" segment, made a significant contribution to the
Cape Breton fiddling tradition through his travels, his recordings, his personal appearances on radio and t.v., and his performances at concerts, dances,
and frequent house sessions. I experienced a bit of this legacy when I visited
the 1996 Annual Highland Village Day concert in Iona, five years after Dan
Joe's death.

The stage on the hill overlooking the beauty and splendour of the Bras
d'Or Lakes gave way from time to time to the artists emerging from the centre stage. Most noticeable on that warm and sunny August day was the list of
young performers — fiddlers, pipers, and dancers — who were able to delight an audience for hours as the day matured into an evening dusk: young
Glen Graham of Judique who played with such poise reminded me of his
uncle, Kinnon Beaton, a well-known Mabou fiddler and composer; Rodney
MacDonald of Mabou, and also Kinnon's nephew, danced the intricate steps
in the Scotch Four like the outstanding dancers of an earlier generation

Harvey MacKinnon and Willie Fraser; and Pat Chafe, the fine pianist and composer from Glace Bay and daughter of legendary Winnie Chafe.

Clearly, the music, the dance, the zest, and the passion to perform, like their mentors, was ingrained and continued among a younger crowd eager to maintain the tradition and establish new traditions. Whatever their mission, these young men and women were having fun and enjoying the day. Would these young artists, however, who are now carrying the torch for Celtic music and dance wonder about its link with the past?

At one point, while somewhat reflecting on the question, I was suddenly enchanted by a performer I had not heard before. Kyle Gillis from Scotsville, Inverness County. I assumed his roots were linked with one of the finest old time fiddlers from Inverness County, Angus Allan Gillis who, with Dan J.Campbell, recorded the "Old Time Wedding Reels" melody, among others, in 1935.[67] (The arrangement for those traditional reels is played to this day like the rendition of other tunes by other great fiddlers. In Cape Breton, the classic renditions are often associated with select fiddlers who continue to pass the test of time, like Mary MacDonald's rendition of "Johnny Cope;" Joe MacLean's rendition of "Donald MacLean's Farewell to Oban;" Bill Lamey's and Joe MacLean's great recording of "Dusty Meadow;" and Little Jack MacDonald's "Star of Robbie Burns." In more recent times, Winnie Chafe's 1980 recording of Scott Skinner's "The Falling Chief" and "Silverwells" and Carl MacKenzie's 1996 recording of "Captain Carswell" are destined to remain as classics. These great tunes which have been played so well by these fiddlers will continue to be an integral aspect of the Celtic music tradition. The fiddlers who are noted for their performance of these selections will always enjoy a special place among the young and aspiring fiddlers of Cape Breton Island.)

Back to young Kyle Gillis and his opening tune, though! Carefully and in mission-like fashion, Kyle ventured into a beautiful slow air despite the likely temptation to open with spirited strathspeys and reels to please the general audience who had gathered in Iona that day and who were encouraging the young performers to "drive 'er." As Kyle finished his selection, which ended with a group of those spirited reels, I made my way down the steep hill to meet him. Knowing the concert staff and organizers very well, including Vince MacLean of Lower Washabuck and Bruce MacNeil of Iona, I was certain I could make my way backstage to get a hot cup of tea and to meet Kyle.

I introduced myself to Kyle Gillis and explained that I enjoyed his rendition of his opening slow air, "Nach truagh mo chas." Kyle explained that he had heard the tune played by Dan Joe MacInnis several years earlier and that he liked it so much he had to learn it himself. He further explained that he wanted to play the tune exactly as Dan Joe played it. This was not unlike what most young fiddlers do when playing the "Old Time Wedding Reels" or "Johnny Cope" or "Donald MacLean's Farewell to Oban" or "Dusty Meadow" — to render them as they were introduced by an earlier generation of fiddlers.

As recent as this year, 1997, one of Cape Breton's young and talented guitarists, Gordie Sampson of Big Pond, contacted me to see if I had a particular recording of Dan Joe's music. Gordie wanted to record the lovely slow air "Caledonia's Wails for Neil Gow," which Dan Joe recorded in 1964. Gordie's intent is to re-record a small bit of Dan Joe's recording performance and to integrate the performance with Gordie's own rendition of the same tune. If Gordie is able to produce this bit of technological magic, it will likely be perceived as a significant tribute by Gordie to Dan Joe's memory.

It is perhaps difficult for musicians to realize how they may impact a young, determined, and aspiring artist still learning the tricks of the trade. But on that day in Iona, I was satisfied that Dan Joe's music had reached the heart of young Kyle for certain. Kyle played the pastoral air, "Nach Truagh Mo Chas," found in the *Fraser Collection*, just the way Dan Joe played it the first time I heard the tune at my home on December 31, 1987. Although Gordie's recording is not available to me at this time, I rather suspect that Dan Joe's interpretation of "Caledonia's Wails for Neil Gow" will emerge in some aspect of Gordie's performance.

Often, some of the more tasteful music played by Dan Joe were those melodies which rendered very personal sentiments he may have felt for certain individuals who were important to his music and to his personal life. His rendition of the old stand-by, "Hector the Hero," was often requested by the Late Father Stanley MacDonald, the former parish priest at Big Pond. Despite Father Stanley's sturdy and ardent Inverness roots, I recall Dan Joe appeared to be one of Father Stanley's favourite fiddlers. In 1963, Dan Joe recorded the beautiful tune, "Bishop MacDonald," in memory the late Father Michael MacCormick, former parish priest at East Bay. On the *Celtic Music of Cape Breton — Volume 1* LP, he recorded "Lord Lovat's Lament" for his good friend, Father John Angus Rankin of the Glendale Fiddlers' fame.

Like some other Cape Breton fiddlers, Dan Joe felt a special relationship with many of the local clergy, especially the Catholic clergy. A.A. Johnston, wrote in his *History of the Catholic Church in Eastern Nova Scotia* about the efforts of the early Highland pioneers to maintain their faith and their determination to keep in contact with the church and with their priests despite the hardships in the new land. A line in A.A. Johnston's description of those efforts might certainly explain that bond between Dan Joe and the clergy to whom he felt close:

The history of the Celtic people, both Irish and Scottish, has shown that their faith remained strong after the loss of their mother tongue, but not after they had been separated for long periods from their priests.[68]

This strong sense of special bonding between clergy and the Cape Breton fiddlers was demonstrated for me most profoundly at the funeral of the late Donald Angus Beaton of Mabou, the renowned Cape Breton traditional fiddler and composer.

The parish priest in Mabou at the time was Reverend Francis Cameron — himself a fine fiddler with Mabou roots. He gave a moving eulogy, and his words gave a special significance to Donald Angus' own beautiful composition "Memories of Reverend Michael Rankin." Donald Angus recorded the tune on his first commercial recording, *The Beatons of Mabou* in 1977. The tune was, without doubt, one of Dan Joe's favourites, and he often played the composition and rendered full marks to Donald Angus for a fine musical piece.

Recently, Reverend Francis Cameron again paid tribute to other fellow Cape Breton fiddlers. On November 11, 1996, he gave the eulogy at the funeral of the great composer, Dan Hughie MacEachern, one of the legends of Celtic music in Cape Breton. On December 21, 1996, Reverend Cameron spoke at the funeral service for Johnny MacPhee in St. Peters. Johnny, like Dan Hughie, was a close friend of the MacInnis family. I was particularly moved by Father Francis' words about Johnny during the eulogy.

Reverend Cameron said that Johnny MacPhee had lived a full life and now, at the age of 92, he would be laid to his final resting place. He also explained that Johnny was not an active fiddler in recent years. He was not an active participant in, for example, the Cape Breton Fiddlers' Association, and many of his close fiddling friends were now deceased as well. Reverend Cameron pointed out in his eulogy that Johnny had maintained a busy dance circuit in Richmond County during his youthful days and that he was always ready to play a tune for his own enjoyment as well as for the enjoyment of others. During the service, I took special note of a fiddle which lay in an open case, which Reverend Cameron had placed at the foot of the altar. It would be one way to symbolize Johnny's musical interest to the congregation. In the absence of other fiddlers at the service, Reverend Cameron took it upon himself to offer a most stirring and compassionate gift. Just moments before the end of the service, he slowly bowed at the foot of the altar, retrieved the fiddle from the case, and then proceeded to play a beautiful "Gaelic Lament." The moment was a quality tribute to all fiddlers but especially, on that particular occasion to Johnny's quiet, humble, and modest life in music.

For Dan Joe, the music of so many of the great Cape Breton fiddlers, Mike MacLean, Winston Fitzgerald, Dan R. MacDonald, Dan Hughie MacEachern, Paddy LeBlanc, Buddy MacMaster, Carl MacKenzie, Winnie Chafe, Donald Angus Beaton, and Duncan MacQuarrie, among many others, from various communities throughout Cape Breton was clearly an inspiration for him. Although, in my adult life, the fiddler whose company he enjoyed most when learning new tunes, recalling old tunes, and simply discussing the music and the composers was his very good friend, Sandy MacInnis, one of the finest fiddlers in Cape Breton who continues to perform at local dances and concerts. In 1975, Sandy composed a jig for Dan Joe as a tribute to their long-time friendship and mutual respect.

Dan Joe MacInnis [left] poses for a photo with his good friend, Sandy MacInnis [right].

Dan Joe MacInnis was born in Sydney in 1922. He died at the Victoria General Hospital in Halifax on August 27, 1991, after a lengthy illness. The final visiting priest to see him the day of his death was my friend Reverend Joseph MacLean, the son of the late Cape Breton fiddler, Joe MacLean. Reverend MacLean and I had not crossed paths since his final visit with Dan Joe until I attended his father's funeral in Sydney in August, 1996. In the eulogy for his father, Reverend Joe reminded the congregation that the legendary trio of Joe MacLean, his father; Bill Lamey, who died in May, 1991; and Dan Joe MacInnis were now reunited. The three fiddlers had shared in so many fine music sessions and exchanged the great traditional tunes of Scotland, Ireland, and Cape Breton.

Notes

1. George Riddell, "Scott Skinner: A Friend's Estimate" (1927), in James Scott Skinner, *My Life and Adventures* (City of Aberdeen in association with Wallace Music, Scotland 1994), (reprinted from *Aberdeen Journal*, 27:4), p. 121.
2. *Celtic Music of Cape Breton — Volume 1*, UCCB Press 1007, 1984.
3. Throughout the early 1970's, more and more people wanted to learn to play the fiddle, Cape Breton style. UCCB, through the Department of Continuing Education, under the Director of Continuing Education, the late Reverend C.W. MacDonald, organized a series of classes and workshops in traditional music. In addition to fiddle instruction, classes were offered in conversational Gaelic, in Gaelic singing, and in Cape Breton style stepdancing.
4. Elizabeth A. Doherty, "The Paradox of the Periphery: Evolution of the Cape Breton Fiddle Tradition 1928-1995," unpublished doctoral dissertation, University of Limerick, Ireland, 1996, p. 55.
5. Mary Anne Ducharme, "Creignish Fiddlers (Interview with Frank MacInnis) in *Celebrate Our Music 1997-98* by Inverness County Recreation and Continuing Education, 18:1, January/February, 1997.
6. John Gibson, "John MacDougall," Article #16, *Scotia Sun*, 1972-73.
7. Ibid.
8. Elizabeth A. Doherty, 1996, p. 100.
9. Virginia Garrison, "Traditional and Non-traditional Teaching and Learning Practices in Folk Music: An Ethnographic Field Study of Cape Breton Fiddling," unpublished doctoral dissertation, University of Wisconsin, Madison, US, 1985.
10. Kate Dunlay & D. L. Reich, *Traditional Celtic Fiddle Music of Cape Breton* (Alstead, NH: Fiddlecase Books, 1986).
11. Kate Dunlay & David Greenberg, *Traditional Celtic Violin Music of Cape Breton*, (Toronto: DunGreen Music, 1996).
12. Elizabeth A. Doherty, *The Music of Cape Breton — An Irish Perspective* (University College, Cork, Ireland: The Traditional Music Archive/The Irish Traditional Music Society, 1994).
13. Mary L. Campbell, "Foreign Element Infringing and Infecting Our Music," letter to the editor, *The Inverness Oran*, July 24, 1996, p. 9.
14. Frances MacEachern, "A Tribute to Dan Joe MacInnis: A Lifetime of Scottish Music," *The Clansman*, Oct./Nov. 1991, p. 9.
15. Ibid.
16. Ibid.
17. Ibid.

18. John Campbell, "Fiddle Festival at Gaelic College Celebrates Our Musical Heritage," *Cape Breton Post*, Aug. 18, 1990, p. 15.

19. John Gibson, "Dan Hughie MacEachern," Article # 16, *Scotia Sun*, 1972-73.

20. Virginia Garrison, 1985, p. 185-186.

21. Kate Dunlay & David Greenberg, 1996, p. 55.

22. Ibid.

23. The tune, "Devil in the Kitchen," was popularized by Ashley MacIsaac on his 1995 CD recording, *Hi How Are You*, and was described by the *Chronicle-Herald's* music critic, Tim Arsenault, as "a straight-ahead Celtic rocker" Arsenault suggested that one should not drive a car while listening to Ashley's version of the tune because the driver may be inclined to apply too much pressure to the gas peddle while keeping beat to the music." [What do you think, Ashley?]

24. James Hunter, *The Fiddle Music of Scotland* (Edinburgh, Scotland: T.A. Constable Ltd., 1979), p. XX1V.

25. Bruce Headlam, "The Devil Went Down to Cape Breton," *Saturday Night*, Sept., 1995, p. 56.

26. See John Shaw's liner notes, *The Music of Cape Breton — Volume 1*, recorded in 1978, Topic 12TS353.

27. Elizabeth A. Doherty, 1994, p. 8.

28. Kenneth MacKinnon, *The Lion's Tongue* (Inverness, Scotland: Club Leabhar, 1974), p. 27.

29. George S. Pryde, *Scotland from 1603 to the Present Day — A New History of Scotland. Vol. 11* (Edinburgh, Scotland: Thomas Nelson and Sons Ltd., 1962), p. 105.

30. Sandy MacIntyre, "Fiddling Cape Breton Style," *Fiddler Magazine*, 3:2, California, Summer, 1996.

31. Kenneth MacKinnon, "Two Peoples or One? The Shared Culture of Cape Breton and the Western Isles," paper presented at the 7th Atlantic Canada Studies Conference, Edinburgh, Scotland, May 5-7, 1988.

32. See Note #26.

33. Kate Dunlay and David Greenberg, 1996, p.3.

34. Elizabeth A. Doherty, 1996, p.6.

35. Alexander MacDonald, "Cape Breton Fiddle Music: Is It Unique? Yes! What Makes It So?" *The Inverness Oran*, July 17, 1996.

36. Ibid.

37. Ibid.

38. Jacqueline A. Dunn, "The Sound of Gaelic is in the Fiddler's Music," senior essay, St. Francis Xavier University, Antigonish, Nova Scotia, 1991.

39. Ibid.

40. Ibid., p. 31.

41. Liner Notes in a recording of Various Artists. (1955). *Songs of Cape Breton Island*. Folkways Records and Service Corporation P450.

42. Jacqueline Dunn, 1991, p. 42.

43. Ibid., p. 45.

44. "MacDonald's Lament . . . Or, Piping and the Competition Straitjacket" [interview with Piper Alan MacDonald], *West Highland Free Press* Scotland, Aug. 22, 1986.

45. David Greeberg, written document called *Dialogue with David Greenberg*, April, 1989.

46. Carl MacKenzie. (1981). *. . . and his Sound is Cape Breton*. World Records WRC11548.

47. John Donald Cameron, compiler and editor, *The Trip to Windsor Collection, The Music of Dan R. MacDonald, Volume 2* (Port Hawkesbury, Nova Scotia: Cameron Music Sales, 1994), p. 1.

48. See recording, *No Boundaries* by Natalie MacMaster, WEA, 1996.

49. Norman MacDonald, "Leading fiddler dies at 94," *Oban Times*, Scotland, March 24, 1979.

50. See liner notes, *Cape Breton Piano — Volume 2* by Doug MacPhee, DMP 6-27, 1979.

51. Mike MacLean visited the Gaelic College in Skye, Scotland in the winter of 1980 to teach fiddling.

52. John William MacInnis, "The Great Outdoors," a weekly article published in the *Cape Breton Post*, June, 1996.

53. Alfred Leblanc, "The Reel Thing," *Equinox*, December 9, 1994, p. 64.

54. Colin Quigley, "Close to the Floor: Folk Dance in Newfoundland," St. John's, NF: Memorial University, 1985.

55. Barbara LeBlanc & L. Sadousky, "Inverness County Dance Project," unpublished report to the Museum of Man, Ottawa, 1986.

56. Frank Rhodes, "Dancing in Cape Breton Island, Nova Scotia," in J.P. Flett and T.M. Flett, editors, *Traditional Dancing in Scotland* (London: Routledge and Kegan Paul, 1964), pp. 267-285.

57. J. Flett & T. Flett, *Traditional Dancing in Scotland* (London: Routledge and Kegan Paul, 1964).

58. George S. Emmerson, *Rantin' Pipe and Tremblin' String: A History of Scottish Dance Music* (Montreal: McGill-Queen's University Press, 1971).

59. John Lorne MacDougall, *History of Inverness County, Nova Scotia* (Belleville, Ontario: Mike Publication, 1972).

60. Frank Macdonald, "Willie Francis Fraser Brings Scotland Close to the Floor," *The Inverness Oran*, July 24, 1996, p. 14.

61. A.A. MacKenzie, *The Irish in Cape Breton* (Antigonish: Formac Publishing Company Limited, 1979).

62. Sheldon MacInnes, "Cape Breton Stepdance: An Irish or Scottish Tradition?" paper presented at the International Symposium on Irish Culture, Louisbourg, Cape Breton, N.S., June 12, 1993.

63. Reverend A.A. Johnston, *A History of the Catholic Church in Eastern Nova Scotia* (Antigonish: St. Francis Xavier University Press, 1960), volume 2, p. 247.

64. Margaret Bennett, *The Last Stronghold: Scottish Gaelic Traditions in Newfoundland* (St. John's, NF: Breakwater Books, 1989), p. 76.

65. Mary MacIsaac, "Valley Gives Warm Welcome to Scots Pipers, Fiddlers," *The Western Star*, Newfoundland, July 3, 1965.

66. Reverend John Hugh MacEachern, Journal of Scotland tour, October 3-18, 1973.

67. John Gibson, "Angus Allan Gillis," Article #11, *Scotia Sun*, 1972-1973.

68. Reverend A.A. Johnston, *A History of the Catholic Church in Eastern Nova Scotia* (Antigonish: St. Francis Xavier University Press, 1972), volume 1, p. 140.

CHAPTER FOUR

The Sons of Skye

The Genesis

One of the highlights of my journey in Celtic music was my association with the Sons of Skye. Between 1974 and 1984, the group travelled extensively and shared some memorable moments as friends, musicians, and entertainers in Cape Breton, in Atlantic Canada, and, eventually, in the grand tour of Scotland.

The idea of forming the Sons of Skye was the result of a number of factors. The seed was likely planted when Cliff Morais, a native Big Ponder with roots in a French Acadian community in the province of New Brunswick, and I were classmates at St. Francis Xavier University in Antigonish in the late 1960's. Given the strong interest in music which Cliff and I had acquired from our Acadian/Celtic heritage, it was inevitable that at some point while attending university, we would be involved in some type of performances. As well, folk music was the in-thing in Canada and in the United States at the time, and students, clad in their folkish and earthy attire, were generally interested in making down-home music or at least listening to it.

On many occasions, Cliff and I gathered in one of the small rooms on campus, usually on a weekend, and assembled several instruments between us; we then settled for an evening of fun with music. Needless to say, those students who were on campus and who were prepared to listen to the music were entertained with a repertoire of melodies played on guitars, or as John Allan Cameron's uncle would say car-tars, of different shapes and sizes. We played music on the more popular instruments of Cape Breton, as well, Cliff on the fiddle and I on my bagpipes. These two instruments, combined with the fun we had making music with them in various locations over several years were most likely responsible for the beginnings of the Sons of Skye.

My pipes, which once belonged to Neil R. MacIsaac, were not fancy. The ivories were a faded, dull yellow color. As a matter of fact, the big drone and the Henderson chanter showed a series of small cracks which often made the playing of these pipes, even in the best of conditions, somewhat strained. They had seen better days and rendered sweeter music in the hands of Neil R., a very gifted piper.

One very cold evening during one of the university's winter carnival celebrations, Cliff and I were providing one of our weekly informal ceilidh recitals. As the evening became early morning, the small group of students (mostly Capers, Ron MacDonald, Steve MacDonald and Angus MacNeil of the East Bay/Iona gang) who had gathered for the ceilidh suggested that we make our way over to Lane Hall, which was located on the other side of campus. The noble objective was to serenade the students in that residence. In those days, the residences at St. F.X. were not co-ed; so some students thought that our music might allow for some honest fun at Lane Hall! Rather than play the part of party-poopers, Cliff and I agreed to meander along. As we were giving a Mockler recital on the occasion, we left Mockler Hall and began a slow march across campus. The march was destined to be a bit awkward because Cliff and I decided we would play some music along the way — or so we thought. Assuming that the authorities, a commissionaire or, worse still, a dean (as some deans lived on campus in those days) might attempt to intervene, we marched with some trepidation. The thick layers of slippery ice and snow were also cause for caution, given the circumstances. However, there were only a few moments of music in the swirling wild winds of the great outdoors on that particularly cold early morning. As we began our march only a few yards outside of Mockler residence, Cliff strumming away on his car-tar while wearing a pair of open-fingered gloves which he had crafted himself in the room before embarking on our journey and I attempting to bellow the old standby "Bundle and Go," a simple 6/8 march from the *Glenallan Collection,* my pipes instantly began to freeze. Suddenly, there was absolutely no sound from the pipes. The yellow drones and the tattered tassels became a resting place upon which the now heavily falling snow settled. The cracks in the big drone and in the chanter were now beginning to fill with ice particles.

The cold weather on that February morning reminded me of the words in the well-known old country song which read, in part, "cool were the winds that swept Glencoe"[1] depicting the tragic historical Glencoe epic of hospitality turned foul — and that's where our excursion was headed. A description of the epic's outdoor elements are rekindled in John Prebble's popular description of the morning of that Glencoe massacre when he wrote: "What remained of daylight was flat, the unnerving pallor that precedes a storm . . .

And by five o'clock the snowstorm was now a blizzard, a swirling white dark-ness,"[2] such was the scene that morning as we ventured across campus in our rather hospitable mood while the winds blew across the mainland and throughout the wild moors of Antigonish, likely heading for the highlands of Cape Breton. Unlike the aggressors at Glencoe, though, the howling winds and falling snow forced this young Caper (me) to retreat to the comfort of my room in the Tompkins Hall residence for the duration of the night. I do not recall whether Cliff continued his journey or if he, too, returned to his room, a matter of some concern because Cliff and I shared the same room. This occasion was certainly reflective of some of the carefree moments in my journey with music while I was a student at St. F.X. University.

When I began piping at the young age of ten, it was with the intent that I would become a serious piper. In fact, Dan Joe expected that I would learn the music with the objective that I play correctly and with feeling. For some people who are close to the music tradition, however, these characteristics were incongruent. What I recall most in my formative years in learning to play were the wonderful pipers I came to hear as I was developing my interest in the pipes. During the time when I had Dan Joe's support to learn the art of piping, I came to know the music of Sandy Boyd, in particular.

Sandy was born in Scotland and when he settled in Cape Breton, he was already a master piper. I came to know him while I was still in elementary school. At the time, Sandy was making his way around Cape Breton and spending the winters wherever he might find a student or a band to instruct. During one of those winter stopovers at our home, my interest to learn the pipes emerged. I learned that in all likelihood, Sandy Boyd instructed hun-dreds of young pipers in his day. He was a remarkable teacher and anyone who was committed to learning from Sandy was sure to get the best instruc-tion (in the formal sense) available. I came to dearly admire Sandy as did so many others who were associated with his music and his generosity. I main-tained a deep respect for his efforts to teach and for his music up until his death. To my ear, though, his music was different than the blend of piping I came to know more intimately, even before I had developed an interest in learning to play the pipes.

Sandy's music was so unlike the music of some other great oldtimers I knew in Cape Breton, pipers who had learned to play among local Cape Breton fiddlers and dancers, both of whom obviously influenced the music of these pipers in a way that was different than the Boyd School or the Shamus MacNeil School of piping. I am not suggesting that one style was superior to the other but rather that the two were just different. These great Cape Breton pipers, however, were peculiar and generally isolated from the mainstream piping, like bands and competitions. At the time, I did not imagine that these pipers of the old stock were being cast aside by some of the more modern-style pipers.

The oldtimers usually wore bib overalls, salt and pepper caps, and burly work boots. Their hands were rough, likely from cutting lumber or working in the mines and their huge fingers were often scarred from cuts and scrapes. Unless they were carrying a set of pipes, one would not expect them to be the super musicians they were. I became familiar with their music in homes and in local halls in the small, rural communities, but by the early 1960's, these seasoned pipers were already confining their performances to select occasions and audiences.

I recall attending a concert in Grand Mira in the early 1960's and hearing the music of Joe Hughie MacIntyre for the first time. To the extent that it was possible, I followed his music carefully. Dan Joe enjoyed Joe Hughie's music and encouraged him to appear in the early Big Pond Concerts. He was then already an elderly man, but he rendered a flavour that was a form of magic in itself; his music was a dance music. I also recollect the music of Peter MacKinnon of Woodbine, Joe Martin MacIsaac of Portage, and Steve MacNeil (Big Frank's son) of Big Pond. Like Joe Hughie MacIntyre, these pipers also had a distinct sound in their music and, like Joe Hughie, the drive in their strathspeys and reels were always suited to dancing. For me, they were simply fiddlers playing the pipes. Their music sounded exactly like that of the local fiddlers I heard at home since I was very young.

Peter MacKinnon and Steve MacNeil were perhaps the first pipers I've observed who sat on a chair while piping; my personal inclination to sit while piping likely developed from watching these pipers. I recall playing for Steve MacNeil on one occasion when he was visiting Big Pond from Boston, and he referred to me as a lazy piper because of my interest in sitting while playing, but when he decided to play a few tunes he, too, sat as he played. I also remember when Peter MacKinnon visited out home. He always made a rather quick entry into the kitchen, and without hesitation, he yanked the pipes from the case, sat on the nearest chair, and began to play. His two feet moved (danced) to the sound of the music, thus rendering a distinct rhythm. Just as quickly, he would then throw the pipes in the case and after a quick cup of tea, he made his way out the door and into his truck, on his way until his next visit!

The piper who gained my attention the most during my youth was Neil R. MacIsaac. Neil R. was a distant cousin of my grandmother's and like Catherine, he was full of the Gaelic. Neil R. lived in a tiny house down the road in Ben Eoin which he built himself, just above his father's house. Neil fished regularly and did some cutting in the woods to make do. He came from a musical family as his father played both the pipes and the fiddle. Neil's father, Ruairidh Shim, received a set of pipes in 1903 which Neil continued to play until he received his own new set in 1953. My mother, Christie, speaks highly of Ruairidh Shim's music as well as Neil's and recalls the many visits she made to his house in Ben Eoin.

I came to know Neil R.'s music long after he had retired from public performances in the wider community. He often encouraged me to visit him at his home, and I played my chanter for him. He was well into his late sixties then. Gradually, my chanter playing progressed to the pipes under Neil R.'s watchful eye and a sharp ear. On occasion, Neil R. gave me tunes which he wanted me to learn. He often corrected the titles of certain tunes with a pencil mark, tunes which he felt were incorrectly titled by the publisher. He also indicated on his different music books whether a tune was good or not good or bad. Neil R. frequently encouraged me to use the written music to learn the correct melody; but, just as often, he tolerated any little embellishments I incorporated in my music. Upon reflection, he was likely encouraging me to play the music in a manner that reflected my individual style first and foremost and was less concerned, initially, with correctness.

Joe Neil in his 1987 publication *Tales Until Dawn* recalls his association with Neil R. and, in particular, Neil R.'s approach to teaching the pipes.

> He had the names of the tunes and he knew so many tunes by heart. He could name hundreds of tunes and tell you in which books they could be found . . . Now when people went to Neil intending to learn to play the pipes, he would test them carefully . . . He was extremely careful about the people who were going to learn music.[3]

Among Neil R.'s prize students was Bernie Gillis of Sydney, son of Margaret and Bernie Gillis and the grandson of Frank MacNeil, Big Pond. My personal times with Neil R. were positive, supportive, and endearing experiences even with Neil's seemingly indifference about tutoring and performing. Neil R.'s instruction was usually brief during my regular visits, but when he decided to play a few tunes on the chanter or on the pipes, that's when I came to know what I enjoyed most in piping. And that sound was not heard just anywhere, although I did hear it in the music of Joe Hughie MacIntyre and Peter MacKinnon. To have Neil R. perform for me was special indeed and I felt privileged and honoured.

The occasion which will always stand out as special for me with respect to Neil R.'s recitals was when he reached into his pipe case and handed me his pipes, for the first time, to play. To this day, I recall playing the Scottish air which Dan Joe had played on many occasions, "Hector the Hero," before breaking into a quick march. My reason for choosing that particular tune was most important and I remember it well. I played "Hector the Hero" by ear as I had never seen the written music for the tune, at least not in the pipe setting, and I wanted to test myself that day to discover whether my playing by ear was up to Neil R.'s expectations. I cannot recall Neil R.'s response, but more visits and tunes followed for some time. Christie often told me about her special moments in Neil R.'s company and how she and others from the community walked for miles, all the way out to Rod S.'s and to Aunt Isabel's in the rear Glengarry, to listen to a young Neil R. play at a house session. Christie explained how his music delighted the stepdancers as well as the dancers in the square sets throughout the night.

Neil R. MacIsaac was one of Cape Breton's old-time pipers. This photo was taken in 1951.

Submitted by Margaret Gillis

Barry Shears, a noted piper formerly of Glace Bay, illustrates in his research[4] the style of piping which prevailed throughout the Cape Breton area in the 1920's, 1930's, and 1940's. He explains that there were many pipers like Neil R. and Joe Hughie and that they did represent the last of a great era in, what Shears calls, Gaelic piping.

> They retained their individual style of playing, the old tunes, and the ability to play for stepdancers. Their playing did not conform with the Army or competition style. Instead of being acknowledged and appreciated [by modern pipers] as exponents of a folk culture, their style of playing was considered inferior and viewed as an anomaly to be corrected.[5]

Several letters published in past issues of the *Clansman*, as well, offer some insight into the piping styles once prevalent in Cape Breton. The 1991 October/November issue reflects the views of John Gibson, a local authority on the piping tradition:

> . . . to ignore Gaelic traditional piping [piping by Gaelic speakers who learned by ear — like Joe Hughie MacIntyre] and to champion as traditional the modern form does an unfortunate disservice to the new world Gaidhealtachd to which we may still turn to find glimpses of music and dance long gone from the Highland Scottish scene.[6]

Gibson was responding to a feature in an earlier issue of *Clansman* concerning the efforts in Antigonish to celebrate the new Antigonish pipe band, which had been developed in the early 1990's. The band was being sponsored by the Antigonish Highland Society, which was then under the direction of Dan MacInnes. Dan was able to give an eloquent reply to Gibson using his usual sense of humour and wit. "If everything I wrote contained the kind of errors that prompted such an articulate and learned response as that provided by John Gibson I would be happy to insert more errors in my writing for the sheer pleasure of reading such an able response." MacInnes continues ". . . I was willing to entertain the notion that the ghosts of pipers from both the Gaelic and modern traditions would welcome the rebirth of piping no matter what the accent. In truth, since they are evoked as ghosts, neither John nor I can comment on their actual sentiments."[7]

In the same issue of the *Clansman*, Gibson contributed a copy of the article "Piping in Cape Breton" by piper Jim MacDonald,[8] which had appeared in an issue of the *Piping Times*. MacDonald describes the linkages between the pipers in Cape Breton and the Scottish pipers prior to World War One. That occasion provided the opportunity for the Cape Breton pipers to learn from the Scottish pipers; hence, Gibson's concerns about the modern era of piping which, he felt, contributed to the demise of Gaelic piping in Cape Breton! MacDonald wrote: "Cape Breton pipers who went overseas in the First World War returned as good pipers due to 'good training' from the Scottish pipers."[9]

I had the opportunity to hear Jim MacDonald play while he was visiting out home in the early 1960's. What I recall most about that session was not so much his style but rather his rendition of the tune, "Dark Island." It was the first time I had heard the tune, and I noticed that the melody caught the attention of Christie who had closed her eyes, as she would so often do while listening to beautiful tunes at good sessions. When "Dark Island" became popular many years later by various folk groups, I recall reminiscing with Christie about the occasion on which we had first heard the tune.

In a subsequent issue of the *Clansman* renowned piper Dr. Angus MacDonald of Glenuig, Scotland published a letter as well, he was living in Cape Breton at the time. MacDonald was responding to the communication of both MacInnis and Gibson. The point Dr. Angus emphasized was that:

> To be literate and to be technically correct does not make one a non-traditional player. Whether one reads the book or not, the most important asset to a musician is his ear for absorbing the music and no less important is technical ability and finger dexterity.[10]

The thoughts and views of these learned gentlemen; Shears, Gibson, MacInnes, and MacDonald; should be examined by individuals who may be inclined to study piping styles in Cape Breton. The current generations of Cape Breton pipers who play their music with the same drive and lift of the early Gaelic pipers include John Morrison, now residing in Ontario, and whose music was influenced by the wonderful Gaelic piper, his uncle Peter Morrison; Jamie MacInnis of Big Pond; and Paul MacNeil of Iona. The music of the latter two young pipers was influenced initially by Danny MacIntyre of Sydney, Joe Hughie's son, and later by the music of the MacDonalds of Glenuig, Scotland, especially Alan, Angus, and Iain.

Playing my pipes at the square dances in the old parish hall in Big Pond, for the "bungalow" people and for the local teenagers, in the mid 1960's, was exciting. Often perched in the same corner and likely on the same old chair on which Dan Joe once placed himself while playing for square sets, and again, with Cliff at my side strumming his guitar, the routine of performing for the public became more entrenched in me. I continued to keep in contact with the music of the island, attending open-air concerts, house sessions, and ceilidhs of different shapes and sizes.

The pleasant moments that I enjoyed in entertainment island-wide, coupled with the lure of the Big Pond Concert stage and my interest in the live performances of Scotland's Na-hoganaich as they toured Cape Breton Island in 1973,[11] provided some incentive for me to organize the Sons of Skye. Na-hoganaich's tour of Cape Breton followed their successful appearance at the National Mod in Scotland in 1972 where they won the folksinging competition and were awarded the gold medal.[12] Believing that Na-hoganaich's tour of Cape Breton would help the efforts of the Cape Breton Gaelic Society to promote and to maintain the Gaelic language of the island, the Gaelic Society organized the event for the summer of 1973. Musically, the young group presented the traditional Gaelic music of Scotland using a variety of acoustic instruments while singing beautiful Gaelic harmonies. As I listened and enjoyed the music of the group, I began to feel that their style of presentation would have some application to Cape Breton Celtic music. As a result, I felt the challenge to introduce a similar concept that would satisfy my continuing desire to both perform and promote the music.

I understood the music of Cape Breton to be largely a series of performances by primarily solo artists. Group performances were not integral to the tradition, at the time. Although, two young Cape Breton performing groups with a solid background in Celtic music within their respective families and communities were already destined to be wonderful group exponents of the music in years to come. The MacNeil Family later named the Barra MacNeils of Sydney Mines were young school students and were actively involved in local concerts and ceilidhs; the original Rankin Family of Mabou was also appearing in a variety of public performances.

As for the Sons of Skye debut, its inception actually began to take shape while I was in Halifax in the winter of 1974. While visiting Big Pond one weekend, I met my former university classmate Cliff Morais and Malcolm MacPhee and explained my interest in forming the group. That meeting with these two gentlemen led to the formation of the Sons of Skye. Blanche (Morais) Sophocleous, a native Big Pond musician and living in Ben Eoin, joined the group later. Blanche was already an established popular artist performing a busy Cape Breton circuit. Eventually, the group was introduced through the media and at different performance venues as belonging to the rural community of Big Pond in Cape Breton Island. Gaelic, English, and French, representative cultures of the Big Pond community, were reflected in the Sons of Skye's music.

Reaching the Public

Actual public appearances were limited, but two major Cape Breton programs were to be an integral aspect of the Sons of Skye's itinerary locally during the next ten years — the Big Pond Festival and the Whycocomagh Summer Festival; the latter was under the direction of Burton MacIntyre who was also a classmate at St. Francis Xavier University. Between these two annual events, the Sons of Skye's appearances were carefully planned and orchestrated. Additional regular Cape Breton venues included the Nova Scotia Highland Village (1975-1978 and 1981); the St. Ann's Mod at the Gaelic College (1979 and 1981); and the Port Hood Festival (1980 and 1981).

In the bliss of these local appearances in Cape Breton, other venues followed in other parts of Nova Scotia and Atlantic Canada, and the Sons of Skye began to give careful consideration to the potential for establishing a professional status for the group. The concern was constant; as the group became more adept at its performances, as the performance venues increased, and as the patron following increased, expectations increased.

Sons of Skye in performance at Dalhousie University, Halifax, Nova Scotia, in September 1979. [Left to right] Cliff Morais, Sheldon MacInnes, Blanche Morais Sophocleous, and Malcolm MacPhee.

Photo by Wamboldt-Waterfield

In addition to select performances in Cape Breton, outside travel became an occasional excursion for fun allowing the Sons of Skye to periodically perform before new and fresh audiences. Several concerts in Codroy Valley in 1975 (some ten years following Dan Joe's appearances with members of the famed McCarthy family in 1965); an appearance at the Musquodoboit Festival (1974) and the Joseph Howe festival (1975); the West River, Prince Edward Island, Folk Festival (1979); and the Antigonish Highland Games (1980 and 1981) were among the exciting performances for the group.

In the summer of 1982, the Sons of Skye took part in the successful Nova Scotia tourism promotion, Old Home Summer, when we were invited to tour the province.[13] The promotion was organized by the Performing Arts Sponsors Organization of Nova Scotia in co-operation with the Nova Scotia Department of Culture, Recreation, and Fitness. The tour took the Sons of Skye to different parts of Cape Breton including Ingonish and North River, and then to mainland Nova Scotia with performances in Halifax, Annapolis Royal, Hemford, and Liverpool for a series of delightful concerts over a seven-day period.

In addition to live performances, the attention by local CBC radio producers was always a special support to the Sons of Skye. CBC Sydney, via the weekly Gaelic programs *Island Echoes* and *Talent Cape Breton*, was a significant booster to local efforts to help launch the professional careers of Cape Breton Celtic artists and to expose the Cape Breton music to regional and national audiences, under the direction of the producers at the time, especially Brian Sutcliff. This effort attracted the attention of other producers in radio and television in Canada and in Scotland. CBC promoted the music of Cape Breton as something unique and special.

Among the highlights for the Sons of Skye with CBC Sydney were the New Year's Eve live ceilidhs, broadcasted for four consecutive years (1976/77 - 1980/81) across Canada from the Confederation Room in the old Isle Royal Hotel in Sydney (now the site of Sydney's Commerce Tower which accommodates, among others, the offices of Enterprise Cape Breton Corporation). The Sons of Skye performed with local fiddlers Carl MacKenzie and Winnie Chafe and pianist Doug MacPhee for the first three years of this production. After the first production, an article in the *Cape Breton Post* stated that: "Canadians from coast to coast were treated to a New Year's Eve Ceilidh that we will long remember. Live from the Isle Royal Hotel, CBC radio sang and played its way through the last moments of the old year and rang in the new. 90 minutes with entertainment was provided by Cape Breton performers . . ."[14]

A member of the local listening audience submitted a letter to the editor of the *Cape Breton Post* on January 5, 1977, which read in part:[15] "I would like to express my thanks to the CBC for the Ceilidh on New Year's Eve. Well done. And let's do it again soon." The series ended with a highly acclaimed performance in 1981.

Other engagements with the media included the April 1982 performance by the Sons of Skye at the CBC launching celebration of the new tower installation in the Mulgrave area. A special fanfare concert was organized to take place at the Strait Area Education and Recreation Centre in Port Hawkesbury, featuring the Sons of Skye. The concert was recorded for CBC and was played over regional radio at a later date.[16] In the autumn of 1978, the group made its first television appearance on the CBC regional program *Who's New*, which was produced by Ralph Waugh in Halifax. Again, in 1983, the Sons of Skye appeared on the ATV television network on the popular program *Up Home Tonight*, featuring Gordon Stoby who was a popular musician based in Halifax.[17] On that occasion, the group was accompanied by the exciting Cape Breton stepdancer Joe Rankin of Mabou, making his first television appearance.

These performing experiences contributed to the group's efforts to present in their shows, a professional presentation of Cape Breton Celtic

music, introducing a variety of acoustic instrument interpretations, folk bal-
lads, Cape Breton Gaelic vocals, as well as some stepdancing and mouth
music. The very essence of the Sons of Skye's performances, however, were
the fun, enjoyment, and pride that the group members felt about the music,
song, and dance which we believed to be reflective of the music we had come
to know at home in the kitchen and, subsequently, in the wider community
of Big Pond. It was important to the Sons of Skye to transmit the pride and
enthusiasm we felt about this music and heritage as we entertained audiences
in live concerts, pubs, or a radio or television production.

One of the most memorable moments of the Sons of Skye's performances
came in 1978, when the group was invited to take part in the first ever trans
Atlantic ceilidh produced jointly by BBC Scotland and CBC Sydney. In addition to the music of the Sons of Skye, the program introduced Gaelic songs
by Reverend Allan MacMillan and stories in the Gaelic by Joe Neil MacNeil
and Donald MacEachern who was chief of the Gaelic Society of Cape
Breton.

Several responses were published immediately following the broadcasted
ceilidh. The following was reported in the April 1979 edition of *College Canada*,
a publication dedicated to serving the entire Canadian college community:

> The live radio hookup (which included the prerecorded material
> featuring the Sons of Skye specifically for the program) was
> masterminded by Norman MacDonald, a recent acquisition to the
> faculty of the College of Cape Breton (now UCCB) where he teaches
> courses in Celtic history and Scots Gaelic. MacDonald began the
> international diplomacy involved in co-ordinating the resources of
> the BBC (in Scotland) and the CBC in Sydney last April (1978).[18]

A Scottish newspaper later reported that BBC's Highland Gaelic Department and the senior Gaelic producer Allan MacDonald, in particular,
regarded the link as an experiment and that they were highly delighted with
the response to the program. The article continues: ". . . the response to the
programme was tremendous, not just from the Gaelic listeners but also from
the many English listeners . . ."[19] Again, in the *College Canada* article, Norman MacDonald referenced the Gaelic content by Joe Neil MacNeil, Donald
MacEachern, and Reverend Allan MacMillan:

> The Scots who emigrated to Cape Breton in the 19th century and
> their descendants have in many ways shown greater devotion to the
> Gaelic language, music, and tradition, than those who have re-

mained in Scotland. Many of the oldest Celtic traditions, and much of the folklore and song, still survive in Cape Breton. This is the ultimate tribute to the devotion to their heritage.[20]

I have always recognized the responses of the Scottish audience and the support of so many BBC people from Scotland. People like Norman MacDonald and radio and television producers like Allan MacDonald and Kenny MacQuarrie provided so much for the Sons of Skye, as a kind gesture towards the group personally, but more importantly, as a sign of sincere interest in the Gaelic connections in Cape Breton overall. The Sons of Skye was only another link in the efforts to further the process and to build a sense of community between the two Celtic regions.

The enthusiasm towards the Sons of Skye by Scotland's media, conveyed later in subsequent correspondence and by community people in general, was a mark of respect to the many individuals in Cape Breton who have persevered in their efforts to maintain the Gaelic traditions through their links with Scotland. Networks between the Gaels of Cape Breton and the Gaels of Scotland were established long before the Sons of Skye were discovered by the BBC. The tireless work of so many people in the Gaelic Society of Cape Breton over the years represents the most profound link with the Old Country. The Gaelic Society's tour of Scotland's islands in 1973[21] comprised no less than ninety-six Cape Breton Gaels, who boarded an airplane in Sydney to begin their journey to the Old Country. That tour of Cape Breton Gaelic speakers, singers, and musicians is perhaps the benchmark for some of the most important links with Scotland, links which continue to this day and extend into opportunities not only for Gaelic language and culture development but also for commerce, tourism, and education.

These Cape Breton Gaels and other like-minded people who visited Scotland made possible the success enjoyed by the first transatlantic ceilidh of which the Sons of Skye were so privileged to be a part. Later, in the autumn of 1979 — following the success of the transatlantic ceilidh and the continuous bridge building already established between Cape Breton and Scotland, the Sons of Skye toured Scotland for the first time!

A Tour of Scotland

The 1979 tour of Scotland by the Sons of Skye gradually espoused a musical mission and a pilgrimage to the Motherland, all rolled into one. The Sons of Skye's tour had two main foci: to participate in the competition at the National Gaelic Mod, and to participate in a series of ceilidhs and concerts in selected islands and mainland locales throughout Scotland, accompanied by musicians Buddy MacMaster, Carl MacKenzie, Doug MacPhee, and Father Allan MacMillan. Completing the fifteen-person tour group were several family members and 71-year old Joe Neil MacNeil of Big Pond, visiting Scotland for the first time.

Active preparation for the tour commenced in early February, 1979. Approaches for funding assistance were made to several public and private bodies in Cape Breton. The arrangements for travel, accommodation, and playing engagements in Scotland were undertaken with the assistance of Scottish native, Norman MacDonald. Official application was made for participation in the National Mod, and traditional Cape Breton Gaelic songs were selected as the Sons of Skye's competition pieces: "Saighdern Cheap Breatuinn" ("Cape Breton Soldiers") composed by Malcolm Gillis,[22] the Margaree Bard; and "Laithean Sona M' Oige" ("Happy Childhood Days")[23] by composer Dan Alex MacDonald of Framboise.

The final itinerary took the Sons of Skye tour group to no fewer than seven Scottish islands — Skye, Harris, Lewis, North Uist, Benbecula, South Uist, and Barra; and to four of Scotland's main cities — Glasgow, Oban, Inverness, and Edinburgh. Participating in eleven official playing engagements, the group travelled over 1,000 miles and made six sea journeys by ferry, ranging in duration from four minutes to seven hours.

The musical engagements invariably consisted of local musicians with whom we shared unique experiences common to our heritage. The Sons of Skye's first public appearance was at the Carbost Primary School where the children were joined by students from Portnalong. During the afternoon, we showed the students a map of Cape Breton, indicating place names which were also used in Scotland. In addition, the group entertained the children with some song, dance, and instrumentals and then presented the school with some Cape Breton souvenirs. The smiling faces of the children that afternoon made the entire tour worthwhile for me. The school visit was followed by an evening concert in the community hall in Portnalong, which included several local entertainers as well. A great deal of joy and excitement ensued in the village hall at Portnalong, Skye, that evening; the concert and the delightful reception proved a reliable indicator of what was to come. The event was reported in a local Scottish newspaper the next day:

> Mr. Norman MacDonald who came over from Cape Breton with the group introduced the chairman, Mr. Jonathan MacDonald. Local singers Mr. Neil MacLeod and Mrs. Ena Macphie of Dun-

vegan, and two Carbost school pupils, Fiona MacKinnon and Kathleen MacLeod started the evening's program, helped by a varied accordion selection by Mr. Alasdair MacKenzie of Portnalong.

In the audience was Mr. Angus Grant, the well-known fiddler from Fort William, and he willingly came forward to play a selection of tunes.[24]

Hence, the first public performance in Scotland by the Sons of Skye took place in Skye and rightly so, as the Isle of Skye was the island from which the group had coincidentally taken its name five years earlier.

Sons of Skye visiting the children at Carbost School, Isle of Skye, Scotland, in October 1979.

Photo by Marlene MacInnes

One weekend in 1974, I was hosting a former classmate from university, Brian Williston (now a judge with the Nova Scotia Supreme Court), at my apartment in Halifax. Explaining that I was planning to form a music group, I indicated to Brian that I was considering the name Sons of Cape Breton for the group. He suggested that a name from the Old Country might be more appropriate and less presumptuous on my part. Digging out a map of Scotland and spreading it across the floor, Brian and I began a paper tour of Scotland. When we came to the Isle of Skye, we agreed that Skye was the place name that would serve the group well.

Now, back to the tour! The Outer Islands of the Scottish Hebrides, which we reached on Tuesday, October 9, obliged by providing unusually warm, sunny weather. The Sons of Skye engaged in an impromptu street music session, in the main shopping area of Stornoway, the capital town of the Western Isles. A postcard sent back home to Cape Breton by Marlene, my wife, to her parents — John J. and Catherine MacDonald in East Bay — read:

We are having a great trip so far. Sunday night, we stayed in Glencoe and Monday night, we stayed in Portnalong, Skye. Today (Tuesday) we are sailing to Lewis for the Mod. The scenery is fabulous and the weather is fantastic — sunny and fairly warm.[25]

In Lewis, the prearranged system of billeting members of the tour group with families in villages close to Stornoway certainly helped to increase the contact between the Cape Bretoners and the Scots.

Catherine and John J. MacDonald (Marlene's Parents).

Preparing for the Mod became the focus for the group during our early arrival in Stornoway. We placed a pre-arranged call to Sydney's radio station CJCB, one of the local sponsors of the trip to Scotland. Cliff Morais and Norman MacDonald gave a brief interview over live radio, conducted by Norris Nathanson, who was the station's owner. On our return to Cape Breton, we learned that the live interview with CJCB Radio generated further interest in the Sons of Skye's travel in Scotland and especially in the Mod competition. (I first met Norris in the summer of 1974, when I had visited his office to explain my interest in doing a radio show for CJCB radio featuring Celtic music. That meeting lead to the half-hour program *Celtic Serenade*. I hosted the progam for one year before going back to university. The program continues to this day and is enjoying success due to the efforts of the popular host Donnie Campbell who took the show over following my departure. The show is now a three-hour production.

Engagements in Stornoway included the Seaforth Hotel where the Sons of Skye performed at a traditional ceilidh in one room while the popular young and dynamic Gaelic rock group RunRig performed a modern version of the Highland music in another room. I recall the members of the respective groups moving from room to room to try and get a partial glimpse of each other's performance. At one point in the midst of that evening, the Sons of Skye were invited to participate in the prestigious West Berlin Celtic Music Festival scheduled for the following July. RunRig went on to achieve international status throughout the 1980's in Europe.[26] In addition to the live performances, the Sons of Skye had an unexpected highlight during its four-day visit to Stornoway; we participated in a thirty-minute television documentary filmed by Cinema Sgire, a community television station. In all, our association with the local residents and our participation in the different concert performances, in the documentary, and in the Folk Song Competition made the first week in Scotland for the Sons of Skye a full and exciting one.

The Sons of Skye's total point accumulation of 166, exactly thirteen points behind the winners, Alchemy, from Stornoway, in the Mod Competition confirmed suspicions that Cape Breton's Scottish music is widely appreciated in the Old Country.[27] It also led to a relaxed and enjoyable second week for the tour group.

The Uists (from whence Dan Joe's ancestors left for Woodbine, Cape Breton, in 1842), Benbecula, and Barra provided more emotive movements for the Sons of Skye and for the local people, as well. In Barra, Marlene retrieved a copy of the local parish church bulletin (for her parents), which had prepared a statement on behalf of a group of children from Barra who had also participated in the choral competition at Stornoway.

> But the children who went from Barra, schooled and guided by earnest and devoted island teachers, gave a presentation of Barra which would do credit to their parents and ancestors. They had a certain bias. They may not have won any prizes but none of you who reside in Barra and Vatersay and rich in the culture which these children carried in your name need be anything but proud of their efforts and of those who tried so hard to coach them. Supreme congratulations to Ann Sinclair, golden girl.[28]

An ongoing stimulus during the tour was the constant attention of the national media in Scotland, with Joe Neil MacNeil, in particular. Joe Neil achieved near-celebrity status with radio appearances in both Gaelic and English and with one famous t.v. appearance, which subsequently led to his instant recognition in every area visited.

One of the more memorable events for me, in the company of Joe Neil in Barra, was when we were visiting the home of the wonderful and talented Gaelic singer, Flora MacNeil. She was a great friend of Cape Bretoners for many years and has often visited Cape Breton. We were invited to visit her home following the concert in the community hall in Castlebay. I remember the occasion well as it was likely one of Joe Neil's proudest moments; he was able to assist Flora, one of Scotland's national treasures, in the recollection of one of the more ancient traditional Gaelic songs. The people who attended this gathering were absolutely amazed at Joe Neil's ability to recall and recite "the" Gaelic — whether it was poetry, songs, or storytelling. Furthermore, the occasion highlighted Joe Neil's remarkable retention and knowledge of the Gaelic songs from Scotland.

On Monday, October 15, the Sons of Skye returned from the islands, and its mini-van was greeted by a welcoming crowd led by a kilted piper at Oban. The three-engagement mainland section of the tour involved travelling north again to Inverness, then south to Edinburgh, and then to Glasgow. The British Broadcasting Corporation were the party's hosts at the Drumossie Hotel adjacent to the historic battlefield of Culloden. The BBC arranged and recorded our concert (and, thankfully paid the hotel's dinner and bed and breakfast rates for the entire tour group for two days!!). At this point, the Sons of Skye and Joe Neil were joined by Cape Breton fiddlers Buddy MacMaster and Carl MacKenzie along with Scottish pianist Doug MacPhee and Gaelic singer Reverend Allan MacMillan. The concert was later broadcasted on BBC Radio, throughout Scotland, on New Year's Day, 1980. An account of that concert appeared in the *Cape Breton Post*:

> The BBC, long acknowledged as pace-setters in standards, have this year decided to devote a full hour of prime time to the best of Cape Breton talent. The show taped in Inverness, Scotland, during the 15-person tour by Cape Breton musicians in October was broadcast throughout Scotland New Year's Day.[29]

The closing concerts took place in Edinburgh and Glasgow and were a fitting climax to an unforgettable experience. The opportunity allowed the group to participate on stage with some of Scotland's leading musical performers, including the Billy Anderson Dance Band and Margaret MacLeod, a former member of the legendary Scottish folk group, Na-hoganaich, who, during their visit to Cape Breton in 1973, had contributed to my interest and enthusiasm to organize the Sons of Skye. The closing events also connected us with the faculty and staff at the School of Scottish Studies at Edinburgh University, who arranged our Edinburgh concert and provided an informal reception. Also appearing at the Edinburgh concert were a group of Shetland and Faroese musicians and dancers, who were on tour for a week of lectures, demonstrations, and workshops on the theme, "Dance and Dance Music of the Faroese and Shetlands."[30] That group was joined by the Shetland's legendary fiddlers Aly Bain and his mentor Tom Anderson. Both musicians are well known to Cape Breton fiddlers.

Prior to the final concert at the City Hall in Glasgow, we were honoured with a reception at the offices of the Canadian Consulate in Glasgow. The Consul, Mr. John MacLaren, presented each member with a token in appreciation of the valuable ambassadorial function fulfilled by the Sons of Skye's tour group. A Scottish newspaper reported the next day the disappointing turnout for the Glasgow Hall program and tried to explain that there were likely a number of contributing factors suggesting that the ". . . closure of the Highlanders Institute and the much bemoaned decreases in attendance at the annual events of the territorial associations are mere symptoms of a deeper malaise within the Gaelic circles in the city."[31] The report also gave a very positive review of the earlier events introducing the Sons of Skye.

> The Glasgow concert was the culmination of a fortnight long visit that had seen the party entertain appreciative audiences at the Mod in Stornaway and at Ceilidhs in Skye, Uist, Barra, Inverness, and in Edinburgh, where the George Square Theatre was filled to capacity.[32]

The initiative taken in organizing the 1979 tour of Scotland by Cape Breton musicians proved to be well justified. In my opinion, the tour was a valuable experience for all those involved and for the variety of contacts that were established, at both professional and personal levels. The tour of Scotland by the Cape Breton Scottish musicians was received with great enthusiasm.

The Home Studio

Before drawing the musical chapter on the Sons of Skye to a close, I would like to introduce the reader to an initiative taken by the group, which was equally as demanding for them as the tour of Scotland, the production of our first and only long-play recording.

There was considerable interest by the media at the time to access the music of the Sons of Skye. The audiences who were hearing the group in live performances were also encouraging the Sons of Skye to produce a commercial album. The decision to do the recording came after considerable thought and a great deal of planning. The time required to prepare the material was a major factor for consideration as were the additional costs for production and then the time and expense required to distribute it. In the end, the Sons of Skye decided by the industry's standards on a rather simple production scheme.

The group was somewhat modest about its expectations concerning the LP moving, as people in the business say. The decision was made not to invest a great deal of money in the technical side believing that the best studio in the world could help only to a point to make the group sound better. To this end, the group engaged the services of Inter-Media Services Ltd., which was owned and operated by Dave Miller of Halifax, to record the LP locally. The same location where I had enjoyed those magical music sessions as a young boy, at home in St. Andrew's Channel, was designated as the studio. This setting saved considerable cost and helped to make the group feel at home during the recording session. Cables, wires, and huge and bulky pieces of equipment were spread across mother's living room for three days.

The album, which actually followed a single recording released in 1980, was recorded in the spring of 1981 and was released in July, 1981. The liner notes, photos, and all the music were selected by the group. The title of the LP was *Both Sides of the Water*,[33] which was the English translation of one of the Gaelic songs on the LP, "Gach taobh dhe'n Uisge." The lyrics were written by Norman MacDonald and the music was set to a traditional Gaelic air from Scotland. The album also contained instrumental selections from several Highland pipe collections as well as tunes from the popular *Skye Collection* of violin music. The instrumental selection beginning with the Gaelic tune "Mo Dhachaidh" was recorded in the memory of the late Mike MacDougall, who passed away in May of the year the LP was released. The Sons of Skye performed with Mike MacDougall on many occasions in Nova Scotia. Mike was native to Ingonish, Victoria County, and was a highly acclaimed fiddler. An international community of friends and musicians were all saddened by his death.

In addition to the Gaelic material, including the Cape Breton songs the group performed at the National Mod in Scotland in 1979, "Saighderan Cheap Breatuinn" and "Laithean Sona M'Oige," the LP presented the Irish ballad "Spencil Hill" as well as a French song "Trois Soirees" which had been written by the Morais family of Big Pond. To commemorate the visit by Joe Neil to Scotland in 1979, the Sons of Skye wrote the song titled "Joe Neil" and recorded the song for the LP. Joe was with us when we recorded the song. I believe he was more impressed with the technical paraphernalia gathered around the house that day and likely wondered why all the apparatus was required to record a little bit of music. The song, "Joe Neil," was recorded again in 1995 by the popular Maritime group, Brakin Tradition.[34]

In the end, the Sons of Skye were satisfied that the recording did justice to the group's music. A release party took place in Ben Eoin in July to celebrate the recording and, over the next few months, the recording was distributed to local stores for sale. The recording was also made available at various concert venues featuring the Sons of Skye.

The Sons of Skye

In April, 1982, Cape Breton's legendary performer Matt Minglewood was preparing for his new recording. Minglewood had become a Canadian legend and by 1981 was getting ready to hit the U.S. market. The time and resources required for Matt to record would certainly be more expansive than the effort utilized by the Sons of Skye. Matt's technical layout and resources were likely typical of the resources required to sustain a superstar. His recording agenda was outlined in a local publication, the *Weekender* in April of 1982:

> With the Canadian market conquered, Cape Breton rocker Matt Minglewood is ready to take on the lucrative rock and roll world of the United States. The Minglewood Band, synonymous throughout Canada with a hard-hitting, country-rock style of music, has signed a five-year contract for five albums with CBS records, which promises American release.
>
> The Minglewood Band has booked a Toronto recording studio to make tapes that will be sent to the company's New York headquarters. Neither CBS nor Minglewood believes in quick albums, so the band will spend about two months in preproduction in a small studio and about a month in a larger studio refining the sound before spending ten days in Toronto or New York for final mixing.[35]

The same publication printed a story about the Sons of Skye including the LP the group had already released. I was hopeful that Matt would not review the featured article detailing the group's recording process at St. Andrew's Channel. The contrast was rather like a David and Goliath story, taking on the recording industry. Matt Minglewood's recording plan, described in the *Cape Breton Weekender*, was indicative of the incredibly wide gap between his recording experiences in the music industry and those of the Celtic artists, especially the efforts by early Cape Breton fiddlers.

Although Matt was promoted as an international star, and rightly so, in the country and rock sphere, one would not likely find a musician in the folk scene (worldwide) who could render better the popular Irish ballad "The Patriot Game" and his much later recording "The Valley of Strathlorne" with Doris Mason, well-known entertainer and recording artist. In my opinion, these songs by Matt Minglewood are two all-time classic pieces of music played by a Cape Breton artist.

My ten-year journey with the Sons of Skye gave me the opportunity to perform and to travel with three very talented and wonderful Big Ponders, Blanche, Malcolm and Cliff! Their trust and confidence in my efforts as group leader were personally rewarding and gratifying. Together, we visited new and wonderful places and met many wonderful people in different communities, in the audience and backstage. The experience introduced the Sons of Skye to world-class musicians and entertainers who often provided support and direction for the group over the years. The media personnel we met in Canada and in Scotland were cooperative and forbearing in our efforts to showcase the music and heritage of Cape Breton, music that the Sons of Skye had striven to replicate.

Notes

1. I first heard the words to this song in the 1960's. The folk group, The Corries, made the song popular. The song probably appealed to the Scottish Nationalists. The Sons of Skye enjoyed singing the song because it has a nice melody. During the group's tour of Scotland in 1979, we stayed in Glencoe on the first night.

2. John Prebble, *Glencoe* (Great Britain: Penguin Books Ltd., 1973), p. 206.

3. Joe Neil MacNeil, *Tales Until Dawn*, ed. Dr. John Shaw (Kingston, Ontario: McGill-Queen's University Press, 1987), p. 222.

4. "The Bagpipe in Cape Breton: From a Conversation with Barry Shears, Piper," *Cape Breton's Magazine*, #52.

5. Barry Shears, *The Cape Breton Collection of Bagpipe Music* (Halifax, N.S.: House of Music, 1995), p. ii.

6. John Gibson, "What Can Be Expected of the Highland Heart of Nova Scotia?" Letter to the editor in *The Clansman*, October/November, 1991, p. 5.

7. Dan MacInnis. (1991, October/November). "MacInnis Replies." *The Clansman*, p. 21.

8. John Gibson, 1991, p.5.

9. Ibid.

10. Angus MacDonald, "In Defence of Scotland's Piping Tradition - Dr. Angus Responds," *The Clansman*, 1991 & 1992, December/January, p. 5.

11. Editorial in the *Cape Breton Post*, August 9, 1973, p. 3.

12. Ibid.

13. Official Program on the Sons of Skye *1982 Spotlight Tour*. Published and distributed by the Nova Scotia Department of Culture, Recreation and Fitness.

14. "Coast to Coast," *Cape Breton Post*, Jan. 5. 1977.

15. "Thanks to CBC," letter to the editor in the *Cape Breton Post*, Jan. 5, 1977, p. 3.

16. John Gibson, "Sons of Skye Solo Concert Part of CBC Radio Opening," *Scotia Sun*, Apr. 26, 1982.

17. Barbara Senchuk, "Sons of Skye Debut on ATV," *Chronicle-Herald*, Jan. 8, 1983, p. 29.

18. Steve MacDonald, "College of Cape Breton Heralds New Year with Live Ceilidh Broadcast to Scotland," *College Canada*, 4:4, April, 1979, p. 14.

19. This quote was taken from an article, "The Canadian End of BBC Highland's Successful Transatlantic Celidh," which was published in a Scottish newspaper, January, 1979 (details unavailable).

20. Steve MacDonald, 1979, p. 14.

21. Reverand John Hugh MacEachern, Journal of Scotland tour, October 3-18, 1973.

22. The following was prepared by the Scottish historian and scholar, Norman MacDonald, and submitted to the National Mod office in Scotland in 1979 as part of an information booklet about the Sons of Skye. "Malcolm Gillis of Margaree was one of Cape Breton's most prolific and talented Gaelic poets. He was born in 1856 and died in 1929 at the age of 73. The song 'Saighdearan Cheap Breatuinn' was written during the 1914-1918 war and laments the fate of the 'handsome, brave lads of Cape Breton' who were in Europe fighting the war. The poem highlights the feelings of the families and villages in Cape Breton as they awaited across from the battle front. The emphasis is on the heroism of the young Cape Bretoners, of the longing at home for their return, and of the certain victory."

23. "Laithean Sona M'Oige" in Dan Alex MacDonald, *Songs from Framboise*, eds. Kay MacDonald and Effie Rankin, 1986, pp. 14-15.

24. "Cape Breton Gaels in Portnalong," *Oban Times*, Scotland, Nov. 1, 1979.

25. Postcard from Marlene MacInnes [who was visiting Scotland with the Sons of Skye] to John and Catherine MacDonald, East Bay, Cape Breton, N.S., October, 1979.

26. Runrig, *The Highland Connection*, 1979, Ridge RR001.

27. "Stornoway Group Wins Folk Contest," *Stornoway Gazette and West Coast Advertiser*, Mod Nan Eilean Souvenir edition, October 13, 1979, p. 2.

28. Parish bulletin, Castle Bay, Barra, October 14, 1979.

29. "Island Talent Featured in BBC: Cape Breton Musicians Hit in Scotland," *Cape Breton Post*, January 2, 1980, p.4.

30. "Canadian Gaels go on Tour." *Weekend Scotsman*, Scotland, 1979.

31. "The Trouble with Glasgow Gaels." *West Highland Free Press*, Scotland, Nov. 9, 1979.

32. Ibid.

33. Sons of Skye. (1981). *Both Sides of the Water*. Inter-Media Services Ltd. IMS-WRC1 -1522.

34. Malcolm MacPhee's brother Cyril sang the song, "Joe Neil," on the most recent recording of Brakin' Tradition.

35. "Minglewood Ready To Tackle U.S.," *Cape Breton Weekender*, April 23, 1982, p.2.

CHAPTER FIVE

Connections

Just Like Home

During my three years of residence in Halifax (1971-1974), I had the pleasure of producing a series of Scottish concerts. My interest is this activity was precipitated by my work on the annual Big Pond Summer Festival. I subsequently challenged myself to deliver a series of concerts, independent of the people and resources to which I had access at home. I soon discovered, however, that my independence didn't last long as I had to revert to my Big Pond roots to acquire some help.

My first effort at an off-island concert was in the spring of 1972 when I introduced several Cape Breton fiddlers, stepdancers, and vocalists in an evening concert at the high school in Musquodobit, Halifax County. Among the performers that evening were fiddlers Dan Joe MacInnis from Big Pond, Paddy LeBlanc from Sydney, and Mike MacDougall from Ingonish; and stepdancer Mary MacDonald (native to Mabou) who was then living in Halifax. In an effort to help, native Cape Bretoners from Inverness County, Big Pond, and East Bay, living in the Halifax area at the time, opened their homes to the entertainers from home, providing accommodations and meals. There was an all-out effort by people like Christie and Lloyd White, Sheila and Angus MacNeil, and Josephine and Jimmy MacDonald to be supportive and hospitable to the performing visitors and to help the 1972 concert and subsequent programs experience success. The support by these people was integral to the efforts to mount worthwhile concert programs.

Building on the networks I had established with the wider community of Cape Bretoners in Halifax and Dartmouth and the positive results of the initial concert, I produced a second concert program in the fall of 1972 and a third in the spring of 1973. The latter was designed to highlight Celtic music performances by youth; it also took place in the school where I had been teaching — Eastern Shore District High, Musquodobit Harbour. The performers were students from various communities in Nova Scotia, students who were interested in Celtic music.

Some of the young musicians appearing in that concert were: pipers Allan Kenny (Dartmouth), Jamie MacInnis (Big Pond), and Kenny MacKenzie (St. Peters);[1] several Highland dancers including Michelle and Melissa White (Dartmouth); as well as stepdancer Mary Gillis from Antigonish whose Port Hood roots were reflected in her steps; and four year old Alvin Gillis of Sydney whose Mira roots were evident in the Gaelic songs he sang that evening. A special attraction to parents from the local communities on that occasion was a choir of young boys and girls from several communities along the Eastern Shore. At their respective schools, they learned music, song, and dance routines which they felt were appropriate to the concert theme. The stars of the concert were, however, the Rankin Family from Mabou. Although very young and still in school, they were very well established entertainers in Inverness County and in the surrounding areas. They performed with the same level of drive and enthusiasm that one sees and hears from today's Rankin Family. At that time, the band consisted of Geraldine, David, John Morris, and Raylene. Dartmouth Cable Television recorded some aspects of the 1973 concert and broadcasted the program at a later date; the program was well received by the Halifax-Dartmouth region.

Fred White, who was then teaching school at St. Peter's High, Richmond County (now on faculty at UCCB) volunteered to provide transportation from Cape Breton for the Rankin Family. Recently, Fred recalled his journey on the morning of May 17, 1973 when he left for Mabou to meet the Rankins and drive them to Halifax. Fred encountered a late winter storm that day, which made travelling conditions difficult.

> I left St. Peter's at about 7:45 a.m. to drive to Mabou, went over to Whycocomagh, and through the Nevada Valley to get to Mabou. The scenery was fantastic with all the silver thaw on the trees as I drove over. I drove quite slowly at times because the roads were slippery in places; I was thankful there was not that much traffic on the road at that time of the morning. I hoped the salt trucks were out on the main road by the time I got to Mabou because I realized I would have someone else's children in the car; I would be responsible for their safety.

When I got to Mabou, I had no trouble finding the Rankin household. It was a white house almost directly behind the firehall. I entered the house and as I recall, there was a crowd of children in the kitchen, and Mrs. Rankin had just finished serving breakfast to the children. It seemed like a typical home, kids having just left for school and lots of younger kids around the kitchen. Geraldine, John Morris, Raylene, and David were the four coming with me. As they were getting their equipment ready, one of the younger brothers was running around the kitchen as though he was getting ready to go, too. His mother scooped him up in her arms, kissed him, and said to him as if to console him, he was going to be the best one of all.[2]

I was fortunate to acquire assistance from the Nova Scotia provincial government to help with the costs associated with the above-noted concert production. It was through those negotiations that I met Lou Stevens, an adult educator and a fine classical pianist. At the time of our first meeting, however, he was working with the Nova Scotia Department of Culture, Recreation, and Fitness, and he maintained some responsibility for cultural initiatives. I continued my association with Lou Stevens for many years following that first meeting and always enjoyed listening to stories about his journey in music and education.

The response to my various Halifax productions was excellent. The concerts' audiences always comprised many Cape Bretoners who settled in Halifax and Dartmouth to find work; this community of Cape Bretoners was well established at the time. The Cape Breton Club was active in organizing dances featuring Cape Breton fiddlers, and the interest generated in the Halifax area at the time for visiting musicians from Cape Breton, who were taking part in the CBC production *Ceilidh*, resulted in excellent opportunities for Cape Breton musicians to participate in a variety of local venues, celebrating the music.

It was clear that the native Cape Bretoners maintained ties with the people at home, and their interest to continue ties with the music from home especially was very important to them. This phenomenon, the need for Cape Bretoners to keep in touch with home, with the music, and with other Cape Bretoners who had settled in large urban communities like Boston, Toronto, and Detroit, became a matter of particular interest to me and later became the basis of my graduate research while I studied in Detroit in 1975-1976.

To Windsor: And Back Again

My research at the Merrill Palmer Institute, an affiliate of Wayne State University, Detroit, Michigan focused on what I described as significant questions about native rural Cape Bretoners living in an urban community. My informants were Cape Bretoners who settled in Windsor, Ontario. These were people who in their native Inverness County community were members of a folk society, a society based on group cohesiveness, commonality, and personal interaction.[3] In an urban society, relations and networks were expected to be different. My research inquiry included such questions as: Do Cape Bretoners establish and maintain secondary and/or primary relationships in the Windsor, Ontario community? What are their communication networks? What facilitates interaction among Cape Bretoners in Windsor? What communication patterns, if any, do they maintain from their native rural Cape Breton? The responses constituted some of the data that I used in my qualifying project, leading to the completion of my graduate studies. In summary, it became clear that the Cape Bretoners in Windsor, Ontario like the Cape Bretoners in Dartmouth and Halifax do establish very close, regular contact. Their departure from home is initiated through what the literature describes as "chain migration,"[4] direct contact before leaving home with other Cape Bretoners, family or friends, who had previously lived in the community. Once there, they build a sense of community which provides support to one another; they organize activities around their church; they intermarry and plan a variety of celebrations together. As quoted in my study:

> Many Cape Bretoners in Windsor frequently gather together . . . The music, the song and the dance are usually a part of this setting.
>
> Tape recordings of their favourite fiddlers and pipers and even Gaelic singers are also played. They relish the opportunity to explain the events which allowed them to record the music of Sandy MacLean or Buddy MacMaster, for example, two of Cape Breton's finest Scottish fiddlers. They take pride in telling of the frequent music sessions in which they participate in Windsor. These sessions may be the result of a visit by a Cape Breton musician whose arrival provides an occasion for either a public dance or concert or simply a large gathering in a home. The event may attract other Cape Breton musicians, not only from the Windsor community but from as near as Detroit and as far as Toronto or Boston.[5]

The Windsor ceilidh experience was relived for me in October of 1996, some twenty years later, in Big Pond, at a delightful session of music at Christie's with Morgan MacQuarrie, an exciting Cape Breton fiddler,[6] who I had met in Windsor in 1976. At the time, Morgan was visiting his native Kenloch from his home in Windsor. He contacted Christie and explained that he and Willie Kennedy, a fine fiddler from Mabou, and Mrs. Elizabeth Beaton, an equally fine pianist, also from Mabou, and Joan Beaton, Elizabeth's daughter, were heading to Big Pond for a few tunes. The reunion proved to be an engaging session of "Coal Mines" music.[7] Until that October, the last time I heard Morgan MacQuarrie play in person was when I was conducting my field work for my graduate research in Windsor, Ontario in 1976. Morgan MacQuarrie and other native Cape Bretoners, including Sandy Beaton (Elizabeth and Donald Angus' son) and family, as well as Jessie Anne Cameron (John Allan's sister) and family, were among those who I had called upon to provide me with an overview of the traditions maintained by Cape Bretoners in Windsor. Morgan is a popular fiddler in the Windsor community and continues the tradition of playing at sessions and at dances.

At an earlier music session in the summer of 1996, and again at Christie's, the Windsor/Detroit music connection resurfaced. Among the fiddlers present was Bobby MacNeil who was visiting home from Detroit. Although Bobby did not grow up in Cape Breton, he visited in the summers and he mastered the Cape Breton music style. Bobby was joined by his three sons, Jimmy, Tommy, and Stephen, all who had grown up in Michigan. They are excellent exponents of the music via fiddle, piano, and Highland pipes respectively. They acquired the music of Cape Breton through their father Bobby and he, in turn, acquired the music through his mingling with Cape Bretoners who had migrated to the Detroit and Windsor areas in the 1940's and the 1950's. The two MacNeil generations had been encouraged to celebrate the music by Bobby's father Bernie who had left Glengarry (Rear Big Pond) in 1917 to settle in Detroit, and by Bobby's mother Ann, who played the piano. Ann often accompanied Judique native Little Jack MacDonald, the "Bard of Scottish Fiddling," who had lived in Detroit in the 1940's,[8] at many sessions as well as on recordings.

Another noted fiddler attending the session that evening with the MacNeils was Carl MacKenzie. Carl's music is magic personified, and he especially enjoys the house session routine and always performs exceptionally well out home. Carl, a well-travelled fiddler, is representative of the Cape Breton fiddlers still living at home and frequently called upon to take his music to other areas in Canada and the United States, always inspiring young musicians with his music, including many individuals who have roots somewhere in rural Cape Breton. Often, Carl and I discuss his travels to distant places with his music.[9]

In the United States, Carl has performed in concert at Kenyan College in Ohio and at the American National Folk Festival in North Carolina and Lowell, Massachussets. In addition, he made three visits to the American Fiddle Tunes Festival at Port Townsend, Washington; two visits to the California Folk festival at UCLA in Los Angeles and the Valley Moon Festival in San Francisco; and two visits to the Fiddle and Dance workshop program in Ashogan in New York. Carl has also performed in Nashville, Philadelphia, Iowa, and Britain, Ireland, and Scotland with the Sons of Skye. Recently, Carl MacKenzie released his ninth commercial recording. I had the pleasure of preparing the liner notes for his 1996 CD *Fiddle Medleys*, and I made particular reference to the fact that Carl has performed his music locally, nationally, and internationally.

Another well-travelled Cape Breton fiddler who released a recording in 1996 is Winnie Chafe. Winnie's exciting and innovative performance of the Celtic music using an appropriate blend of classical interpretation on her CD *Legacy* is reviewed by Kate Dunlay in the Celtic newspaper *Am Braighe*.

> It is satisfying to see an artist take an experiential leap and land successfully. Quite a number of Cape Breton musicians have done this recently, all going in different directions, finding their own niches. For fiddler/violinist Winnie Chafe, *Legacy* was a natural step in the development of her own style and presentation . . . Winnie's own basic style sound is born in the romantic era, except when she is playing strictly Cape Breton style.[10]

Indeed, Winnie and her music have moved in countless directions over the years. On a personal note, I had the pleasure of appearing as a guest on her CBC national *Ceilidh* program in Halifax, which aired in the early 1970's, when she invited me to play a few selections on the Highland bagpipes. This was rather an awkward occasion for me because I had acquired the habit of sitting while playing the pipes. As well, I had also become accustomed to including back-up accompaniment like piano and guitar in my performances. This would have been a rather unorthodox manner to play the pipes, by CBC's standards. Winnie assured me that the set and the style of presentation would be to my satisfaction; so it was! As a matter of fact, after the show's taping, I learned that Winnie had some delight in requesting CBC to prepare for this unusual piper from Cape Breton. That CBC session with Winnie Chafe and the many other talented musicians she was directing as part of the program was a pleasurable musical moment for me. Several months later, the Sons of Skye's first public appearance in Sydney was at the Sydney Bandshell, as guests of Winnie Chafe.

As I noted earlier, Winnie Chafe, like Carl MacKenzie, is a well-travelled fiddler. In addition to her CBC program and her many recordings, Winnie has performed in festivals and in concerts throughout Canada, the United States, and the British Isles. While living in the United States, she was a member of the California Ventura Symphony. In 1974, Winnie organized a group of musicians from Cape Breton and Eastern Nova Scotia and toured the Maritimes, performing for large audiences.[11] In 1975, Winnie Chafe and several other Nova Scotia artists participated in the ceilidh which took place at Edinburgh Castle in Scotland. In advance of that historic Ceilidh production journalist, Linden MacIntyre stated in his article that:

> We have here musicians from Nova Scotia, who are among the finest exponents of the province's Scottish tradition. Winnie Chafe, will move a Canadian High Commission to the brink of poetry with her slow airs and laments.
>
> Buddy MacMaster from Judique will generate a heartbeat in this room as academics, lords and ladies, sleek businessmen, diplomats, politicians, and simple folk from remote places, move their feet shyly in time with his strathspeys and reels.
>
> Dougie MacPhee from New Waterford and Joey Beaton from Mabou will defy the pure traditionalists of Scotland with demonstrations of how the music of the bagpipes and violin have been adapted to the piano at home.[12]

The program was hosted by the Canadian External Affairs Minister, Allan J. MacEachen, and the Scottish Secretary of State, the Honourable William Ross following some high level diplomacy since only the Queen and British ministers had been hosts in the castle before that particular ceilidh.[13] The program also introduced the Scottish musicians: Duncan Morrison (pianist), Calum Kennedy (Gaelic vocalist), and the highly celebrated accordionist John Carmichael who rendered, among other selections, the tune "Allan MacEachen's Welcome To Edinburgh Castle" which John had composed for the Cape Breton host.[14] For her performances in many productions like the Edinburgh Castle Ceilidh and her many other contributions to the music and culture, Winnie Chafe was awarded the degree, Doctor of Letters, by the University College of Cape Breton in 1995.

Official public appearances by Cape Breton musicians like Carl

MacKenzie, Winnie Chafe, Buddy MacMaster, Doug Macphee, and Joey Beaton, who travelled extensively throughout the 1960's, the 1970's, and the 1980's, have played a major role in introducing Cape Breton Celtic music to many quality musicians, for example, American musicians Frank Farrell, Kate Dunlay, Mark Connor, and David Greenberg; Irish musicians Liz Doherty and Tony Smith; and Scottish musicians Allister Fraser and Hamish Moore. They have all been inspired by the music of travelling Cape Breton musicians. These American and Irish musicians, who have acquired a thirst for the Cape Breton music through their association with select Cape Breton musicians, are accomplished artists in their own right within their respective communities of music. They view the Cape Breton stuff as value added.

Some keen musicians outside the tradition would depict the traditional music in new and innovative ways, as was the interesting result of Daniel Goode's collaboration with several traditional artists in Cape Breton, beginning in 1975 and culminating in a performance by several fiddlers together with piano player Joey Beaton in New York 1982.[15] The fiddlers, Kinnon Beaton, Donnie LeBlanc, David MacIsaac, Theresa MacLellan, John Morris Rankin and Brenda Stubbert, made up the "Cape Breton Concerto." Their New York performance highlighted Daniel Goode's concerto which had been scored for six violins, piano, and symphonic band. The score was tailored to the special talents of the soloists. The concerto was described in the following:

> In one continuous movement, the work features old fiddle tunes played by the violins and piano, combined with accompaniment patters in the band derived from the tunes.[16]

Along with the Cape Breton music, there were classic selections by such composers as Tchaikovsky, Siberlius, Strauss, and Püer. Daniel Goode's own work with the Concerto was an inspiration and was appreciated by those who were able to hear the performances. Goode is himself a clarinetist and composer and at the time of the visit by the Cape Breton Concerto to New York, Goode was director of the Electronic Music Studio of Livingstone College-Rutgers in New Jersey. He is a native New Yorker and received his training at Oberlin and Cornell.[17] The Cape Breton Concerto gave a UCCB sponsored performance in Sydney in June, 1982 before travelling to New York.

The Concerto's work may have helped lay the groundwork for later initiatives like the 1985 Celtic/classical fusion "The Octet" resulting in Scott MacMillan's concert piece "Songs of the Cape" — a suite in four movements. The music features a classical string quartet with four rhythm players performing in the traditional style. The Songs of the Cape was recorded by the

UCCB press in 1985.[18] In 1996, David Greenberg released his popular recording *Bach Meets Cape Breton,* which also features an exciting blend of classical and Cape Breton traditional music.[19]

The Tours: UCCB Connections

Upon completion of my graduate studies in 1976, I returned to Cape Breton. I was given the mandate by UCCB's Continuing Education Office, under the administration of Dr. Ora McManus, to organize a series of collaborative activities with groups, like the Cape Breton Gaelic Society or the An Tulloch Gorm Society, or institutions like the Gaelic College in St. Ann's. Dr. McManus was hopeful that through UCCB and different community-based networks, including the media, the community would create a greater interest in celebrating the Celtic heritage.

McManus promoted the idea of greater collaboration and networking among groups and individuals, island-wide, to effectively celebrate the music, song, and dance of rural Cape Breton. In doing this, McManus believed that the increased community co-operation would help foster the sense of pride already entrenched in the exponents of the music. Furthermore, they would acquire a process, through education, to transmit the culture and the spirited features of the tradition which were still contained largely within select rural communities of Cape Breton. McManus' thinking was not unlike that of the Antigonish Movement, described in Michael Welton's *Knowledge for the People.*[20] McManus, like Dr. Moses Coady, founder of the movement, wanted to nurture what Welton calls "a program of adult education, self-help, and co-operative development." But unlike Coady, McManus wanted communities to nurture culture (music) in the interest of economic development and, thus, the greater good. He wanted the resources of public institutions, like UCCB, public school education, and community development agencies, to embrace the culture in a positive and constructive manner and to allow for mentors and bards within the music tradition, for example, to emerge and to seek opportunities to help develop, among other things, an entrepreneurial spirit centered around the music. McManus wanted the local bards and mentors to be part of educational initiatives that would help them to teach and to train effectively and with confidence in the community. Subsequently, initiatives by individuals and families from the community would ensure that the traditions would be maintained and this would generate opportunities for the whole community, at the local, national, and international levels.

The musical links made by many travelling Celtic musicians to and from Scotland especially, and to some extent Ireland, became more a part of my work. In the late 1970's through to the late 1980's, a number of initiatives were embarked upon to foster greater links between the different Celtic regions. Believing that the Celtic links were important to our respective communities locally, nationally, and internationally, I deemed music to be the most effective catalyst for bridging those links in economic development, in history, in social issues, as well as in culture, particularly with Scotland. I felt assured, indeed zealous, about the need to keep music always at the forefront. The foundation for moulding these musical links at UCCB was through Continuing Education by establishing a modest but effective music program emphasising quality performances.

Although McManus encouraged activities at UCCB, like Dan Joe's fiddle class and Reverend Eugene Morris' dance class, he believed that it was important for the role models and mentors to continue their function in their respective communities, in efforts they may engage to proffer the music tradition, for example. He believed institutions like UCCB should not displace the role of the community and the family in teaching the tradition but rather lend support through publications, concert performances, and general support to the would-be teachers at the community level. He wanted the areas with an already intense interest in the music and the dance among the smaller rural communities to be available to any one person or community in Cape Breton interested in the traditions. There is exciting evidence that the spirit of bonding and nurturing and sharing is alive and well, especially within the music and dance tradition of Cape Breton in the 1990's.

The initiatives to include the Gaelic College, for example, included the successful 1983 Closing program for the Gathering of the Clans and a most memorable 1983 St. Andrew's Day celebration in the Great Hall of the Clans. The St. Andrew's Day celebration featured the music of Winnie Chafe and friends and a talk by Iain Noble, Isle of Skye, Scotland (who was instrumental in assisting with the Sons of Skye tour in 1979) and culminated with a splendid evening of music and conversation and homemade food prepared and served under the direction of Muriel Morrison, Paul Hanna, and UCCB's hospitality students. (The menu was scotch broth, bread, fresh country butter, marinated herring, roast beef, mashed potatoes, turnip, peas, strawberry skye, tea and red/white wine). It was a wonderful St. Andrew's Day celebration in Cape Breton, a joint effort by the Gaelic College, UCCB, and individuals from the community.

In addition, I had the pleasure of being involved in the extensive concert series organized by the Gaelic College as part of its summer school program in 1984[21] and again in 1986. During the time of these events, the Gaelic College was administered by Norman MacDonald, with the exception of the 1983 Clan Closing program, at which time the Gaelic College was administered by Leonard Jones.

UCCB also introduced an in-house concert series to provide a venue for guest fiddlers, usually two fiddlers for each concert, to render a nice arrangement of special tunes, including pastoral and Gaelic airs. The fiddlers were offered time to play solo and to play in unison, thereby highlighting the spontaneity and brilliance of the music; this allowed the performers to share the depth and power of their presentation to an attentive audience.

UCCB's concert productions were considered to be a change from the usual local dance settings and from the popular variety concerts which often featured a litany of performers. The concert series became a popular attraction for the community, mainly because the small and intimate setting (usually in the Little Theatre at UCCB), and the entertainment format closely modelled the home-kitchen sessions. Local fiddlers, including Kyle MacNeil, Howie MacDonald, Kinnon Beaton, and Gordon Cote performed. Several of the UCCB concerts were recorded by CBC radio for local and regional programs.

The concert series format later evolved to the wider community, beyond UCCB's facilities. Such was the case in March, 1982 when fiddler Donald MacLellan was asked to perform in the series. Donald was living in Toronto, and has been since 1947, but he maintained close contact with the music in Toronto and in Cape Breton. I especially recall Donald's visit that March. It was likely one of the most electrifying music sessions I have ever experienced. That particular session did rekindle for me some of the same intensity I would often garner at a typical house session out home.

Donald was invited to play in a two-part performance at the newly established Co-Op Pub in Sydney. The establishment needed a little kick-start at the time and I had been asked if I might consider placing one of the campus-based concert programs at the pub. I agreed and, believing that Donald MacLellan's visit would generate a great deal of excitement, asked him to participate.

Donald's music has a unique quality and a very distinct MacLellan sound. I personally enjoy how he renders the full range of the music, marches, jigs, and reels, as well as the slow airs. However, when Donald decides to make that special effort for an attentive audience of good listeners who appreciate the music, it appears to me that Donald's strathspeys are the tunes which can make everyone take particular notice and most effectively evoke strong feelings of passion for his music.

During those performances on that March weekend, Donald's performances were remarkable, and his strathspeys were plentiful, which is a sign that
the fiddler is comfortable and ready to give a quality performance — and so
it was! At the Saturday afternoon performance, he drew five standing
ovations. For two of the ovations, he was accompanied by Doug MacPhee on
piano; for the final three, he was accompanied by his sister Theresa, a wonderful fiddler in her own right, and his sister Marie at piano. The tunes were
like signature tunes, "The Braes of Auchteyre," "Able Banks," "Devil in the
Kitchen," "Duke of Gordon's Birthday," "Dusty Meadow," and "Blair
Drummond." For those close to the music, the combination of musicians
and the drive and the lift in the tunes brought back many wonderful
memories of the famed MacLellan Trio, [22] who appeared at many concerts
in Cape Breton in the 1960's and the 1970's. My journal noted records that
the atmosphere around the Co-Op Pub that weekend suggested that the occasion was not only a session of music for all who attended to enjoy, but
also a tribute to one of Cape Breton's finest teams of old time traditional
musicians.

Eventually, the concert series format also served as an effective drop-in
for the occasional outside artist wanting to perform in Cape Breton. Groups
from Scotland like the popular Boys of the Lough and Battlefield Band participated. As is usually the case, members of these professional groups often
change and sometimes the past travelogue of the bands is not always passed
on to the new members. This was clearly the case with the Battlefield Band.
I was humoured to read in a summer 1996 edition of the *Inverness Oran* an
interview with the young fiddler from Scotland, John McCusker. He explains
in the interview that:

> . . . he has toured the world, including Canada, a number of times
> with the Celtic group, Battlefield Band, he was in Cape Breton
> (himself) for the first time at The Ceilidh Trail School of Celtic
> Music. The band itself, has been around longer than the young
> fiddler has been alive, 27 years, recording more than 20 albums.
> McCusker said "We toured the world, but never Cape Breton"[23]

In fact, The Battlefield Band appeared at the UCCB Playhouse on April
4, 1984, as part of a concert series, some twelve years before McCusker's first
visit. During that 1984 visit, the band went on to tour several Cape Breton
rural communities after its UCCB appearance.

In the case of the Boys of the Lough and the Battlefield Band, the two
groups had planned a North American tour, and a call from their respective

agents revealed that the group members felt that it was necessary to appear in Cape Breton because of all the attention the Celtic music from this area was continuing to acquire internationally. The respective groups were invited to take part in separate programs.

*B*oys of the Lough arrive from Scotland to perform at the UCCB Concert Series.

Photo by Owen Fitzgerald

In 1985, still with UCCB, I had the pleasure of helping to introduce to Cape Breton a program which was promoted as "The Road to the Isles" tour, featuring the magnificent voice of the BBC broadcaster and author, Finlay J. MacDonald from Scotland, who I had met during the Sons of Skye's tour in 1979. (Finlay hosted the concert, which was recorded by the BBC, at the Drumossi Hotel with the full group of Cape Breton musicians involved in the Sons of Skye tour.)

Six years later, Finlay J. toured Cape Breton with Kathleen MacDonald, an acknowledged star of radio and television in Scotland. By this time, Kathleen's career included performances in France, in Ireland, and in other parts of Canada. Finlay J. and Kathleen were joined by Rhona MacKay, who is a harpist of international reputation and trained at the Royal Scottish Academy of Music. She was the principal harpist with the Scottish national orchestra under Sir Alexander Gibson.[24] Also participating in the tour was Dr. Angus MacDonald, who is a piper from Glenuig, Scotland and who, at the time, was living in Cape Breton. In addition to the Scottish performers, Mary MacLean Gillis, from North Sydney and a celebrated pianist in Cape Breton joined the tour. The interest by the Cape Breton Gaels in maintaining a close link with Scotland as well as the interest by the Scotland artists in the Cape Breton music were the main forces which made it possible for these talented professionals from Scotland to visit Cape Breton through their respective tours.

The "Road to the Isles" program was scripted to present a historical journey in music. It utilized music that illustrated the state of the Highlands before Culloden, taking songs and bagpipe music from the great days of Clan Chief patronage, music from Dunvegan and Duntulm. Some Jacobite songs were included, plus songs from the beginnings of evictions, the potato famine, and the songs of the postwar revival. These were some of the themes depicted in the music. The Cape Breton tour by these artists took them to Sydney, Loch Lomond, Big Pond, Margaree, St. Ann's, and then mainland Antigonish.

In addition to the Finlay J. tour, Dr. Angus MacDonald was instrumental in the now internationally acclaimed Capercaillie tour of that same summer (1985).[25] Capercaillie's performance was a distinct contrast to Finlay J.'s. The latter presented a very traditional style of program in a low key but entertaining format, rendering mostly stories and unaccompanied Gaelic vocal solos as well as the haunting instrumentals. The Capercaillie band was dynamic in presenting an upbeat version of traditional music. The two styles are now depicted in popular film productions like *Rob Roy* and *Braveheart*, two successful productions about the struggles, the strife, and the conflicts among the early Highlanders. The Capercaillie band had established an interest in Cape Breton music even before their tour was announced.

Capercaillie's first recording, *Cascade*, which was released in 1984,[26] the year before their visit to Cape Breton, included the great Dan R. MacDonald composition, "Trip to Windsor,"[27] as well as tunes from other great Scottish composers like Neil Gow. In 1985, Capercaillie was described as fresh and innovative. Their Cape Breton visit included performances in Louisbourg, Margaree, East Bay, Ingonish, St Ann's, Sydney, Whycocomagh, Port Hawkesbury, Big Pond (the annual Big Pond Concert), and one very memorable house ceilidh in Big Pond. The fall 1996 issue of the *Green Linnet* catalogue, commemorating the 20th anniversary of the record distribution outlet, presented Capercaillie's music with the following note — more than ten years after their visit to Cape Breton:

> When the groundbreaking Scottish band Capercaillie interprets traditional music, it demolishes ancient boundaries. Walking songs become Scottish funk; a Scots Gaelic ballad breaks the UK Top 40. Called the most exciting and vibrant band in Celtic music today, Capercaillie has performed for ecstatic audiences globally and set new standards in contemporary Scottish music for over a decade.[28]

The Cape Breton audiences, for which they performed in 1985, were witness to the introduction of one of Scotland's most exciting and dynamic entertainment groups. Capercaillie continues to pay tribute to the music of Cape Breton as they make their way around the globe.

The Capercaillie tour, like the Finlay J. tour, received funding from the Sydney Bicentennial Commission, which was under the chairmanship of George MacNeil. The commission was established to celebrate the 200th anniversary of the city of Sydney. The last major birthday celebration in Sydney was its 175th anniversary, July 24-30, 1960. The official program for the week-long activities in 1960 suggests that the planning committee offered only a modest recognition of the Celtic music and its activities. As a matter of fact, the closest the organizing committee came to fiddle music in its 1960 celebration was the inclusion of a performance by Don Messer in the old Sydney Forum, July 27.[29] According to the official program, the music of Cape Breton fiddlers was not an integral part of the celebration. Yet, this was at the time when the Cape Breton fiddler had already acquired international attention through countless recordings and through special appearances in Canada, in the United States, and in various parts of Cape Breton. The introduction of the full range of Celtic music from Scotland and from Cape Breton during the 200th anniversary of the city of Sydney, under the chairmanship of the late George MacNeil, helped to correct what I consider a major oversight on the part of the 1960 organizing committee.

The Media: UCCB Connections

The activities centering around Cape Breton Celtic music began to attract increased attention by personnel in Scottish radio and television, especially in the 1970's and the 1980's. The increase in Cape Breton concerts, ceilidhs, and open-air festivals, the increase in recordings by fiddlers, the Gaelic language revival in Scotland, and the efforts, especially by the Cape Breton Gaelic Society in Sydney and by the many local chapters throughout Cape Breton, like the Mabou Gaelic and Historical Society, to mount a similar campaign in support of Gaelic retention in Cape Breton are evidence of this revival. Perhaps most importantly, however, are the results of the personal visits, exchange of correspondence, and regular contacts between different groups, organizations, individuals, and families that helped develop a series of special initiatives by interested parties from Scotland with respect to the Celtic music, song, and dance of Cape Breton.

I personally enjoyed a series of special contacts with the Scottish media primarily because of my association with Norman MacDonald, who was previously a faculty member at UCCB and who is now living in Skye and working with BBC Scotland. From these networks with the Scottish media emerged opportunities for me to assist the BBC and some independent producers from Scotland to depict the music of Cape Breton for an international audience.

In February, 1985, I received a letter from Douglas Eadie of Pelicula Films Limited,[30] Scotland, announcing the company's interest in producing a film celebrating the far-travelled fiddler. The company was interested in visiting several centers in North America where threads of Scottish fiddlers were available socially. The letter stated that: "Clearly, Cape Breton has to be a part of the story — fiddle playing, piping, and Gaelic song and culture."[31]

Their nine-day visit, which had been altered from an original three-day visit, to Cape Breton took them to Eskasoni, Baddeck, St.Ann's, Glencoe, and Cheticamp. Under the direction of Mike Alexander, the crew filmed ceilidhs, dances, and milling frolics in a variety of venues, including community halls, beverage rooms, and private homes. In the *West Highland Free Press*, January 31st 1986 edition, Chris Frew wrote his review of the program:

> This music, its travels and its exponents on both sides of the Atlantic form the subject of an interesting short documentary series to be shown on Channel Four in March called *Down Home* . . . Originally commissioned as a three-part series — "From Shetland to Texas"; "From Appalachia to Nashville"; and "From Cape Breton to Quebec" — the result pleased Channel Four so much that they asked for extra program to be made up from the embarrassment of riches the producers, Pelicula Films of Glasgow, had to cut out to keep to the limits of time and theme (originally set).[32]

In the fall of that same year, Gordon Menzies, Executive Producer with the BBC in Scotland, contacted me to assist in the making of *The Celts*.[33] The objective of the television program was to "reflect something of the way of life, the traditions, and the language of the Scots in Cape Breton." This particular production took the BBC crew to Irish Cove, where they were able to visit the Woolen Mill industry owned and operated by the Cash family; to Soldiers' Cove where they were able to film the Sutherland Farm; and the Gaelic College where they filmed that wonderful bard of Highland traditions, Archie Alex MacKenzie.[34] In addition, the travel log took the crew to several other communities in rural Cape Breton to record music, song, and dance. This effort was followed by several initiatives by international media to spend time in Cape Breton, including the very well-known documentary, *The Blood is Strong* (1988), produced by Ted Brocklebank.

The most recent visit by a Scottish tour was the contingent from the

Highlands of Scotland, who were visiting UCCB in October 1996, to share their interest in building a university in the Highlands,[35] a university with a role and purpose in education and training and links with the wider community which would be much like that at UCCB. I had the pleasure of meeting with these people at a luncheon arranged by UCCB President, Dr. Jacqueline Scott. I met with these people on the same day I had delivered a farewell eulogy to Joe Neil MacNeil at his funeral mass at St. Mary's Church, East Bay at which time I explained to the congregation that Joe Neil's many visits to Scotland and Scotland's interest in Joe Neil helped to pave the way for links between Scotland and Cape Breton, like the meeting I would attend later that day at UCCB with the Highlands' Convenor and several educational authorities from the Highlands.

At the same time, UCCB was hosting a visit by well-known Scottish historian, Jim Hunter, and BBC producer, David Young, who were producing a five-part series for radio on the "Scottishness" of the "Americas."[36] UCCB's Dr. Mary K. MacLeod and Dr. Terry MacLean had arranged for Hunter and Jackson to visit different parts of Cape Breton and to talk to several people. Hunter had visited Cape Breton first in 1981 to deliver a short course on the parallels of the two Celtic regions, Cape Breton and the Hebrides of Scotland.[37] The course been arranged by Norman MacDonald through the Continuing Education Office at UCCB.

The Tributes: Saying Thank You

The UCCB activities were only part of an effort by the wider community to promote the Celtic music of Cape Breton. Among the other leaders, as mentioned earlier, was the Gaelic Society, which introduced a series of annual concerts in the 1970's to celebrate and to recognize Gaelic Bards. These popular tributes engaged a different format in 1978 when Dr. Charles MacDonald, Professor of Religious Studies at UCCB, chaired a committee of UCCB and New Dawn Enterprises representatives, and people from the wider community to a organize a special tribute to Cape Breton entertainer John Allan Cameron. The event was to recognize John Allan's successful career as an entertainer in the Canadian music field.[38]

In August of 1980, the New Waterford Gaelic Society organized a tribute for pianist Margaret MacPhee and, on the occasion, Dr. Charles MacDonald was guest speaker. Dr. MacDonald justified the event honouring Margaret when he stated: "Margaret used her talents for the enjoyment of thousands of people. She has played throughout Cape Breton, never turning down an invitation, whether a benefit for a needy cause, a picnic at Big Pond or Johnstown, or at the hundreds of other occasions where her presence was so much desired."[39] As master of ceremonies for the afternoon and evening, I was able to introduce many of Margaret's special musical friends who had gathered for the tribute, fiddlers John Campbell, Buddy MacMaster, Carl MacKenzie, Dan Joe MacInnis, Mickey Gillis, and Reverend Angus Morris, among others. The tributes continued entering the 1990's when the dance community honoured stepdancer Margaret Gillis. On that occasion, I had the distinguished task of addressing those who had gathered in Sydney for a delightful evening's ceilidh with music, food, and friendship as a tribute to Margaret for her many years as a stepdance teacher.[40]

These community-based tributes prompted UCCB's Continuing Education Department to organize a series of additional tributes including one for Dan Hughie MacEachern of Queensville, Inverness County, in 1980.[41] In addition to the music and the congenial gathering of friends and family, the evening was a reflection on the wonderful musicianship of Dan Hughie over several decades. The guest speaker for the evening was Reverend John Angus Rankin, who was parish priest at Glendale and who had been actively involved in setting up the Cape Breton Fiddlers' Association. Reverend John Angus had established a very close friendship with Dan Hughie and on the occasion said: "It is our prayer, Dan Hughie, that God will bless you with better health and leave you with us awhile so we may benefit from your knowledge of music."[42]

Cape Breton fiddlers perform at the Dan Hughie MacEachern Tribute, 1980. [Left to right] Reverend Francis Cameron, Buddy MacMaster, Carl MacKenzie, Reverend Angus Morris, and Doug MacPhee at piano.

Raytel Photography

One of the many surprises prepared for Dan Hughie that evening was the presence of his six sisters.[43] The sisters, who had travelled great distances, were seated at the head table, awaiting for Dan Hughie to enter the auditorium. The applause during their meeting and greeting was magnificent. It was the first time "his sisters had been together on Cape Breton for forty years,"[44] a special event which I enjoyed immensely in my journey of Celtic music; the pleasant memories of that evening will stay with me for many years.

In 1982, the Buddy MacMaster Tribute[45] and Ceilidh was organized at UCCB, introducing Buddy as one of the more significant exponents of music in the Celtic world. Like the Dan Hughie tribute, the program was well attended as people gathered from Canada and the United States to applaud the creative and musical genius and the many years of performance and generosity demonstrated by Buddy. In his address to the large assembly, the guest speaker for the evening, Reverend Malcolm MacDonell, past president of St. F.X. University, spoke the following words with respect to Buddy MacMaster and his place in the unique culture of his native Judique and the wider Cape Breton community:

> One of the most distinguished artists in this distinctive cultural expression is Hugh Allan (Buddy) MacMaster. He is a gentleman in whom we find this cultural artistry deeply rooted in an exemplary Christian character. He is a man with a responsible sense of citizenship, witness his years in the municipal council and our school board, not to mention the many other services he performs for our community. When you blend character and culture and citizenship and categorize them together with generosity, happy the community adorned and served by such a person.[46]

Buddy MacMaster received an honourary Doctorate of Letters from St. F.X. University in 1996.[47]

These UCCB celebrations were followed by a special tribute to Reverend Eugene Morris[48] for his tireless effort to promote and to teach the Cape Breton style of stepdancing, resulting in an original "Train the Trainer Program." Eugene Morris' students are continuing the tradition across Cape Breton through a wide variety of programs offered in conjunction with community and provincial agencies to promote and to teach Cape Breton stepdancing.

In the late 1980's I initiated contact with a provincial agency to determine whether it may be possible to procure some support for the local efforts in teaching dance. I contacted the office of Dance Nova Scotia (DANS) in Halifax — an arm of the Nova Scotia Cultural Federation — and met with Dianne Milligan, the executive director. That contact resulted in DANS, though the work of Dianne, collaborating with several of the popular local dance teachers and performers to organize workshops to improve their personal techniques for teaching stepdance and for efforts to train would-be dance teachers. The effort has reached dance teachers across the island.[49] In addition, several instructors recently completed a teaching guide for square dance — Cape Breton style. *Just Four on the Floor* has been approved for use in the public school system as part of the physical education program. In addition to the written guide, professionally recorded cassette tapes of the local music, rendered in a slow tempo (the reel and the jig) to better assist the teaching of the different square dance routines, are also available (the musicians: Buddy MacMaster and Dave MacIsaac). The production has been introduced in several workshops to local teachers, and the response has been excellent.

By 1989, my role in Continuing Education at UCCB, with respect to Celtic music changed, and my work to engage a process to link with the wider communities, especially rural communities, assumed a renewed priority — one more reflective of the wider educational interests of the community and UCCB's mission to introduce the full range of expertise and resources of UCCB to rural Cape Breton. Prior to my current responsibilities at the Beaton Institute, researching Celtic music, I brought closure to my Celtic connection in the wider community through Continuing Education. As if by way of a finale, although not planned as such, I produced a concert at Holy Angels High School auditorium in October 1989, presenting an exciting cast of local and visiting Celtic artists. Appropriately, as if through some intervention by some Celtic spirit, some of the performing artists, fiddlers, pipers, dancers, and vocalists, with whom I had developed a special rapport through my work at UCCB beginning in the mid 1970's, took part in one of the most successful concerts I had ever produced.

Stepdancers Reverend Eugene Morris and Betty Matheson; fiddlers Carl MacKenzie and Dan Joe MacInnis; pianist George MacInnis; the Cape Breton Gaelic Choir under the direction of Mae Cameron; Gaelic vocalists Kay MacDonald and Joe Murphy; folk singer Donnie Campbell; and pipers Jamie MacInnis, Paul MacNeil, and Dr. Angus MacDonald all performed. Among the performers were many individuals who had instructed stepdance classes, Gaelic language classes, and beginner's violin classes at UCCB, and all had been involved as performers in many of the concerts and ceilidhs I had produced over the years. Also appearing was the popular Scottish group, Ossian, who were on a world tour at the time of their visit to Cape Breton and were eager to perform in the concert. In addition, Cape Breton's own world-class act, the Barra MacNeils, made a special appearance. On the occasion, the Barras rendered a vocal selection in memory of their uncle, Charlie MacKenzie who had passed away the day before. Charlie, like his brothers Carl, Hector, and Simon and his sister Jean, was a gifted musician. He was especially celebrated in the community as a fiddler and as an outstanding vocalist, and as stated that evening, Charlie had been a special inspiration and support to the Barra MacNeils for many years. Two well-known radio personalities in Cape Breton, Rosemary McCormack of CBC's *Island Echoes* and Dave Reynolds, formerly of CJCB, were the hosts for the evening.

Notes

1. While attending staff orientation at Eastern Shore District High School (ESDH), Halifax in 1972, I was introduced to Mimmi MacKenzie. It was our first meeting. Mimmi explained her interest in "the music." She proceeded to explain that there was music in her family and that the pipes are of particular interest to her brothers. She also explained that she had often attended some good sessions of music with fiddlers like Alex Francis MacKay and Donald Angus Beaton and that was a very good indicator of interest in music, I thought. Later I would meet two of her brothers who are excellect pipers: Kenny (who performed at the ESDH concert in 1973) and Allan. A third brother, Ian, plays guitar and Mimmi plays piano.

2. I approached Fred White recently, and I asked him to recount his journey from Mabou to Halifax on May 17, 1973.

3. Robert Redfield, "The Folk Society," in *The American Journal of Sociology*, 3:4, Chicago: The University of Chicago Press, Jan., 1947, p. 23.

4. David W. Hartman. *Immigrants and Migrants*. (Detroit: University Thought Publishing Company, 1974), p. 31.

5 Sheldon MacInnes, "Folk Society in an Urban Setting," unpublished master's thesis, Detroit, Michigan: The Merrill-Palmer Institute (affiliate of Wayne State University), 1977, p. 46.

6. Morgan's music is on his father's side. Morgan's grand-uncle, William MacQuarrie from Orangedale, was a violin player. Another grand-uncle, Hector J. MacQuarrie, won a silver cup in pipe competition in 1891. Morgan's aunt Christy MacQuarrie played the violin as well. These notes are from John Gibson's 1972-1973 research (*Scotia Sun* article #22).

7. There are several explanations attributed to the sound in the Mabou "Coal Mines" music. For some, it is the "Gaelic" lilt and can only be rendered by violinists who speak the language; for others, it is a peculiar technique in the use of the bow; and still for others, it is a particular repertoire and an emphasis on specific notes throughout the tunes. Yet, for others, it is all of the above. Whatever the explanation, it takes years to master. The music is distinctive and delightful to hear and especially to dance to.

8. One of Little Jack's closest friends was Bernie MacNeil, formerly of Rear Big Pond. Each summer, Bernie visited my home in Big Pond and shared stories about the Detroit music sessions. Little Jack and his music were central to the stories.

9. John Campbell, "Cape Breton Music: Carl's Magic Carpet," *Cape Breton Post*, August 30, 1988, p. 15.

10. Kate Dunlay, "Review by Kate Dunlay" [of Winnie Chafe's *Legacy* recording], *Am Braighe*, Winter, 1996/97, p. 10.
11. Winnie Chafe citation which was read at UCCB's 1995 graduation ceremonies, at which time Winnie received a Doctor of Letters.
12. "Evening of Merriment, and Tension." I received the article from Joey Beaton, one of the musicians who took part in the ceilidh. The article was written by Linden MacIntyre.
13. "Nova Scotia's Claim to Castle to be Reasserted." I received this article from Joey Beaton.
14. See Note #12.
15. The official program for the 65th Guggenheim concerts.
16. Ibid.
17. Ibid.
18. *The Songs of the Cape*, recorded by Octet, UCCB Press 1008, 1985.
19. *Bach Meets Cape Breton*, recorded by David Greenberg/Puirt a Baroque, Marquis ERA 181, 1996.
20. J. Lotz and M. Welton, "Knowledge for the People: The Origins and Development of the Antigonish Movement," in Michael Welton, ed. *Knowledge for the People* (Toronto: OISE, 1987), p. 97.
21. Gaelic College's Summer Institute Brochure, 1984.
22. *The MacLellan Trio of Cape Breton*, recorded by Theresa, Donald, and Marie MacLellan, Breton Books and Music BBM5-003.
23. Frank Macdonald, "Scottish Fiddler Finds Cape Breton Musical Landscapes a Lot Like Scotland," *Inverness Oran*, July 17, 1996.
24. Official brochure for the "Road to the Isles program," which was prepared by Finlay J. MacDonald in collaboration with Dr. Angus MacDonald, 1985.
25. Official brochure for the "Capercaillie tour," 1985.
26. *Cascade*, recorded by Capercaillie, Etive SRT4K178, 1984.
27. See Note #47, chapter 3.
28. *The Green Linnet Records* catalogue, Danbury, USA, CT06810, 1996, p. 9.
29. Official program for *Sydney's 175th Anniversary Week,* July 24-30, 1960.
30. Douglas Eadie, Co-producer, Pelicula Flims Limited, Glasgow, Scotland. Letter to Sheldon MacInnes, February 12, 1985.
31. Ibid.
32. Chris Frew, "Travels with a Fiddle," *West Highland Free Press*, January 31, 1986.
33. Gordon Menzies, Executive Producer, British Broadcasting Corporation, Glasgow, Scotland. Letter to Sheldon MacInnes, Sept. 11, 1985.
34. In 1990, Archie Alex was named Bard of Mod Ontario. He was described by patrons of the Mod as an ambassador for the Highland heritage of Canada when he went to the National Mod in Scotland as the Lieutenant

Governor's Award winner in 1988. [according to Mod Ontario 1991 official program booklet]

35. Norman MacDonald, "A Highland University: Some Lessons in the Politics and Planning of Higher Education in North and Northwest Scotland, 1829-1992" (published paper available from Barail, the Centre for Highlands and Islands Policy Studies, Sabhal Mor Ostaig, Teangue, Sleat, Isle of Skye IV44 8RQ), 1992.

36. John Campbell, "Cape Breton Not Only Home for Scots in North America," *Cape Breton Post*, Nov. 2, 1996.

37. *Cape Breton Island and the Scottish Highlands: Two Celtic Societies and their Parallel Development*, a short course and staff development seminar, July 6-15, 1981. Course outline and brochure, designed by Norman MacDonald.

38. Steve Mills, "Cape Breton's Singing Ambassador John Allan Cameron Returns Home," *Cape Breton Post*, Oct. 21, 1978, p. 4.

39. "Margaret MacPhee Guest of Honor," *Cape Breton Post*, Sept. 5, 1980, p. 24.

40. As guest speaker for the occasion, I spoke about Margaret's contribution to the dance community. I reminded the audience that the teaching of dance is a tradition with the Gaels in Cape Breton and in Scotland.

41. Margaret (MacEachern) Dunn, "Dan Hughie MacEachern: A Family Profile" in *MacEachern's Collection: The Music of Dan Hughie MacEachern - Volume 11*," published by Margaret Dunn, Antigonish, Nova Scotia, 1993.

42. Ibid.

43. In reference to #41, there is a beautiful picture of Dan Hughie with his six sisters, that was taken at his testimonial on November 15, 1980.

44. Ibid.

45. See Official Program for the Buddy MacMaster Testimonial at the Beaton Institute, UCCB.

46. I quoted directly from the Beaton Institute's archival video, *Buddy MacMaster Testimonial* (restricted access), which was filmed by Cyril MacInnis.

47. St. Francis Xavier University convocation program, 1996.

48. I produced the *Tribute to Reverend Eugene Morris*, which took place in October, 1989.

49. A discussion paper presented by Sheldon MacInnes to the Inverness County school teachers, in Mabou, at a workshop sponsored by DANS regarding a rationale for teaching square dancing in the Inverness County school curriculum, physical education program, Spring 1995.

CHAPTER SIX

The Early Industry — Mixed Reviews

The Many Roads "Taken"

The increased lure to Cape Breton music, song, and dance has become more widespread among the general public in recent years. A contributing factor to the surge of interest in the music is the desire by some musicians and entrepreneurs to promote the music as a cultural industry. These efforts have given rise to some incredible success stories for some Cape Breton performing artists, especially as seen in their commercial recordings, in television and radio appearances, and in their travels throughout Canada, the United States, and Europe. Historically, the Celtic music of Cape Breton had penetrated national and international regions through the travels of, and recordings by, musicians from rural Cape Breton, at a time when the music industry itself was less sympathetic to the Cape Breton performing artist.

Public interest in the Cape Breton Celtic music is longstanding and widespread and was actually an integral force in keeping the music tradition alive. Research shows that among those interventions to help sustain the public interest were the personal efforts of individuals representing various interests: the research and collection by academics and scholars in folklore and musicology, especially from the United States and Britain (like Charles Dunn, S.R. Cowell, J.P. Hughes, John Lorne Campbell, J.P. Flett, and T.M. Flett); the early research in Cape Breton and subsequent publications by Nova Scotia personalities (like Major C.I.N. MacLeod and Helen Creighton); [1] the publication of local fiddle music composers, in *Cape Breton Melodies*, compiled and arranged by Gordon F. MacQuarrie in 1940;[2] the appearances by exponents of the music and dance at national and international festivals like Laughie Gillis' and Harvey MacKinnon's participation in a 1961 Quebec Folk Festival;[3] the 1952 participation by the "The Grand Mira Chorus" in

Halifax;[4] and the vast array of early competitions among local fiddlers including those by Michael MacInnis of Rear Big Pond.[5] Dan Joe competed in a
program sponsored by the Cape Breton Dairymen's Corporation Society in
1942 at which he won the Old Time Fiddler's Championship trophy.

The local media also have a history of involvement in producing programs that depict the Celtic music of Cape Breton. The July 15th and July
18th editions of the 1938 *Post Record* describe the local ceilidh, *Celtic Forum*,
which hit the Canadian airwaves at that time.

> *Celtic Forum* makes it bow to Canada radio audiences tonight, when
> a completely new program will be presented from Sydney at 8:00.
> The program will be broadcast over the Canadian Broadcasting
> Corporation network and through the United States mutual
> Broadcasting Company.[6]

Performing artists for the ceilidh included Malcolm R. MacLeod, Gaelic
singer and conductor for the program, and fiddlers Mary MacDonald and
Gordon F. MacQuarrie.[7] The program received a positive response across the
country.

Additional opportunities to promote the music developed among trans-
planted Cape Bretoners, including musicians living away and keenly
interested in the music, as a way to celebrate culture and to extend the music tradition beyond the home boundaries, like Bernie MacNeil's music
sessions in Detroit in the 1940's, Bill Lamey's concert and dance activities in
Boston in the 1950's, and Steve and Rita Broley's music sessions in Toronto
in the 1960's. These gatherings likely emerged as a result of the tradition of
widespread travels by Cape Bretoners, including several noted fiddlers. John
Gibson in his research in 1972-1973 recorded some of the detail about the
travels of several legendary Inverness County fiddlers.

> [Sandy MacLean lived at Foot Cape, near Strathlorne, Inverness
> County]. He visited that city [Boston] on many occasions and at a
> competition held there in 1929 in which 21 fiddlers competed,
> Sandy playing Strathspeys, Reels, and Hornpipes, took first prize.
> But he was also out west three times during the 20's . . . It mightn't
> be fair to say that he played mostly for Westerners, for hundreds of
> Cape Bretoners went west looking for work.[8]
> [Angus Allan Gillis lived in South-West Margaree, Inverness
> County]. In 1926 and 1927 Angus Allan was down working in
> Boston and naturally his fiddle went with him. He played for a

local radio station, WHDH, and regularly he and some other celebrated Cape Bretoners did their share in many musical get togethers, particularly in dances in the Winslow Hall near Dudley. Another Margaree-er, Alex Gillis, was there, so was Ronnie Gillis from Judique . . . [Angus Allan explains to Gibson.] "In 1933, I had occasion one time to visit Ontario, to Alexandria in Glengarry County to fiddle [to compete]." [Gibson explains:] He [Angus Allan] won the St. Finnans' Centenary Cup.[9]

[Donald Angus Beaton lived in Mabou, Inverness County.] Donald Angus performed at the Orange Hall in Brookline, Mass. in 1966, 1968, 1969, and 1972. While in Boston in 1972, he recorded a radio program for WTBX (sic) in Cambridge, Mass. In 1967, Donald Angus performed at the Saxon Club Hall in Windsor and St. Mary's Hall in Toronto, Ontario. In 1971, Donald Angus performed at the VFW Hall in Waltham, Mass.[10]

[I had the pleasure of attending Donald Angus' performances in Boston in 1972 when I travelled there with Doug MacPhee to attend those activities which featured Donald Angus particularly].[10]

An important factor in the mainstay of the music has always been its relevancy or its place within the local area as a means to building community and to nurturing pride and tradition among families and different community-based networks, and this is likely true today as well. A classic illustration of this are the early parish picnics, like the 1902[11] Iona Parish Picnic which likely contributed to the founding of the now popular annual Highland Village Day Concert in Iona. Events like Highland Village Day in Victoria County and the now legendary Broad Cove Concert in Inverness County, which got its start in 1957,[12] have been significant forces in helping to maintain the Celtic music tradition in Cape Breton.

Like the community of Iona, the people in St. Margaret's Parish organized the Broad Cove concert around the volunteer spirit and the community pride ingrained in the local talent from Victoria and Inverness Counties to raise funds for local parish activities. After forty-plus years, the Broad Cove concert continues to attract an audience from various parts of North America and is seen as a model to other local areas to foster citizenry and to help sustain community pride and tradition. Proceeds continue to support the parish needs.

Of the few hundred in the parish, it seems everyone turns out to either park cars, sing, dance, sell hot dogs, or collect money at the concert which is their major fundraiser for the parish.[13]

Also important in sustaining an interest in the music was the emergence of the square dance activity throughout Cape Breton not only in the rural communities but also in Sydney at the Carpenter's Hall, the Old Army and Navy League Hall, and the Venetian Gardens.[14] These popular Sydney dances together with the early Sydney Scottish Concerts[15] emerged and developed with the arrival of the dance fiddlers from the rural communities to live and to work in the Sydney area in the 1940's and the 1950's, dance fiddlers like Bill Lamey and Joe MacLean. Local radio continued to play the music through regular programs; together with a series of commercial recordings and eventually through television, additional productions emerged in Sydney. Each of these venues provided a forum for the music from rural Cape Breton.

These initiatives represent the longevity of interest in the Cape Breton Celtic song, dance, and music and may well have been the seeds to the current activity in local Celtic music, which is so integral to the East Coast music industry today. These earlier developments flourished primarily because of personal contacts and friendships within the community of artists despite the seemingly lack of interest by the mainstream industry to engage the artist in a professional manner and by the artists who held a guarded view towards tinkering in the interest of commercializing the music. Accordingly, the efforts in the 1970's and 80's culminating in the 1990's, of some of the Celtic artists of Cape Breton embraced the industry side of the music. Consequently, the business aspect and success of the local music have now become one of the incentives for some of the local Celtic artists to expand their boundaries.

The February 1997 East Coast Music Awards (ECMA)[16] highlighted two fiddlers from Inverness County as representative of the Atlantic region's finest musicians: top female artist of the year, Natalie MacMaster, and top male artist of the year, Ashley MacIsaac.[17] These awards represent only two of the eight awards received jointly by both performers in several competitive categories. Since the early 1990's, awards received by Cape Breton musicians, like the Barra MacNeils, the Rankin Family, and John Allan Cameron, are symbolic of the interest in the Cape Breton Celtic performer.[18]

As a result of the Celtic craze, the music industry sometimes forfeits the temptation to resist labelling everything and anything as Celtic. Although understandable, it may not always be appropriate. Rita MacNeil, for example, has usually chosen not to label her music as Celtic, or even Folk, Country, or Blues. Yet, writers and reporters take the liberty to sometimes describe her music as belonging to a particular strand, and the Gaelic label is sometimes ascribed, probably because of her Cape Breton roots. In a review of her 1988 Calgary concert, Wendy Dudley, a reporter with the *Calgary Herald*, wrote:

"Much of the songwriter's material has a Gaelic spell, no doubt borrowed from her hometown of Big Pond, Cape Breton."[19]

Some people build a description of Rita's music on structure and form; other people on the message and emotions expressed in the lyrics and in the interpretation. A review in the October 1995 magazine, *Saturday Night*, described Rita's music as: ". . . music with a downhome flavour and songs that became anthems for doers and dreamers. Hope-filled lyrics about family, faith, and Cape Breton, coupled with a voice any gospel singer would die for. . . ."[20] Yet, on the occasion when Rita decided to visit her Celtic roots in Barra, Scotland to perform, culminating her performance with her inspiring song "The Crossing," Rita was taken to task in a local Cape Breton publication because she introduced a Celtic connection in her music.

On the other hand, urban folk musicians like Kenzie MacNeil, a well-known singer/songwriter from Sydney, consciously link their artistic endeavours with the Celtic music tradition of Cape Breton. Kenzie once explained in an interview that the tempo, for example, in his popular song "The Island" was inspired by John Allan Cameron's guitar rendition of the highland pipe tune "Farewell to the Creeks."[21] John Allan has likely inspired many urban folk musicians and writers from the Sydneys like Kenzie, Ronnie MacEachern, Al Bennett, and Fred Lavery — all gifted writers or performers or producers and in some cases a combination of all three. Musically speaking, these artists appear to be closely associated with the Celtic stuff. In fact, Al Bennett is an accomplished Celtic fiddler in his own right.

The urban folk musicians' interest in being associated with efforts to promote the rural heritage inherent in the music of the Cape Breton fiddler, the Gaelic songs, and the traditional dance has helped to foster their individual musical careers and as a result, these musicians are quite often perceived as representing the traditional Celtic music of Cape Breton, thus receiving some widespread media attention.

The initiatives by the many urban folk musicians through public institutions like UCCB, or CBC, or the music industry in general through commercial recordings, theatre, and drama, and the successes enjoyed because of their respective accomplishments have sometimes been referred to as a benchmark for luring increaed attention to the local music scene. This may have been Ken Donovan's view when he states in *The Island*:

> Cape Breton music and humour received its wider exposure in 1977 with the production of a musical comedy entitled the "Rise and Follies of Cape Breton Island."[22]

Merle MacIsaac in his article "Cape Breton Hitparade/Traditional Music Goes Top Ten" in *Bluenose* links the interest in Celtic bands like the Chieftains as all-inspiring to local artists, and this is likely the case. After all, Scotland's Nahoganaich had a profound influence on shaping the Sons of Skye in the early 1970's. MacIsaac writes:

> Bands like the Chieftains of Ireland, for example, have demonstrated the larger appetite for traditional Celtic music. Meanwhile, the pull of distant folk concerts and their exuberant audiences have no doubt stoked the confidence of young Cape Breton musicians.[23]

What MacIsaac may not have realized and Donovan may have viewed in diminishing returns was the depth of the real hidden treasure, the popular legacy and tradition of the Cape Breton fiddler as probably the single most significant factor in generating attention towards the musical genius of the wider community.

These past treasures have given rise to the current generation of Cape Breton solo fiddlers, Ashley MacIsaac, Wendy MacIsaac, Glen Graham, Jackie Dunn, Kyle Gillis, Rodney MacDonald, John Morris Rankin, Howie MacDonald, Kyle MacNeil, Dwyane Cote, Stephanie Wills, and Natalie MacMaster. These artists now take their rightful place on the industry's stage and many people see their mentors as the leaders of an earlier era.

Over several generations in many small Cape Breton rural communities, the fiddler emerged as a continuing source of inspiration and genius for many individuals and families associated with the music. These idols, seemingly detached and isolated, were very much well-travelled musicians and were often revered as living legends despite the lucid interest among the early fiddlers to view the music as an industry. That is to say, the earlier fiddlers saw the music not as a market-driven commodity but rather as a way of life.

One of Cape Breton's most celebrated personalities is Senator Allan J. MacEachen. In addition to his recent Honorary Doctorate of Letters from the University College of Cape Breton (1997), he has received recognition from several other universities and colleges in Canada as well as from a wide variety of sectors in the community for his achievements as a member of the House of Commons, where he first took his seat for the riding of Inverness in 1953. Allan J.'s presence in the circle of Canadian and international diplomacy was felt almost immediately after he took office. Several years ago, during his early tenure in the House of Commons, he and a friend were travelling the coast of Inverness County. In the hopes of getting directions to a particular home in the area, they approached a high school student. During the conversation, the strong sense of presence of the local fiddlers among the people of Inverness County was reaffirmed for Allan J. He shared the following story at a St. Andrew's Day function sponsored by the Cape Breton Highland Society in, 1968:

> Those of us from Cape Breton pride ourselves deservedly on our appreciation of higher education. But sometimes I believe that we love music, we love the pipes, and we love the fiddle more . . . I was travelling on the coastline of Inverness County with a friend of mine . . . We stopped this day on the side of the road and we met a young man and we asked directions to the house we were seeking. He was about in high school. We asked him his name. He reluctantly told his name; he was a true Scot. And, he of course, seeking an exchange, he asked us our names. So my friend said, "This is Allan MacEachen." And there was no reaction. My friend thought that he ought to know me. He said, "This is Allan MacEachen; he's on the radio all the time." The young man looked at me and his eyes flashed in wonder as he asked, "And do you play the fiddle?"[24]

The "78's" Turn "33 1/3"

Perhaps more than anything, the early recording experiences of the local fiddlers represent one of the more significant contributions to the mainstay of the music and at the same time reflect the state of the cultural industry, or lack of it, in Cape Breton in the 1950's. Among my most vivid recollections of Dan Joe's interest in performing in the public domain are my conversations with him concerning his own early recordings. His stories concerning the recording industry revealed both positive and negative aspects about his experiences. [25]

Dan Joe's recording experience in the late 1950's through to the mid-1960's was not unlike the recording experiences, for example, of Angus Chisholm, Angus Allan Gillis, and Dan J. Campbell who travelled from Cape Breton to Montreal in 1935[26] to record music on the Decca label. These early recording sessions resulted in a large collection of popular records, which were available at select stores in different parts of Canada. It is estimated that over a hundred recordings were made and several thousand records were pressed and sold. "In the sixty years since the issue of the first Cape Breton fiddle record on 78 rpm disc in the 20's, over three hundred commercial recordings featuring Cape Breton fiddlers have been produced on forty different labels."[27] Many individuals credit these recordings as an important source of transmitting the music.

Like other Cape Bretoners who recorded in the 1950's, Dan Joe did not expect a large monetary return for his labour. Some airtime over local radio stations in the region, like CJFX and CJCB, was a mark of recognition for his efforts. His recordings enjoyed airtime at radio station WBOM in Boston, as well. This was often described by Mike MacDonald, a native Big Ponder living in Boston, and by the Irwin Family who have Irish Cove roots and who often visited during the summer months and took part in music sessions at Dan Joe and Christie's. Members of the musical Irwin family often performed with many of the Cape Breton fiddlers who lived in Boston in the 1950's and 1960's.

In the early 1960's, Dan Joe's interest in recording continued, but the old 78 format was on its way out. The technology had changed and the long-play records, or LP's as they became known, offered an opportunity to sustain Dan Joe's interest with respect to recording. Dan Joe recorded on the Celtic and Banff labels which were owned by George Taylor of Rodeo Records in Montreal.

One can only presume that the industry's interest in further recording the music of the Cape Breton fiddler was accelerated for a number of reasons, not the least of which was the continuing popularity of the music which had been recorded on the 78. It was now less likely that the vinyl recordings would be damaged if minimal care was taken and, therefore, the potential developed to distribute a greater number of recordings since the packaging and merchandising became more user-friendly for shippers, retail outlets, merchants, and the consumer. By this time, there was an increased usage of phonographs in households throughout Canada and the United States, and this offered increased potential for sales of recordings in both Canada and the United States.

Certainly, from Dan Joe's perspective, the important features of the new recording format were that it increased the number of selections that could be recorded on one disc, and the tempo of the LP recordings was closer to the natural timing. Most important to Dan Joe was that he could now put more effort into arrangements and new tune groupings for the extended recording format. The average length of a long-play recording was about thirty-three plus minutes, which accommodated about fifteen to eighteen minutes of music on each side of the LP. The music was presented in a series of cuts of about three minutes each; this translated into about five or six cuts or groups per side. Now, Dan Joe could more effectively present the groups of tunes in a manner closer to the way he played them in public venues.

A major variance in the vinyl format from the earlier 78 was that the LP's were packaged in a sleeve, which provided the opportunity for liner notes, printed information about the music and about the recording artist. However, Dan Joe was not encouraged by the recording companies to design a sleeve or to include liner notes. At that time, the recording industry made the decisions regarding the sleeve's content, and one can only presume that the industry did not deem the additional time and expense to include this information to be significant.

Consequently and unfortunately, information about Dan Joe's music, about the various music collections, and about local composers and mentors were void in the industry's packaging of his music. The recording process did not give him an opportunity to share his stories and his personal recollections about the music. It did not give Dan Joe, for example, an opportunity to share the story behind the jig, "The Council Gathering," which he recorded on his second LP, *The Scottish Canadian Fiddle of Dan Joe MacInnis*, in 1963. Dan Joe had been invited to play at the home of Joe MacDonald in East Bay on the evening of MacDonald's successful win of a local council seat in a Cape Breton County municipal election. At the time, Dan Joe was preparing to release his second LP. During the evening of celebration, Dan Joe decided that he wanted to record a particular jig on the LP to recognize Joe MacDonald's success in that year's election. As Dan Joe was not able to determine the correct title of a certain jig, he took the liberty of naming the jig, "The Council Gathering Jig." The tune was later recorded by Mabou's Donald Angus Beaton at a session in January 1976 and released on his *A Musical Legacy* recording which Joey Beaton produced in 1985 using the same title Dan Joe had given the tune in 1963. As the entire process of depicting Dan Joe's music and the culture and community it represented was handled by the recording industry and was fostered only to the extent that the recording industry thought it was important, stories like this add human interest and a behind the scenes view of the performer.

When I reviewed the various LP cover designs of the Cape Breton fiddlers of the early 1960's, I learned a great deal about the recording industry's approach to the music and to the community of the Cape Breton. On some occasions, for example, photographs of the fiddlers were used to enhance the sleeves; often, the same photo of the artist was used by the recording company for the artist's subsequent recordings. Such was the case with Dan Joe's recordings. In his second LP, cited earlier, Dan Joe supplied a black and white photo for the back sleeve. The same photo appeared on his final solo LP, recorded in 1964, but as a smaller version.

The use of stylized caricatures depicting the fiddle instrument on the albums' sleeves was also a popular feature, which was the case in Dan Joe's third LP. The fiddle caricature depicted a Scottish or tartan association with the music rather than the promotion of the Cape Breton interpretation of traditional music.

In addition to the use of caricatures, perhaps one of the more bizarre practices employed by the recording industry at the time, with respect to the cover designs of LP's, was dressing the front cover with an attractively coloured picture, which was often supplied by the Nova Scotia Tourist Bureau, of a provincial site depicting a typical tourist destination anywhere in Nova Scotia.[28] Such was the case with Dan Joe's albums in 1962 and 1963. What is noteworthy about this situation is that in many cases, the pictures on the fiddlers' albums had little, if anything, to do with the featured fiddler or even with the community in which the artist lived. For example: the recording by Little Jack MacDonald displays a picture of Peggy's Cove in Halifax;[29] a recording by Winston "Scotty" Fitzgerald actually displays a front photo of Citadel Hill in Halifax and a panoramic view of the city of Halifax.[30] Little Jack MacDonald was from Creignish and actually was living in Ontario when he recorded his only LP. "Scotty" was from White Point, Victoria County and was living just outside of Sydney when he recorded his LP's.

It appears that the recording companies lacked an interest in promoting Cape Breton Island, even on the cover of an album which featured the music of a recording artist from Cape Breton. Obviously, they didn't recognize the marketing value of indigenous photos. Clearly, there was little effort to try to include a photo of the artist's community or even a photo of the area in Cape Breton representative of the fiddler's respective community.

Coupled with the sleeve design, the distribution and marketing of the material were also managed by the recording companies, as was the case with the early 78's, and Dan Joe accepted this practice as the acceptable way to do business. Despite the fact that the new vinyl format was more durable and user-friendly, Dan Joe was not enticed to become personally involved in the marketing aspect which would allow him to distribute some LP's, at least locally, so that he could realize some share of the profits from sales. In summary, the only aspect of the recording which involved Dan Joe was his actual performance of the music — everything else was left for exploitation by the recording industry itself. Dan Joe simply did not ask questions about the business side of this enterprise, and that was fine with the industry representatives!

Occasionally, despite the availability of these records, some people requested homemade recordings of Dan Joe's music, and this was always an interesting aspect of the local music. In the early 1960's, while I was still at home, several American folklorists arrived during a rather quiet Sunday afternoon to record Dan Joe's music; these researchers used a small recorder.

Dan Joe and the family members who had gathered to experience this moment were curious about the interest shown by these researchers from the United States. During the afternoon, they recorded plenty of Dan Joe's music and some conversation with Dan Joe about his music. The recording session ended after a couple of hours. There was no more communication with these people after that day except by way of the mail several months later. As a gift for Dan Joe's music, he had been issued a year's subscription to the *National Geographic Magazine*, a magazine that, Dan Joe learned later, was a prestigious publication restricted to only certain sectors of the populace.

Not all home recording sessions were so comforting. On many occasions, the recording techniques were not effective and the people who were compiling personal collections often distributed the material randomly. The use of inadequate equipment and the poor recording conditions resulted in many homemade recordings that were very disappointing to the artist. On the other hand, many people will say, including the fiddlers, that many of those recordings are priceless today as they do provide the only recorded music of some fiddlers.

By 1965, Dan Joe, like other fiddlers, began to lose interest in the recording studio, probably because of his busy performing schedule of concerts and dances, which consumed much of his time and provided him with a great deal of satisfaction; the negative experiences surrounding the use of personal recorders; and the lack of monetary return from the commercial recording industry. This caused a dislike and even mistrust of the recording industry by many fiddlers who had recorded earlier.

The earlier recording sessions were, in retrospect, negative experiences for the fiddlers. Without written contracts with mutual benefits, there were no royalties and little or any financial return for the recording artists. Furthermore, recording companies re-packaged the earlier 78 recordings to conform to the LP format[31] without any consultation with the fiddlers and again with little or any financial benefit to them. The fiddlers developed a sour taste for the recording process and began to distance themselves from any commercial recordings. This attitude continued for about a ten-year period, 1965-1975. However, the approach by the recording industry, beginning in the early to mid-1970's, started to change.

A quiet determination by the Cape Breton fiddlers to take control of their destiny in the industry emerged long after Dan Joe had left the studio. Many local fiddlers began to take responsibility for initiatives associated with production and marketing in the recording industry. This new effort enabled some of the fiddlers to be become successful entrepreneurs with their music.

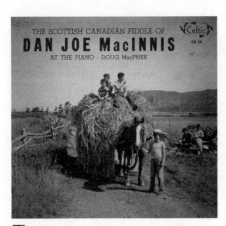

The front sleeve of Dan Joe's second long-play album, recorded in 1963.

[Right] Dan Joe MacInnis, 1963.

Photos by Celtic

Among the more exciting entrepreneurial fiddlers in Cape Breton is the ever-so-popular Howie MacDonald. He has been a member of the versatile Rankin Family since the group hit the road in the early 1990's. Howie has performed at concerts, ceilidhs, dances, and pubs in his own right through-out North America and has acquired a tremendous following of fans wherever Celtic music is performed. As a full-time musician, he also takes re-sponsibility for managing his own business affairs.

In addition to touring, Howie has produced six solo recordings. He is also featured on a number of recordings backing up other musicians and he has collaborated with other musicians in producing their recordings as well. Among his innovative recordings are *Live and Lively*, which he recorded at a dance in Sydney and *The dance last night*, his most recent. On this particu-lar recording, Howie effectively introduces a comedy skit featuring several true to life characters, played/narrated by Howie himself, who supposedly at-tend a dance somewhere in rural Cape Breton. The behaviour of these true to life characters on the way to the dance as well as at the dance is one which might accurately represent the old-time dances in the good old days.

In addition to his own business side of the music, Howie MacDonald actively supports a variety of initiatives to promote the local music. In many of his efforts, he often engages members of his family, including his extended family, as guest musicians. For example, his support and encouragement for Marilyn MacDonald (Mar, his sister) resulted in her title recording, *My Love, Cape Breton and Me*, featuring her wonderful rendition of the song, "The

Hills of Home," one of my favourites. Between his extensive tours and busy studio work, Howie takes some time to perform at local stepdance classes in Sydney where his music is greatly appreciated by the aspiring dancers.

A couple of years ago, Howie appeared at a benefit ceilidh in Toronto to raise money for the Finlay Walker Art Collection. The ceilidh was sponsored by the Friends of Finlay Walker to purchase the collection for the University College of Cape Breton, as a memorial to Finlay's memory.

Howie later explained that he enjoyed the trip to Toronto immensely but was alleged to have said, using a deep brogue accent, that he would never again accept a "free" airline ticket from Sheldon MacInnes. I had arranged for Howie's airline ticket to Toronto; the ticket was complimentary in support of the project. Unfortunately, Howie experienced some turbulent flights and in the final analysis, it took him almost the full day to reach Toronto from Sydney. As usual, though, Howie's remarkable sense of humour is revealed as he told this story to one of my family members.

The young fiddler has a remarkable sense of humour which, coupled with his musical talent, has contributed significantly to his popularity. Howie MacDonald is likely one of the most talented individuals I know personally. His spirit to be creative and more or less in control of the business side of his music might have developed as a direct result of the pioneer work by Rounder Recordings.

The "Rounder" Experience

Rounder Records of Massachussets arrived on the scene in the early 1970's with a determination to lure fiddlers to record after having researched the earlier recording efforts of the Cape Breton fiddlers. This intervention by Rounder followed some positive experiences by the local fiddlers who were invited to record for CBC radio and television in the early to mid-1970's. Certain practices and procedures, as well as personable staff at CBC, helped to encourage the fiddlers to return to the studio and to regain a level of trust and satisfaction. The material recorded by CBC was subject to strict regulations with regard to air time; the recording sessions were more of a collaborative process and were often replayed for the fiddlers for final approval before going to air; and copyright laws prevailed. As well, the local musicians' union began to scrutinize the interest in the music of the Celtic artist moreso than in the past.

The recording industry was beginning to discover the musical genius of the Cape Breton fiddlers which resulted in an extended interest in the fiddlers' music in the United States, Canada, Scotland, and Ireland. Rounder's approach was to instill in the musicians an entrepreneurial spirit in their recording efforts. This new philosophy was maintained and eventually, the fiddlers learned new and innovative ways and techniques to engage in the business of recording their music and to assert almost complete control of the process. This approach continues to prevail among many Cape Breton fiddlers today.

Rounder Records' representatives personally met with several fiddlers and encouraged them to record their music. Their goal was simply to persuade the artists to record with Rounder and to explain that all other details, marketing, distribution, cover design, and even the liner notes, would be influenced by the artist. Rounder Records also allowed the artist to review the recorded music material after the mix had been completed. This was a new feature in the commercial process as far as the Cape Breton fiddler was concerned. The artists decided, after hearing a demo of their recording, whether or not they wanted to take that final step, the pressing process leading to the production of the record. The fiddler was now finally an active partner in the process, the reverse of earlier recording practices! Unlike Dan Joe's earlier experiences, the fiddlers were now encouraged to submit camera copy information for liner notes. These notes became a feature of Rounder Records' recordings. In these notes, the fiddlers had the opportunity to publicly recognize their mentors, their family, their family genealogy, their communities, and the many local composers whose music was so integral to the uniqueness of the music of the Cape Breton fiddlers. These matters were of extreme importance to the local fiddlers. It also gave them an opportunity to identify the many great collections of music from which the fiddlers extrapolated their tunes including those collections composed by Scotland's Hunter, Gowe, Marshall, and Skinner. Great collections like the *Skye*, the *Atholl*, and the *Kerr's* were among the prize possessions of these fiddlers, and they were eager to proclaim this fact. The fiddlers often turned to a friend or to a family member with good writing skills to prepare the information for the liner notes accurately and professionally. In the event that the information was prepared by a Rounder representative, it was always returned to the artist for proofreading.

To grasp Rounder's approach, one needs to study some of the company's initial productions. Rounder's first commercially released recording of a Cape Breton fiddler was in 1974.[32] The recording was by Cheticamp native Joe Cormier whose LP consists of three sleeves of detailed information and photos about the music and its origins, the performers, and the mentors. The information introduces his family and his native Acadian community in a very tasteful and informative manner.

Joe Cormier's account of his music is an excellent source of information to help one understand the nature and importance of the music to the Cape Breton fiddler and to the community. Joe explains the role of community fiddlers like his uncle, the classically-trained Marcellin, and the popular Placide Odo and neighbouring fiddlers like Winston "Scotty" Fitzgerald and Angus Chisholm, information which adds to the importance and the value of the recording. Joe Cormier has lived in Boston since the early 1960's, and he recorded his LP in Boston.

The same liner note format applies to John Campbell's[33] first recording in 1976. His father Dan J. recorded a 78 rmp with Decca, which was released in 1936. John's LP, in contrast to his father's 78's, provides a treasure of information about John and his music as well as about his father's music.

Among Rounder's gems is the first recording ever of Cape Breton's *The Beatons of Mabou*.[34] The recording features the music of Donald Angus Beaton and his wife Elizabeth together with their sons Joseph and Kinnon. Donald Angus was in retirement age when he recorded the LP in 1977. The liner notes by Revered Hugh A. MacDonald provide an indepth presentation about the music of Mabou and its link with the Coal Mines' music using the traditional Gaelic titles.

Donald Angus' followers in Cape Breton, in other parts of Canada, in the United States, and in Scotland were delighted with the outcome of the recording. It features, in a professional and dignified manner, one of the most prolific traditional performers and composers of the music, for the community to add to their collection of Cape Breton violin music.

One of the cornerstone features of the Rounder Record approach was to offer the fiddler the opportunity to purchase the final product completely packaged for sale in units of a thousand and, later, in units of five hundred, following the initial pressing. The result was that the fiddlers received a manageable supply of records, equivalent to an equally manageable budget; the fiddlers then marketed their albums at their different performance venues and at local retail stores. As a result of their record sales and their personal involvement in the process, the fiddlers realized a greater share of the financial return. In most cases, the scheme involved the entire family in the merchandising process at concerts, at dances, at conventions, and even at weddings and house ceilidhs. A modest but viable industry, which had missed earlier opportunities, emerged and is carried on today at concerts and ceilidhs. The fiddlers finally realized significant control over the process and directly benefitted from their efforts.

Interestingly enough, however, among their most competitive variables were those earlier recordings, the 78's which were now converted to vinyl and the early LP's which were continually repackaged and released by individuals who controlled the Celtic and Banff labels, recordings which included *The Fiddlers of Cape Breton — A Collectors Item, Twenty-Four Cape Breton Fiddle Medleys*, and *Cape Breton Violins*. Later, these same recordings appeared in the new cassette format, in the 1980's, and in the CD format, more recently, unlocking new commercial opportunities for sale purposes. Unfortunately, the local fiddlers featured on these repackaged recordings still did not receive their fair share of financial returns; the photos from the earlier recordings depicting Citadel Hill and Peggy's Cove and the incomplete information about the artist and the music prevailed, as well, on the repackaged recordings.

In due course, the fiddlers learned that they could negotiate with other recording companies and studios to record their music; they could also negotiate to have the material pressed at different sites, as well, like World Records in Ontario. Mobile recording and studio work in other locales like Halifax followed. This had some impact on setting the current trend to construct studios in Cape Breton. The process has evolved to an interesting music recording industry in Cape Breton today.

Breaking New Ground

Ken Donovan's 1970's renaissance described in *The Island* offers a summary perspective of the attention to the music by a wide range of sources representing commercial recordings, publications, film, and video. The notice by the music industry to engage the Celtic musicians, for example, as one aspect of the music deserving of recognition opened up opportunities for many Cape Breton musicians and for other performers from all facets of the performing arts.

It is exciting today to see the media celebrate excellence in the Cape Breton entertainer. I was delighted, for example, to observe the response to the Rita MacNeil performance on CBC national television in October, 1994. The premiere show, *Rita MacNeil and Friends*, was acclaimed a hit by critics and by those who simply enjoy Rita and her music as a hit. As Roger Abbott stated on the first show, Rita is truly a national treasure. Although the show is no longer broadcast on CBC, Rita is expected to appear in some national format again in the near future.

As Canadians continue to celebrate the achievements in the cultural industry of many outstanding Cape Breton performers and to savour their triumph, one might also remind oneself of those individuals who originally nurtured the groundwork for the Cape Breton artist within the Canadian music industry — individuals like John Allan Cameron who entered the music scene when the music industry in Canada, including the Maritime region, was not so interested in the musicians of Cape Breton.

John Allan's first major public appearance was in the early 1960's on CJCB television in Sydney and I recall the occasion very well. My family was glued to a small black and white television set because Dan Joe had heard that Dan R. MacDonald's nephew was going to be a guest on a local program. As the program began and the name Cameron was mentioned, Dan Joe darted from the kitchen where he had been shaving and quickly explained the young man's background. Dan Joe did not know John Allan personally at that time but had heard great things about John's music and also that John had spent some time studying to become a priest. With that bit of information, the entire family settled to watch the program and to listen as John Allan performed the tune "Kitchener's Army March" on his six-string guitar. Shortly after that evening, John was introduced to his first music session at our home in Big Pond. Subsequently, John Allan married Dan Joe's niece (my cousin), Angela Broley. This close association with John Allan allowed me to observe his career with some personal interest.

John Allan's brother, John Donald, also a fine musician explains that he and John Allan got an early start in the music.

> For the first public appearance on violin and guitar, John Allan and John Donald played for a dance at the Dunmore School on June 1, 1953 . . . their first stage (concert) appearance took place in Port Hood on July 29, 1953.[35]

John Allan's first television presentation in the early 1960's led to a series of performances in local parish halls in Cape Breton, in Antigonish, and in Halifax. With the support and encouragement of Gus MacKinnon at CJFX radio station in Antigonish, John's music became well known throughout the Maritimes, in concert appearances and on recordings. His first LP, *Here Comes John Allan Cameron*, was an instant success, but like the early recordings of the fiddlers, I would speculate that the answer to the question of how many recordings were sold may not be certain. His vibrant, live presentations and his recordings included Gaelic songs, stepdancing, and lively melodies on the guitar. In addition to his success as an entertainer, John Allan's significant contribution may have been his determined effort to introduce the music of the Cape Breton fiddler to a wider audience via the media and the music industry in general. This effort helped clear the way for opportunities, now enjoyed by many of the Cape Breton fiddlers and entertainers.

When John Allan introduced himself to CBC Halifax in the early 1970's, he created a sense of magic among the producers, directors, and even the floor technicians who, understandably, had been enthralled for many years with the music of Don Messer and *Sing Along Jubilee.* The Messer program, which aired from 1952 to 1969, and *Sing Along Jubilee,* which aired from 1961 to 1972, were popular throughout the Maritimes.[36] Unfortunately, CBC personnel who were making decisions about showcasing local performers on the *Don Messer Show* or in any other context presumably had only limited knowledge about the Cape Breton fiddler. However, fiddlers who did appear with Messer include Winston Fitzgerald,[37] Elmer Briand,[38] and Carl MacKenzie.[39] Although John Allan viewed Messer as "the original Canadian superstar" and "his show (Messer's) was equivalent to Ed Sullivan's show in the U.S.,"[40] John Allan wanted to change the Messer style when he arrived on the Halifax stage with his version of the "Mabou Shuffle," a form of Inverness stepdance.

John Allan's strategy was calculated to simply entice CBC television to further introduce a blend of music, song, and dance more seasoned and alluring than New Scotland itself. This resulted in the national production, *CEILIDH*, a progeny of the Maritime regional program *Let's Have A Ceilidh*, featuring John Allan Cameron, which originally aired nationally in 1972.[41] Virginia Beaton and Stephen Pederson explain Dr. Neil Rosenberg's understanding of John Allan's musical style:

> Cameron was one of the first folk/country performers from the Maritimes to emphasize heritage and origins, and to work with musical literature that was indigenous to the area . . . [42]

In addition to his unique guitar interpretation of prodigious compositions like Dan Hughie MacEachern's "Trip to Mabou Ridge" and his Uncle Dan R. MacDonald's "Glencoe March," he introduced a national audience to prominent fiddlers like Angus Chisholm, Buddy MacMaster, Cameron Chisholm, and Theresa MacLellan who were among the original CBC *Ceilidh* Fiddlers.[43] My most memorable moment of many visits to the CBC set in Halifax to watch John Allan's program in production was the time I was able to spend with these fine fiddlers. Their lively tunes, especially their strathspeys, were as foreign to the CBC Corporation as the music collections from whence they came — the *Atholl*, the *Skye*, the *Fraser*, the *Edcath*, and the *Marshall*, to name but a few from the old country; and the jewel, *Cape Breton Melodies*, compiled by Gordon MacQuarrie of Cape Breton. It was truly gratifying to watch the CBC production staff work the set. I could see the enjoyment and pleasure they were receiving from working with these recently discovered stars from Cape Breton.

From a personal point of view, it is puzzling that the CBC could promote regional programming like the Messer show for so many years while at the same time almost completely neglecting to introduce a regular quantity of the music of Cape Breton fiddlers. Popular programs like the *Don Messer Show* were established institutions at CBC for almost three decades before the Cape Breton fiddler appeared on the set in Halifax with John Allan. The music of the Cape Breton fiddler was an institution on Cape Breton Island and in some respects beyond, long before CBC began regional programming. The Cape Breton fiddlers engaged a busy dance and concert circuit on the island; they also made special appearances in Toronto, Boston, and Detroit; they participated in local radio and television productions like *Celtic Forum* as early as 1938[44] and later programs like the *MacDonald Lassie Program* (Dan Joe MacInnis), and the *Cape Breton Barn Dance* (Winston "Scotty" Fitzgerald).[45]

To fully appreciate the popularity and interest among many Cape Bretoners in the fiddle music, one needs only to recall the journey by Angus Allan Gillis, Dan J. Campbell, and Angus Chisholm who made their way by train to Montreal in 1935 to do a recording.[46] This initiated a myriad of popular recordings produced in the 1940's, the 1950's and the 1960's, featuring Cape Breton fiddlers.[47] This legacy, organized at the local level, was the inspiration and the incentive for John Allan's mission to further promote the Cape Breton fiddler.

I sometimes wonder if the current CBC producers in Halifax and in Toronto, who are now actively involved in promoting and encouraging Cape Breton music, ever question where their predecessors were in the 1960's. At that time, many Cape Breton fiddlers were household names in most of Cape Breton and in select pockets in various parts of Canada and of the United States where many Cape Bretoners had settled. In fact, the documentary, *The Vanishing Cape Breton Fiddler*, which was produced in 1971, gives one account of how CBC viewed the state of the local fiddlers.[48]

Ray MacDonald of CJFX radio station in Antigonish explains his view on the above-mentioned documentary:

> As far as the Scottish music, it was being promoted by CJFX when it wasn't the popular thing to do. When CBC began dabbling it was a little more permissible. But CJFX never really varied from when they started . . .
>
> You know that I never believed in the myth of the "Vanishing Fiddler." I don't think it was true because CJFX never stopped playing (music of the Cape Breton fiddler). And that was in the heart of it.[49]

And that is the way I remember it growing up in Big Pond! One could tune into CJFX each morning and get a good blast of tunes from Buddy MacMaster or John Campbell or Cameron Chisholm or Donald Angus Beaton before heading off to school. Again, just before the six o'clock news in the evening, a good selection would be played to close out Clyde Nunn. In the early evening, my school work was put on hold for a few moments while the ever-popular *Scottish Strings* radio program on CJFX rendered music by many of those fiddlers who did not record commercially, fiddlers who lived in Margaree or in Mabou or in Boston or in Detroit and made special recordings for CJFX to play over the long winter months. CJFX's contribution to keeping the music at the forefront in the 1950's and the 1960's is an integral part of the tradition. And Ray MacDonald continues that tradition today . . . thank you, Ray!

Nevertheless, in response to CBC's, the documentary called the *Vanishing Cape Breton Fiddler* which suggested that the fiddler was something of the past, a festival was organized in Glendale, Inverness County in 1973.[50] It was spearheaded by a committed group of individuals to demonstrate that the music was every bit as strong in the 1970's as it was in earlier decades. Thousands of people witnessed the extraordinary event, the first Glendale Fiddlers' Festival, a three-day event at which one hundred plus fiddlers of all ages performed. And, yes, CBC and many other representatives from the media and from the music industry were also there to experience the magic! The contrast from an earlier era with the present day regarding coverage by CBC television and radio and the music industry in general is a taste of personal satisfaction for Cape Bretoners, like John Allan Cameron, who have persevered for so long to promote the music, song, and dance of Cape Breton. The results were most satisfying as well for the charter members of the Cape Breton Fiddlers Association, some of whom were Frank MacInnis, Reverend Eugene Morris, Burton MacIntyre, Joey Beaton, Reverend John Angus Rankin, Anne Marie MacDonald, Jeanette Beaton, and Rod C. Chisholm. In 1998, the association, now under the direction of Betty Matheson, will celebrate twenty-five years of support to the music, an opportunity for the association to promote the music, to foster fellowship among local fiddlers, and to help establish a network among fiddlers worldwide who are interested in the Celtic music.

Meanwhile, as the CBC *Ceilidh* production evolved in the 1970's, John Allan left the show, and CBC then engaged several additional fiddlers from Cape Breton under the direction of Winnie Chafe, who had already attained international celebrity. The production, however, now focused on introducing Scottish professional entertainers from Scotland, like the Alexander Brothers, Calum Kennedy, and Allister Gillies, or entertainers from Scotland

and living in Canada. There was now less of an emphasis on the local per-formers, i.e., Cape Breton talent; subsequently, the program was cancelled and likely for a host of reasons. Meanwhile, popular productions like the *Tommy Hunter Show* continued to control the Canadian content on CBC variety programming, always providing opportunities for many of the Ameri-can country music artists to appear on national television, but, once again, did not include the Cape Breton performers, with the exception of Hughie and Allan. Following a short series with CTV, 1975-76, John Allan began his own show on CBC national television by 1979, called the *John Allan Cameron Show.*[51]

John Allan Cameron at a session in Big Pond. [Left to right] Al Bennett, guitar; John Allan, guitar; Dave MacIsaac, guitar.

Photo by Cyril MacInnis

Among John Allan's guests on his new show was Cape Breton fiddler Winston "Scotty" Fitzgerald, who had actually retired from a vigorous mu-sic scene in Cape Breton. John Allan was determined, without apology or malice, to set the record straight and to place "Scotty" among Canadian leg-ends. Although the music of Winston "Scotty" was second nature to many households, especially in rural Cape Breton and wherever clusters of Cape Bretoners collaborated off-island, it was John Allan who gave Winston "Scotty" Fitzgerald who, by this time, was in his 60's, his rightful place in the national broadcasting fraternity in Canada.

Subsequently, Fitzgerald along with Cape Breton fiddlers Jerry Holland, Wilfred Gillis, and John Donald Cameron, originally touring as the Cape Breton Symphony, performed in Canada and parts of Europe with John Allan.[52] It became clear that this music was special and was destined for prominent recognition. With John Allan's tours featuring many of the Cape Breton fiddlers throughout the 1970's and the early 1980's, a surge of interest by the music industry in the Cape Breton music developed. Material that was recorded in kitchens, in dance halls, in concert halls, in theatres like the UCCB Playhouse, at major festivals which have been in place in rural Cape Breton since the early 1960's and some as early as the late 1950's, and in sessions recorded in the studio for CBC's local productions *Island Echoes* and *Talent Cape Breton* received air time on regional broadcasts on CBC radio and television. Many of the Cape Breton performers who took part in these regional shows gained new opportunities to appear on national productions for special occasions.

By the 1980's, BBC television and independent film companies from Scotland and from the United States made increased visits to Cape Breton to record local Gaelic material, including the music of the Cape Breton fiddlers, for broadcast in Britain and in the United States. Major festivals across Canada and the United States were showing more interest in the music of the Cape Breton fiddlers.

Local composers and writers were being encouraged to publish more tunes and related material; thus emerged collections like those by Dan R.MacDonald, the Beaton Family, Jerry Holland, and more recently the second of Dan Hughie MacEachern's music collections. Reprints of older collections, like Scotland's *Fraser* and *Skye* collections, were initiated in Cape Breton through the efforts of Paul Cranford. Paul also released a number of his own compositions in the *Lighthouse Collection*. Information about the fiddlers and their music was in demand, and this resulted in Allister MacGillivary's two popular publications, *The Cape Breton Fiddler* and *Cape Breton Ceilidh*. These publications represent some of the endeavours which have had an important impact on the music and cultural development of not only the Celtic music of Cape Breton Island but also of other cultural expressions.

Initiatives in the early 1990's that reflect the ongoing national and international interest in the Cape Breton Celtic music, in particular, include the 1993 visit by a BBC film crew from Scotland to record Cape Breton Celtic music, song, and folklore for six television programs (part of a series recorded by the BBC over many years); the Buddy MacMaster music video which was broadcasted on national CBC television and also made its way through international commercial markets; the Balnain House museum project in Scotland which now includes a presentation on the history and development of Cape Breton Celtic music; the visit by sixteen Cape Breton traditional musicians to Cork, Ireland in February '93 to take part in an annual Irish music festival; and the recognition of outstanding Cape Breton fiddlers at the East Coast Music Awards including Jerry Holland, Ashley MacIsaac, Howie MacDonald, Natalie MacMaster, Winnie Chafe, and Dave MacIsaac. The

1993 summer tour to the Scandinavian region by the Scumalash Family band; as well as the continuing popularity of some of North America's leading entertainers like the Rankin Family, the Barra MacNeils, and John Allan Cameron, keep Cape Breton Island on the world globe of quality entertainment.

1. Helen Creighton and Calum MacLeod, *Gaelic Songs in Nova Scotia* (Ottawa: Queen's Printer, 1964).

2. Gordon F. MacQuarrie, compiler and arranger. *The Cape Breton Collection of Scottish Melodies for the Violin.* edited and published by Joseph Beaton, Medford, M.A.

3. Helen Creighton and Calum MacLeod, 1964.

4. Laughie Gillis. (1985). *Gaelic Songs from the Mira.* CR1-8137.

5. Allister MacGillivary, *The Cape Breton Fiddler.* (Sydney: UCCB Press, 1981).

6. "Celtic Forum on Air Tonight Over CBC Network," *Post Record,* July 15, 1938.

7. Ibid.

8. John Gibson, "Sandy MacLean," Article #6, *Scotia Sun,* 1972-73.

9. John Gibson, "Angus Allan Gillis," Article #11, *Scotia Sun,* 1972-73.

10. John Gibson, "Donald Angus Beaton," Article #12, *Scotia Sun,* 1972-73.

11. Roddie C. MacNeil et al., *The Story of St. Columba Parish* (Sydney: City Printers, 1994), p. 23.

12. See Note #2, Chapter 2.

13. Frances MacEachern, "The Broad Cove Concert - The Best Gift of All," *The Clansman,* October/November 1991.

14. In addition to the many stories told to me by Dan Joe and Christie about the early dances and dance halls, I often heard Marlene's parents Catherine and John describe in detail how they enjoyed attending these programs. Catherine actually worked with Bill Lamey at Eastern Bakery in Sydney in the 1940's. Bill was certainly one of the more active participants in these early concerts and dances in the Sydney area. Doug MacPhee often talks about one of the final fiddle competitions held at the Lyceum in Sydney in the early fifties which was organized by Bill Lamey and Reverend Hugh A. MacDonald. John often spoke about Tena Campbell, perhaps his favorite fiddler, and her dance circuit in the Sydney and East Bay areas.

15. Ibid.

16. Robert Martin, "Sonic Boom: Nova Scotia Open to the World," *Atlantic Progress,* May 1996, pp. 6-11.

17. Ken MacLeod, "Cape Breton Rocks at ECMA Weekend," *Cape Breton Post,* February 21, 1997, p. 25.

18. Robert Martin, 1996.

19. Wendy Dudley, "Rita Has Audience Flying On Its Own," *Calgary Herald,* December 1, 1988.

20. David Napier, "Lovely Rita, Ratings Queen," *Saturday Night*, October 1995, p. 100.

21. Recently, I spoke to Kenzie MacNeil about his interest in the Celtic music, and he explained that the tune "Farewell to the Creeks" inspired the rhythm for his very popular song, "The Island."

22. Kenneth Donovan, "Reflections on Cape Breton Culture: An Introduction" in Ken Donovan, editor, *The Island: New Perspectives on Cape Breton's History 1713-1990* (Sydney, N.S.: UCCB Press, 1990), p. 7.

23. Merle MacIsaac, "Cape Breton Hit Parade," *Bluenose First Anniversary Issue*, November/December 1993, p. 30.

24. Elizabeth M. MacDonald, *To the Old and the New Scotland* (Sydney, N.S.: City Printers Ltd., 1981), p. 142.

25. Ian MacKinnon, "Fiddling to Fortune: the Role of Commercial Recordings Made by Cape Breton Fiddlers in the Fiddle Music Tradition of Cape Breton Island," unpublished master's thesis, Department of Folklore, Memorial University, NF, 1989.

26. Ibid.

27. Ibid., p. 1. [This information includes recordings to 1988.]

28. Ibid.

29. *The Bard of Scottish Fiddling* by Little Jack MacDonald, Celtic CX. 23, n.d.

30. *Winston "Scotty" Fitzgerald and His Radio Entertainers* by Winston "Scotty" Fitzgerald, Celtic CX. 34, n.d.

31. Ian MacKinnon, 1989.

32. *Joseph Cormier* by Joe Cormier, Rounder 7001, 1974.

33. *Cape Breton Violin Music* by John Campbell, Rounder 7003, 1976.

34. *The Beatons of Mabou* by the Beatons of Mabou, Rounder 7011, 1977.

35. John Gibson, "John Donald Cameron," Article #21, *Scotia Sun*, 1972-73.

36. I retrieved this information from the CBC archives, Halifax, in October 1994.

37. Allister MacGillivary, *The Cape Breton Fiddler* (Sydney: UCCB Press, 1981), p. 103.

38. *Elmer Briand and His Cape Breton Fiddle* by Elmer Briand, Celtic SCX58.

39. Official brochure for *UCCB's 20th Anniversary Celebration*, 1994.

40. Silver Donald Cameron, "John Allan Cameron, Entertainer," *Atlantic Insight*, November 1980, p. 47.

41. "Ceilidh," *Dartmouth Free Press*, January 3, 1973, p. 1.

42. Virginia Beaton & Stephen Pedersen, *Maritime Music Greats* (Halifax, N.S.: Nimbus Publishing, 1992), p. 94.

43. Ibid.

44. Refer to Note #6.

45. Ian MacKinnon, 1989, p. 91.
46. Ibid., 1989, p. 49.
47. Ibid., p. 58.
48. Ron MacInnis, producer, *The Vanishing Cape Breton Fiddler* (Halifax: Canadian Broadcasting Corporation, 1971).
49. "A Visit with Ray "Mac" MacDonald, In Honour of the 50th Year of CJFX Radio," edited from Conversations with Marjorie MacHattie, *Cape Breton's Magazine*, #64, p. 75.
50. Ibid.
51. Virginia Beaton & Stephen Pederson, 1992.
52. Ibid.

CHAPTER SEVEN

The Gaelic: The Second Solitude

The Circle — Catherine's Kitchen

While attending university in the late 1960's, I was introduced to Charles Dunn's popular *The Highland Settler* first published in 1953.[1] I recognized that Dunn's work presented what I considered to be an accurate picture of the Gaels I had come to know in my home community of Big Pond. I was impressed with the eloquent and simplistic manner in which he described the Gaels of Cape Breton following his visits throughout Cape Breton in the 1940's. Later, I came to appreciate the work of Scotland's John Lorne Campbell in the same way and in particular, his book *Songs Remembered in Exile*.[2] Although not published until 1990, the book highlights Campbell's historical journeys to Cape Breton over fifty years ago.

In the accounts by Dunn and Campbell, I was struck by the apparent void in their information with respect to the music of the Gael like the fiddlers and the pipers. I wondered why there was so little written about the music of the Cape Breton fiddler, in either of these highly acclaimed publications. While growing up in Big Pond, I had come to know the fiddle music and the pipe music as the most significant aspect of the artistic genius among the Gaels with whom I felt a special bond in Cape Breton. Clearly, the purpose of the research of the two esteemed scholars was the Gaelic culture generally and the language and the Gaelic songs, in particular, and only in a minor way, the music.

My point in raising the matter is to highlight that there are two distinguished authors, whose research work in Cape Breton and subsequent publications almost exclusively highlight the Gaelic language and the Gaelic songs to illustrate the intensity and authenticity of the Gaelic culture retention in Cape Breton. I believe that any account about Gaelic culture retention in Cape Breton must also include referencing the level of intensity within the music as maintained by some fiddlers and some pipers. Personally, I can appreciate how one can become consumed with one aspect, the music, for example, and sometimes at the expense of the others.

Any journey in Celtic music in Cape Breton will have some direct link to the Gaelic language and song, for some, an absolute link. My own experiences in the music were often of great intensity because of my family's close association with so many musicians who were involved with the music as if creating their own solitude in time and space. Almost just as often, my experiences with the music did not involve the Gaelic language or the Gaelic song. Conversely, those who did become involved with the songs and the language with the same level of intensity as I did with the music may have experienced the same degree of solitude with respect to the Gaelic. Upon reflection, I wonder to what extent the Celtic music of Cape Breton as I know it today, and the Gaelic language and song were able to fuse during the period of time devoted to my journey? I know there has been an enormous effort on the part of some people to try and keep the Gaelic language and the Gaelic songs alive, but in my view the language and song and the music of the fiddle, for example, may represent two solitudes.

Significant efforts, historically, to grasp support for the Gaelic from institutions of assorted descriptions rendered a focus to the Gaelic unlike that for the music. By the 1970's, some efforts to teach the indigenous fiddle music outside the home prevailed and with success, through the efforts of individuals like fiddlers John MacDougall, Winnie Chafe and Stan Chapman especially.[3] Although, to a larger extent, the music continued to be nurtured in the home and within the family and extended family, with the support of and encouragement from mentors in the community. This home environment is described by Liz Doherty in her 1995 dissertation, "The Paradox of the Periphery — Evolution of the Cape Breton Fiddle Tradition."

> In the active home environment, parents or siblings traditionally are active participants in the tradition (of the music), or at least provide constant exposure to the music and encouragement to the younger generations.[4]

Doherty has clearly depicted my personal experience and the experience of other members of my family who are also involved with the music. Unlike my association with the music, my association with the Gaelic was different. I did not acquire the sense of passion for or awareness of the emotions inherent in the Gaelic language as I did in the music. The Gaelic language and songs were an integral part of the kitchen of my two grandmothers, Mary D.P. MacInnis, Alexandra Street and Catherine MacIsaac, St. Andrew's Channel. Yet, the experience was not so different that I couldn't maintain a bond for and an appreciation of special Gaels like Jessie Campbell or Annie Jack MacInnis or Johnny Hughie MacInnes or Kate MacDougall or Joe Neil MacNeil. After all, they were special people and in my youth, I came to know them as friends and neighbours and relatives, not for the language they spoke. My memories of these native Gaelic speakers are pleasant and endearing.

In my youth, Joe Neil was known to me as "Mechanical Joe" so named because of his skill in several trades. Joe had become a living legend by the 1970's because of his vast knowledge of and passion for the old Gaelic traditions. I was deeply saddened when I heard of Joe Neil MacNeil's death, on October 14, 1996. At the time of his death, I recalled my friendship with Joe Neil and especially that wonderful tour of Scotland he had taken with the Sons of Skye exactly seventeen years earlier, to the day of his death. As part of the tour, we travelled to Glencoe where the tour's participants spent the first night; we later travelled to communities like Skye, Lewis, and the Uists. Needless to say, Joe Neil was in his glory. The 1979 visit, which was Joe Neil's first sojourn to the Isle of Barra, was an experience that Joe Neil cherished and faithfully reminisced until his death.

I had been asked by Joe's family to offer the eulogy at Joe's funeral. I explained to the congregation who had gathered to say a final goodbye at the small white church at East Bay, overlooking the parish cemetery, that I often recalled the Joe Neil who would visit my grandmother monthly in her tiny country kitchen some thirty-five years earlier. There, Joe Neil joined a small circle of friends from the neighbouring community of Ben Eoin to converse in the Gaelic.

Catherine MacIsaac's circle, Theresa MacPhee and Dan J MacPhee, Neil R. MacIsaac, Kate MacDougall and Joe Neil, spent several hours reminiscing about the old times and the old ways. Their passion, so it seemed, recalled in story the romance, the hardships, and the anguish of their lived experiences — depicting joy and sadness, tragedy and hope, loneliness and jubilation — which would be introduced only as legends and folklore to future generations.

The circle often rendered the old Gaelic melodies — the lyrics and the "Peurt-a-Beul" (a form of mouth music) — that depicted the crofters from distant islands — crofters who they knew only in songs but would not likely see or embrace. The circle quoted from the poetry of bards from Scotland and from Cape Breton because they seemed to effectively describe the beauty of the glens and the valleys, the mountains and the streams, and the glory and the waste of the ancient battles and the modern wars. They shared a personal view and a commentary on the decline of community, their feeling of abandonment as a result of the departure of their loved ones to places far and away to search for work, the feelings of loss at the passing of friends and family, and the sense of confusion felt by the subtle efforts of authorities to encourage the seemingly lack of interest among the youth in the traditions and the customs of the rural Gael.

It appears that this precious circle was their final stronghold on the Gaelic tradition. They recognized that the times in the twilight of their life's journey were different from their youth and emerging adulthood. The language was spoken only by a few people outside their circle.[5] Thus, the gathering symbolized the last of an exceptional generation of Cape Bretoners who had managed against all odds to retain the language in their quiet, simple, humble, but just as often, difficult lifestyle embedded in their Gaelic traits. They realized that the Gaelic world they experienced in that warm and intimate circle would become something less by day's end.

Their struggles to simply survive hardships and to endure adversity, suffering, affliction, and even scorn were the motivating factors to persevere and to reconvene so that the joy and bliss they felt from each other's company could linger just a bit longer. Yet, the Gaelic spirit that they cherished and to which they adhered would later, in only two generations, be a struggle to grasp and the effort to grip and to hold that spirit of even a recent past would, by the 1970's, become the Celtic Revival. This revival which emerged, to try and sustain a mastery of that spirit, is still apparent today but not likely destined to be quite like the spirit so enthralling within that precious circle. At 88, Joe was the final participant from the circle to depart this world.

What would Joe Neil now share with the old-time circle, reconvened once again to celebrate his arrival? Joe Neil would likely describe the communities of Ben Eoin, St. Andrew's Channel, and Big Pond as different than the one experienced by the members of the circle while they were alive. What is this Celtic revival, they would ask of Joe Neil? They would ponder on all the fuss and activity to try and recapture the past including the Gaelic language.

Among their recollections about the plight of the Gaelic language in Cape Breton, their stories about the neglect experienced by their offspring while attending local schools, like the old Bracks Brook elementary school, would be that teachers were visiting and wanted to remove the Old Country's ways including the Gaelic from the students and the community.[6] John Lorne Campbell in *Songs Remembered in Exile* paraphrases the view held by *Mac-Talla's* Jonathan G. MacKinnon:

Gaelic, said Mr. MacKinnon, had been a permissive subject in the schools since after the war, but no way had been found yet to introduce it into the curriculum. The Premier of the Province of Nova Scotia (Angus MacDonald) was a Gaelic man, and no doubt his administration would have been willing to accede to any united demand, but the difficulty was to hit on a scheme that would get the support of all the different sections and denominations.[7]

MacKinnon also made a reference to the issue of out-migration so prevalent in rural Cape Breton at the time. Charles Dunn wrote in *The Highland Settler*:

At that time many Gaels did not wish their children to waste time on the language. They wished them to learn English well so that they could succeed in the world, and to study all the "practical" subjects available. Stern realism was more important to them than sentiment and intangible cultural motives.[8]

In his research for the Mabou Gaelic and Historical Society in the early 1970's, J.J. MacEachern, a school teacher in Mabou, identified the factors he believed resulted in the demise of the Gaelic language in rural Cape Breton. He explains that the:

. . . failure of the schools to value it and instill it in the students was primarily responsible . . . that the teachers, clergy, and inspectors spoke to parents about not speaking Gaelic in front of their children.[9]

In the final analysis, the out-migration from the rural communities and the strategy among the public education authorities to discourage the children from speaking Gaelic contributed to the decline as described by Campbell, Dunn, and MacEachern.

Nevertheless, despite all efforts to facilitate change, the first generation of students from the old Bracks Brook School and from similar one-room schools in rural Cape Breton retained a great deal of the language. Albeit, that retention of the language was inflicted with a feeling of inferiority, especially when they gathered with individuals who were more fluent in Gaelic or, even worse, with individuals who were descendants of the Celtic heritage who refuted the value and beauty of the Gaelic and who added to the mockery and the scorn directed to those who spoke the Gaelic, sang the songs, and performed the music.

Not having persevered at acquiring the Gaelic language at any point in my life, despite my close proximity to Catherine's circle, does not personally leave me in good stead to complain about the decline of the Gaelic language. This, I believe, is better left with those who are now committed to learning the Gaelic and to those who want to speak the language in the way it was spoken and valued by people like Kate MacDougall, Neil R. MacIsaac, and Joe Neil MacNeil, and for some there are standards.

The circle: Kate MacDougall, Theresa MacPhee, Dan J. MacPhee. [Left to right]

Submitted by Michael MacIsaaac

A few years ago a young man (in his mid twenties, I would guess) came to visit me at UCCB as he was in the area. He explained to me his enthusiasm about wanting to learn the Gaelic language. He presented himself as a determined individual. I do not recall seeing him any more following that visit. Subsequently, I learned that the young man, Brian MacLeod of Baddeck, initiated a series of contacts among some Gaels in his local community and around his home who gave him a good start. As a matter of fact, Brian grew up in a Gaelic environment. His father Neil, a fiddler, "is a fluent Gaelic speaker and his grandfather, the late Danny Kenny MacLeod from North River, was a noted Gaelic singer and a member of the North Shore Gaelic singers."[10] Brian later went to Scotland where he studied at and graduated from Sabhal Mor Ostaing. I recently reviewed an article Brian had submitted to the *Clansman* concerning his efforts to learn the language which indicated that he had aspired to some high standards along the way. He not only acquired the language, but it would appear from reading his article that he has developed a passion for the quality of the Gaelic language being spoken in Cape Breton and Scotland today. Although I will quote only a small sample of his article, the complete information will be of interest to anyone concerned about the Gaelic language.

> In the case of idioms there is equal cause for concern. Gaelic, like other languages, makes use of indigenous phrases, expressions, and figures of speech which are central to the language and its proper expression. Their meaning would be lost in any attempt to translate them into another language. It is indicative of the prevailing influence of English over Gaelic. For better or worse, they are becoming part of the fabric of Gaelic as it is used today.[11]

As for the future of the Gaelic in Cape Breton, Brian offers the following comment:

> The prognosis for the future is far from clear. Opinions run the gamut from optimism to pessimism. Given the evidence of the language's decline thus far, it would seem more probable to say that Gaelic's demise is inevitable, but human nature being what it is, this is no way a certainty . . . although it would seem a lot depends on the attitudes of people, individually and collectively, within the language's community.[12]

I am certain that Kate and Neil R. would have been impressed with this young man's respect for and value of the language.

Rejoining his circle and trying to respond to their curious questions, Joe Neil, in his soft voice of despair and loneliness, would likely explain as he did so often in my company that the old Gaelic traditions of Cape Breton are quickly eroding and are likely lost forever. He would indicate that the Celtic revival, however, did take the time to recognize his retention of the ancient Gaelic traditions. The result was the publication of his book in 1987, entitled *Tales Until Dawn*[13] (edited and translated by Dr. John Shaw), which records a series of Joe's recollections of ancient stories, proverbs, and songs. He would then show them the Marius Barbeau Medal he and Dr. John Shaw received in 1989 from the Folklore Studies Association of Canada (FSAC) for their contribution to ethnic and folklore analysis.[14] He would also take special delight in telling this circle of ancient souls about the honourary Doctorate Degree of Letters he received from St. Mary's University in 1990.[15]

Perhaps, though, as he describes his travels in Canada and in Scotland — sharing Gaelic stories and talking about the oral tradition — his description about his first visit to Barra in 1979 would likely bring about his charming and gentle smile, tears in his eyes, and a slow quiver in his lower lip. He would tell of the wonderful people he had met on that journey and how he had been hailed a treasure as if from the "Ark" itself.[16] Once the excitement would settle, however, I'm sure that he would ask Kate to sing a song and would invite everyone to join the chorus; subsequently, Joe would then ask Neil R. to tune the pipes and render one of those beautiful slow and haunting Gaelic airs, just as Neil R. did a generation earlier.

Early Seeds: Sustained

Through my extension work at the University College of Cape Breton I would often engage many who were and continue to be determined in their efforts to provide educational leadership to the Gaelic language problem in Cape Breton. This coupled with my personal quest to promote the Celtic music, would allow me to encounter some remarkable individuals among the Gaidhealtachd like Joe Neil. They engaged their own circle of opportunity in their own journey and grasped the Gaelic language and the Gaelic songs, particularly. They, too, persevered in their quest to retain the language and, subsequently, to help foster research, teaching, and publication in Gaelic from the 1960's to the 1990's. Their story of perseverance is now the basis upon which current efforts prevail to build a strategy to try and maintain the Gaelic language and song in Cape Breton today.

Such was the case with Cape Breton native, Dr. Margaret MacDonell, for example, who was appointed chair of the Celtic Studies Department at St. F.X. University, Antigonish, in 1977[17] and whose research resulted in the culmination of her 1982 publication, *The Immigrant Experience: Songs of Highland Immigrants of North America*.[18] The publication has been well received in Canada, in Scotland, and in the United States. Under Dr. Margaret MacDonell's direction, the St. F.X. Celtic Studies program grew to eventually reach an increased student population, followed by a process to build closer links with the wider community of Antigonish in the interest of Gaelic retention in that area of the province.

Other Cape Breton native Gaelic speakers were also actively involved in efforts to help promote a recognition of the Gaelic language in their respective communities, like Kay MacDonald of New Waterford, a Margaree native. Kay was employed as a researcher at the Beaton Institute, University College of Cape Breton; she retired in 1981. Kay was also one of the hosts on the popular CBC Gaelic program *Island Echoes* until 1985. She was active at the community level with the Gaelic Society of Cape Breton and through her work as a Gaelic teacher in New Waterford's continuing education program. Even in retirement, Kay continues to teach Gaelic under the auspices of the Cape Breton Gaelic Society.

A more recent development involved Cape Breton native Hector MacNeil who was appointed on a part-time basis as a member of the adjunct faculty at UCCB where he now teaches Introductory Gaelic and Advanced Gaelic. Perhaps most significant is that Hector received a full-time appointment as Gaelic language programmer at the Gaelic College, St. Ann's, in 1996.

Dan Joe MacInnis and Doug MacPhee survey Celtic music collections at the Beaton Institute, UCCB.

Photo by Raymond Fahey

Gaelic instruction in the Continuing Education program at UCCB for children and adults was also among the evening and weekend classes offered within the adult education programs administered by school boards in Inverness, Cape Breton and Antigonish counties in the 1970's which encouraged native Cape Breton Gaels to teach Gaelic. Native Gaelic speakers from the Cape Breton community with little or no formal teacher training were active in instructing many of these programs. Sydney residents such as Helen Howatt, Malcolm Campbell, Margaret Chaisson, and Kay MacKenzie with the support and encouragement of Jim Kelly were instrumental in the programs located in the industrial area of Cape Breton while Josie MacNeil, Jessie MacKenzie, and Tena Morrison were instrumental in rural Cape Breton. Similar efforts were instrumental in the wider mission to promote teaching Gaelic and to provide an environment to build upon the earlier efforts to encourage the youth, in particular, to acquire the Gaelic singing as well as the language.

Mae Campbell Cameron, who supervised the Sydney school music program in the 1950's and 1960's[19] and organized a school choir singing Gaelic songs supported efforts, during her retirement as well, to promote Gaelic singing. In the 1970's, Mae Cameron together with Kay MacKenzie and Sister Hazel Power and Shauna Doolan instructed a successful children's choir which was sponsored by the Gaelic Society of Cape Breton. Mae continues to direct the all-Gaelic adult choir "Oranaiche Cheap Breatuinn," which she founded in 1983[20] with Kenna MacDonald, a native Gaelic speaker from Lewis who was living in Cape Breton at the time. In 1996, Mae Cameron received an Honourary Doctorate of Letters degree from the University College of Cape Breton for her contribution to music in Cape Breton.[21]

Sister Margaret Beaton was inspired by Dr. M.A. MacLellan to establish Cape Bretoniana. She became in turn the inspiration for an attempt by grassroots Gaels including Hughie MacKenzie, Joe Gillis, and Jimmy Charlie MacNeil to begin Gaelic language instruction at Xavier College, now the Beaton Institute at UCCB. This early work gave rise to the Gaelic Society of Cape Breton.

Like many others involved in promoting Gaelic in the 1970's these individuals and their initiatives received widespread support throughout the Gaelic community of Cape Breton. That support was expressed in a variety of ways, promoting Gaelic interest organizations in the local communities, attending classes, producing Gaelic content programs for radio and publication, hosting exchange visits between some Gaels in Scotland and Cape Breton as well as special concerts and ceilidhs featuring performances in the Gaelic by the young and the old alike.

There is no question that the early passion among some to keep the language alive continues. That passion beginning in the 1970's particularly would continue to seek support for the Gaelic from a variety of individuals and representatives with different agencies and public institutions.

Leadership: "From the Outside"

The presence of the Cape Breton native Gael in key positions to promote Gaelic in Cape Breton and the surrounding region was not always the case. The urge by some people who were not native to the area but who settled in Cape Breton acquired an interest, indeed a passion, to help to rekindle a strategy in support of Gaelic in Cape Breton emerged. Their efforts are a feature of the Cape Breton Celtic revival story over several decades.

The initial seeds to revitalize the Gaelic and to foster a Celtic revival in Cape Breton may have been planted first, with the arrival of the Gaelic College at St. Ann's in 1939, through the pioneer work of a Presbyterian minister, A.W.R. MacKenzie, who arrived in Baddeck by way of Skye, Montreal, and New York in 1935.[22] His dream was to establish "a school to teach both young and old the traditional Scottish arts: the language, music, crafts, and culture." He believed that his parishioners' pride in their unique Highland Scottish heritage was the key to their survival as a community."[23]

MacKenzie's dream may have been a sequel to the efforts by the American Presbyterian, John C. Campbell, who was born in Indiana of a Scottish immigrant in 1867.[24] Following his graduation from the seminary, Campbell decided to go to the southern mountains to help with the distressed social conditions, with the assistance of the Russell Sage Foundation.[25] This resulted in "the opening of the foundation's Southern Highlands Division office in Ashville, North Carolina, the organization of the conference of Southern Mountain Workers in 1913, and the posthumous publication of the *Southern Highlander and His Home* in 1921."[26] Campbell's wife, Olive D., directed her attention to "the music she heard in people's homes and churches, the quilts and the coverlets on their beds, the baskets and the tools they made and used."[27] As David Whisnant illustrates in his 1983 publication, *All That is Native and Fine*, the germ of the idea for the Campbells' initiatives is directly linked with the early American interests in the Grundtvitg Danish School program founded in Denmark in the mid-1800's and promoted "as a response to the problem of educating and enlivening Danish farmers and rural people . . ."[28] This trend within the United States may have had a profound influence in helping MacKenzie conceptualize his dream in Cape Breton, to depict the Cape Breton Scot as one representative of the popular stereotypical modern Highland dancer clad in tartan kilts and the kilted piper as well rendering a music (fostered through the summer visits of Shamus MacNeil) to suit the Highland dance forms of Old Scotland.[29] This image was not unlike the case at the John C. Campbell School in the U.S. where, according to Whisnant (and in the interest of preserving a local culture), "Danish traditions in music and dance were freely introduced, frequently in direct conflict with and in preference to local traditions." [30]

A review of the early programs at the Gaelic College will show that there was little or no effort to include the exponents of local fiddle music and the local stepdancing, in the regular activities let alone the Gaelic style piping which prevailed in Cape Breton during and even following A.W.R.'s tenure at St. Ann's.[31]

James Lamb points out in his 1992 publication *The Celtic Crusader — The Story of A. W.R.*[32] that MacKenzie turned to Scotland to recruit instructors in piping, Gaelic, and highland dancing believing that this was the way to bring credibility to the Gaelic College.[33] One could also speculate that MacKenzie wanted to let the local tradition flourish in its natural setting rather than to try and package the tradition at the college and that his decision to distance the college from the local culture may have been one contributor to allowing the traditional music and the traditional dance, in particular, to survive the test of time. The popular view, however, is that it was because of MacKenzie's interest in promoting a tourist market to support the local economy that the tartan image prevailed at the college.

Lamb continues to explain that conflict emerged during MacKenzie's tenure. The influx of public money would make it necessary that some outside intervention prevail in running the affairs of the college. Some were strong advocates for a college dedicated to the teaching of the language while others demanded an entertainment centre to satisfy the interest of the travelling public. "It was a conflict that was never — could never be — resolved, and it was to bedevil college affairs down to the present day."[34]

However, there is ample evidence today that the Gaelic College, now under the direction of Sam MacPhee, is actively interested in celebrating a mix of music and dance unique to Cape Breton, together with the popular programs which continue to have appeal to the visiting students from the United States and Canada. This, together with the appointment of a Gaelic language programmer, will help the efforts for the language and the music in the wider community. The Ceilidh School in Inverness County was established in 1996 by Jeannie Rendall. According to Rendall, it offers a program in music which is more reflective with what one may find in an Inverness County kitchen.[35] Unlike John MacDougall's program in Inverness and the UCCB experience with Dan Joe in the early 1970's teaching the fiddle music, the Gaelic College and the Ceilidh School are well-positioned to include some interesting data and materials with respect to the local music, which should help in the transmission process, especially with respect to traditional fiddling as well as piping.

A.W.R. MacKenzie's work with respect to the Gaelic language was likely cultivated in the efforts by Major Iain MacLeod, with his arrival in Nova Scotia from Scotland in 1950[36] that is, the process for Gaelic language retention was now to become entrenched in the institutional setting and the home environment would be a less likely place for future generations to learn the language.

Such was the case for Christie MacInnis who, as a child, was scorned for speaking the Gaelic at the old Brack's Brook School in Big Pond and who, in the 1950's, as a young woman living in Sydney, enrolled in an adult education class to try and expand her fluency in the proper manner. The instructor, Major Iain MacLeod, a member of the staff of the Department of Education for the Province of Nova Scotia, had been encouraged to settle in the area after his arrival from Scotland to help promote the use of the Gaelic language following what was described by some as the period of ridicule. MacLeod recognized the ridicule experienced by country folk like Christie because education authorities in his native Scotland had engaged their own tactics to discourage the use of Gaelic in rural Scotland. Kenneth MacKinnon in his book *Gaelic — A Past and Future Prospect* provides the following account of the Scottish or Old Country experience.

> The passing of the 1872 Education Act marks an important turning point for the recognition and the use of Gaelic within the education system. Under the new regime, the use of Gaelic was actively discouraged in the schools. The device of "maide-crochaidh," a stick on a cord, was commonly used to stigmatise and physically to punish children speaking Gaelic in the schools. It was reported in use as late as the 1930's in Lewis.[37]

MacKinnon further explains that there was little or no support, either, in Scotland's subsequent Education Acts, 1892, 1901, and 1908 respectively, and that the 1918 Education Act referenced the Gaelic with "vagueness and brevity."[38] MacKinnon explains that the Committee on Bilingualism of the Scottish Council for Research in Education, however, was reconstituted in 1956[39] with a mission to maintain the Gaelic. It is likely that MacLeod viewed the Cape Breton experience to eradicate the Gaelic to be like the Scottish experience. But he could see worth and value as well as opportunity in any efforts to rekindle an interest in the Gaelic in Cape Breton as well.

MacLeod was appointed head of the newly created Celtic Studies Department at St. Francis Xavier University, Antigonish, by President D.H. Somers in 1958 and retained the post until his death in 1977.[40] As a member of the faculty of St. Francis Xavier, MacLeod became one of the more influential individuals in the efforts to teach Gaelic and to engage research about the traditions of the Scottish Gaels, in Cape Breton especially.

I met Major MacLeod while studying at St. Francis Xavier University in 1968 and, by that time, he had settled into a state of retirement, although he was still in the classroom teaching many Cape Bretoners, among others, the Celtic Studies courses. My good friend Joe MacLean from Sydney, who attended St. F.X. with me, had registered for several of MacLeod's courses.

While Joe MacLean spoke highly of the Major's classroom antics to teach the language, Joe explained that when visiting the Major and Iona, the Major's wife, in their kitchen, he could more effectively learn the Gaelic language in this informal setting. The classroom was only a place to meet and to set appropriate times and schedules for the next home ceilidh, while the real learning took place in MacLeod's kitchen. I shared with Joe that my early recollections of hearing the Gaelic in conversation and song go back to the circle of the oldtimers in my grandmothers' kitchens.

Sheldon's graduation from St. F. X. University, 1970. [Left to right] Dan Joe, Christie, and Major MacLeod.

Photo by Marlene MacInnes

As a result of my stories, Joe had made several attempts to entice me to change my study interests in History and Psychology to Gaelic. I often said to Joe that I intended to learn the language the old-fashioned way at home in the kitchen, between semesters, with my grandmother and her circle of friends. However, despite my personal interest in the Celtic traditions, especially in the music, song, and dance, I did not go back to learn from the circle. Now, that opportunity for me to learn the language from those wonderful people is lost forever.

Conceivably, the history with respect to the Gaelic language retention in Cape Breton and MacLeod's efforts will be recorded as the beginnings of the strategy to pivot outward to seek leadership in support of Gaelic. A review of the efforts to retain Gaelic in the 1950's, through the 1970's, that will show the individuals like MacLeod from Scotland and others from the United States, took command of some local initiatives within public institutions with a mandate to promote the Gaelic language. This was the case at the

Gaelic College in St. Ann's, the Canadian Broadcasting Corporation in Sydney, the University College of Cape Breton and St. Francis Xavier University in Antigonish. Many of the individuals appointed to key positions in the interest of Gaelic programming at these institutions in education, research, and broadcast service — beginning in the 1950's through to the present — were from away, and they became leaders in efforts to foster an interest in the Gaelic language.

In 1973, a concerned group from Sydney prepared a submission to the Xavier College (known now as UCCB) President, Dr. Donald F. Campbell, urging that a program be established in Gaelic language.[41] The submission was part of a community-wide effort to mobilize an appeal for more Gaelic to be taught in the different public institutions, especially at UCCB. This was precipitated by the work of the Gaelic Society and its interest in establishing training sessions for would-be Gaelic instructors. Through their initiative, Jake MacDonald of Jordon Hill College, Scotland, visited Cape Breton in 1973 and conducted a program for Gaelic teachers.[42]

By the late 1970's, UCCB (then College of Cape Breton) had engaged Norman MacDonald, also from Scotland, on a full-time basis to teach Gaelic. Through his efforts, some working links had developed between UCCB and the Gaelic College, St. Ann's, whose summer faculty continued to be mostly individuals from away teaching Gaelic, piping, and Highland dancing. In 1986, the American-born scholar, Dr. Ken Neilsen, was appointed Chair of the Celtic Studies program at St. Francis Xavier University, Antigonish.[43] Among the popular hosts of the CBC production, *Island Echoes*, in the 1980's was Rosemary McCormack, also a native Gaelic speaker from Scotland and popular Gaelic singer. Today, Rosemary co-manages R&B Heritage Enterprises in Iona, Victoria County with her husband, Brian. The business promotes Gaelic singing recordings and research.[44]

The public education authorities instituted a school program in Inverness County in the early 1970's with Marjorie (MacDonald) Beaton and Effie (McCorquodale) Rankin, both native to Scotland and employed to teach Gaelic.[45] Based on my own research and observations, I believe that these two appointments, in particular, were among the most significant to try and revitalize the Gaelic language in Cape Breton. The efforts to lobby the local school authorities to keep the language in the schools continue today. A recent observation by one individual suggested that if the program had been maintained in the manner as originally established and had not faced early cuts, then the nineties would have seen some of the graduates from the local communities in Inverness County return to the local school system and beyond to teach the Gaelic.

In addition to the Inverness program, the Nova Scotia Highland Village Society established a Gaelic teaching program in 1984 [46] with Jim Watson, an American-born who learned the language in Cape Breton. The Highland Village program is designed for the volunteers and the professional staff associated with the Village activities.

The above and similar initiatives created a greater awareness of the Gaelic language in the wider community throughout the 1970's and the 1980's. A younger generation of Cape Bretoners acquired some Gaelic, several individuals learned the Gaelic songs, like Mabou's the Rankin Family who are now acclaimed as excellent entertainers on the world stage and who sing "in the Gaelic." Other individuals like Brian MacLeod (Baddeck), Beth MacNeil (Beaver Cove), Jeffery MacDonald (Queensville), and Mary Rankin (Mabou) became fluent in Gaelic conversation. The latter three also visited Mod celebrations in Ontario and in Scotland to compete in Gaelic singing.[47] Mary Rankin won Solo Under 16 at the North American Mod in Ontario in 1987.[48] Like her sister Rita, Mary participated in the popular Gaelic singing group from Mabou, Calleagan Mhabu, under the direction of Gaelic speaker Maureen MacKenzie who is also from Mabou. I had the pleasure of assisting this group in releasing a beautiful recording of Gaelic songs in 1989.[49] In 1995, Mary and Rita released their own CD recording, *Lantern Burn*,[50] which features some beautifully rendered Gaelic singing as well.

> The girls (Rita and Mary Rankin) started singing in public school concerts in grade primary and they were often asked to sing solo as early as grade five. In grade three they started taking Gaelic and it was there they learned to sing Gaelic songs.[51]

In addition to the Gaelic tutoring, research and publications in support of Gaelic emerged. Programs, like the Donald Ferguson Essay contest at UCCB, were developed to encourage further research and review by university students.[52] Achievements by personalities from an earlier era like those of Jonathan G. MacKinnon (1869-1944) emerged for study and discussion. MacKinnon founded the Gaelic newspaper, *Mac-Talla*, in Sydney, Nova Scotia in 1892 and continued publication until 1904. Again, Charles Dunn, author of *The Highland Settler*, writes about *Mac-Talla*: "No other entirely Gaelic periodical, even in Scotland, has run for so long as did *Mac-Talla*, and perhaps none has contained such varied material or appealed to a public so widespread" — Canada, Britain, United States, and New Zealand.[53] Through the initiative of Norman MacDonald, UCCB's Beaton Institute sponsored the Jonathan G. MacKinnon memorial lecture on April 6, 1979. The guest lecturer was Reverend Roderick MacLeod from the Island of Berneray, North Uist who spoke on "The Gaelic Language Today."

Other legendary personalities and their achievements in Gaelic also came to the forefront, for example, Laughie Gillis' contribution to promoting Gaelic singing and the "Grand Mira Gaelic Chorus." Neil MacPhee, a Gaelic learner initiated the Laughie Gillis Memorial Scholarship at UCCB[54] which was supported, in part, through the proceeds from the 1985 recording *Gaelic Songs from the Mira*[55] featuring the voice of Laughie Gillis, which Neil and Reverend Norman MacPhee produced. Recognition was also given to Archie Alex MacKenzie of Christmas Island who, like his father, was a noted writer, singer, and storyteller; he was named the "Bard" of Mod Ontario. In addition, Archie Alex represented Mod Ontario at Scotland's 1988 National Mod.[56]

The people associated with community-based organizations, like the Gaelic Society of Cape Breton, the Mabou Gaelic and Historical Society, and the Iona Connection (and their long-standing campaign to lobby the province of Nova Scotia to legislate a Gaelic language policy — whose efforts likely resulted in Resolution No. 563),[57] believed that it was imperative that the Gaelic language be restored to at least a reasonable level of fluency. The dreams to maintain the Gaelic are noble and endearing, but the strategies to help realize those dreams are sometimes ineffective and cling to an extremely frail culture, in the best case scenario.

Networking

In a bold move to wake up Scotland (again) to foster Gaelic in Cape Breton, a project to engage An Comunn Gaidhealach of Scotland developed. In 1981, discussions took place between Norman MacDonald of UCCB and Finlay MacNeil, a member of the management committee of the Highland Association (An Comunn Gaidhealach) of Scotland concerning the possibility of the Scottish National Mod coming to Sydney.[58] By 1982, an island-wide committee, on which I served, was established to organize the project. The plan was to host the Mod as part of the 1985 Sydney Bicentennial Celebrations.

A written proposal was sent to An Comunn in Scotland, for review. The mission was dauntless and daring but surprisingly, the idea received a positive response in Scotland and, not so surprisingly, a jubilant celebration in Sydney.[59] Following the commitment by An Comunn to hold the Mod in Sydney, Scotland's *West Highland Free Press* described the idea as "brave and imaginative."[60] The May 31st edition of the *Cape Breton Post* wrote: "it will stir the blood of every Cape Breton Scot . . . that Scotland's great Mod is coming to us in 1985."[61]

By 1984, however, the idea for Sydney to host the Mod ran into considerable difficulties, locally: with planning detail and funding; followed by the deteriorating, eroding, and eventual collapse of support for the idea in Scotland. The immediate outcome is described privately by some people as Cape Breton's own "Battle of Culloden" and may have interjected renewed life to the old cliché war of words. This was followed by calm and reason and some soul searching on both sides of the water. In the end, the idea of the great Mod leaving Scotland to become a showcase among the Gaels in exile (like the victims at Cullodon Mor in 1746) died a slow and painful death. The official decision for Sydney not to host the 1985 Mod was made February 28, 1984.[62]

With the Mod experience behind, it became apparent to some people that the single most pressing initiative required among those interested in working and trying to maintain the Gaelic language within the communities was the absolute need to work collectively. Progress would not materialize in the interest of Gaelic maintenance without a sustained commitment by every community-based group and publicly-funded institution with a mandate to support Gaelic to work collaboratively. To this end, UCCB, through Continuing Education and the Beaton Institute, began a strategy to assist the community to determine a process of collaboration and co-operation in Gaelic programming.

As stated in the article prepared by Jim Watson:

> If Gaelic language is to remain as a positive, affective feature of life quality in Cape Breton, it must be realistically supported morally and financially by all of our social institutions — the school system, media, church, Legislative Assembly, and bureaucracy. Otherwise, Gaelic will writhe in Nova Scotia to its ultimate death . . .[63]

With the support and encouragement of UCCB administrators, Dr. Ora McManus, Director of Continuing Education, and Dr. Robert Morgan, Director of the Beaton Institute, representatives from the wider community were invited to advise UCCB on an international conference dealing with "Language and the Politics of Maintaining Culture in Modern Society." In a paper I presented to the Gaelic Society in 1987, at their annual meeting, immediately following the conference, I explained the rationale for the conference plan in the following manner.

> It appeared a number of island-wide struggles have emerged in an effort to provide leadership to the Gaelic language and culture maintenance. The struggles were evident at institutional levels as well

as at the community level. These struggles became emerged in a number of matters including personality issues, institutional and philosophical differences and financial concerns. It was clear to some that the time had arrived for an attitudinal change. There was a need for diplomacy and a constructive exchange of ideas concerning Gaelic language maintenance. A conference with an international scope was seen to be the best way, for the short term, to try and bring about a "renewed collective commitment" to Gaelic maintenance. [64]

Dr. John Shaw, Gaelic speaker, researcher, and author, who at the time was associated with Cape Gale Associates,[65] would be the driving force behind the program's agenda. Shaw's contacts throughout the Celtic regions in Scotland, Ireland, Wales, and other parts of Canada would culminate in an impressive list of keynote presenters like John MacInnis, Edinburgh; Diarmuid O'Tuama, Belfast; Marjorie Beaton, Mabou; Gordon MacLellan, Ottawa; and Ken Neilsen, Antigonish. In all, over thirty specialists in the field of Celtic language and Celtic tradition would gather for the three-day conference in Sydney.

Topics introduced at the conference included: "Language Education of Children," "Music and Gaelic Culture," "Gaelic Language and Cultural Politics," "Publishing Gaelic Culture," "Museums and Cultural Presentations," "Invention of Tradition," and "Tourism and Gaelic Culture."[66] Throughout the conference, the written and the electronic media coverage was widespread. The good will that prevailed during the conference demonstrated a sense of community and a sense of pride among the people who assembled. The mix among the over 100 delegates was ideal: people from community-based organizations, educators from schools and universities, politicians, writers, administrators, researchers, clergy, teachers, musicians, native Gaelic speakers, and learners. There were ceilidhs and more ceilidhs and more ceilidhs!!

A series of resolutions were endorsed in the interest of maintaining the Gaelic language. These emerged in response to the dialogue and encouragement from the many delegates attending the conference. During a series of meetings and discussions following the conference, the local delegates agreed that the idea of establishing a council to represent the community-wide interest in Gaelic language should be organized, thus taking its cue from a talk by one of the conference's guest speakers, Gaelic Language activist, John Alex MacPherson, a North Uist native.

The impetus for the preservation of the Gaelic language in Canada must come from the grassroots, says John Alex MacPherson, a former chief of the Gaelic Society of Cape Breton. He said the grassroots organizations like the Gaelic Society and the Toronto Mod Ontario (of which he is chair) have provided the stimulus for Gaelic revival . . . MacPherson warned that organizations acting unilaterally "can easily become filters and depressants. Together, in common cause, they can be expeditors and motivators."[67]

Following several months of further discussion leading to a concept for a working structure and a criteria for appointing representatives to the council, a public meeting was called for November 18, 1989[68] in Iona to formally establish the council. It was approved, and a press release to the media reported that "those in attendance were unanimous in saying that the council with such a wide range of representatives from Cape Breton will play a significant role in providing encouragement and support to existing and new initiatives." [69]

The first meeting of the council, which was expanded to include all Nova Scotia, took place on February 6, 1990[70] and began to formulate the by-laws. Some people were and continue to be skeptical whether the process will be able to meet its objectives. There is evidence that the council lacks cohesion and commitment, and the idea of the council providing a catalyst and unifying voice on behalf of Gaelic programming may be eroding.

The present state of affairs with respect to the retention of the Gaelic language and the workings within the Gaelic Council, in particular, may be effectively tallied by local activist, author, and historian, Jim St.Clair, when he is quoted in Silver Donald Cameron's essay, "The World Which Is At Us:"

> . . . the dissensions are so deep, and the wounds are so painful, there's no unity of approach . . . a few years ago an attempt to establish an island-wide Gaelic council ended with great hostility over issues like whether the meetings should be conducted in Gaelic. These conflicts keep good people away. We need to name the divisions among the Celts, and set them aside.[71]

I read, again, in Jim St.Clair's words, the sentiments of Jonathan G. MacKinnon which MacKinnon expressed to John Lorne Campbell in 1937 about the decline of Gaelic in Cape Breton.

Unfortunately, the initial work on the part of the council may have lacked cohesion; thus, the objective to work together, which was so badly needed in the effort to have the council work effectively on behalf of Gaelic retention, may not in the final analysis be realized. However, the council continues to meet and to plan initiatives in the interest of Gaelic programming. Without unity and a common agenda, however, meaningful and sustainable action among the key participants will not be possible, and the resources and wider-community support will not materialize, and it must, if any long-term results are to be realized and maintained.

A Rationale for Gaelic Retention

The current initiatives with respect to community and economic development in Cape Breton, especially in rural areas, will help to keep select sectors within the community, some provincial and some federal funding agencies, and the bureaucrats from their respective sectors on side in efforts to help provide support to the culture and the Gaelic language. Some view strategies linked with community development and economic renewal as a viable rationale for promoting the language.

In 1989, the Sydney conference, Options For the 1990's, embraced a series of discussion groups and workshops to focus on the community initiatives for Gaelic language and cultural development in Nova Scotia.[72] The conference organizers described "The current status of Gaelic language in Nova Scotia is in part symptomatic of the larger problem of a down turned economy and its consequent contribution to social dissolution."[73] This was followed by a similar conference in Halifax in May, 1991 presenting the Gaelic language as an economic asset to Nova Scotia requiring a collective support and direction.

In 1993, The Scottish Societies Association of Nova Scotia's concept paper, entitled "Turning a Way of Life into a Way of Living," again emphasised the need to visit Gaelic culture and language retention in a context of "sustainable economic development."[74] Viewing Celtic culture as a cultural industry received approval from Scotland's Roy Pederson of the Highlands and Islands Development Board. While attending a conference in Sydney in early 1990 on economic development, he acknowledged " . . . the dangers of commercializing culture but says the more the community involves itself and knows about its heritage and culture, the better it can avoid the worst excesses."[75] The prospects concerning the financial viability of cultural industries held by some people in the cultural community of Cape Breton generally, including some involved with Celtic culture interests, is reflected in the 1995 research by Weldon Bona culminating in the 1996 report to ECBC "Cape Breton Culture Industry Strategy for Growth:"

> Based on our study, we estimate that there are almost 1,500 full-time and almost 2,000 part-time jobs in the culture industry in Cape Breton. We estimate that 80% of these jobs are seasonal. The

industry annually generates almost $80,000,000 in revenues and has infrastructure estimated at over $333,000,000.[76]

The activities I have outlined are less than a thumb-nail sketch of the wide range of concerted action beginning in the 1950's, continuing through to the 1990's, to maintain the language. They represent a wide range of initiatives by professionals and volunteers in education, research, economic development, and local community-initiated projects. The complete list of initiatives for Gaelic language revival in Cape Breton over the period of time concurrent with my journey in Celtic music is beyond the parameters of this publication. To give adequate commentary to the full review of the history and analysis of past and current efforts to maintain the Gaelic language would take a collaborative initiative among many people. Suffice to say, and for a wide range of reasons, by the mid-1980's, the efforts to revive the language were extensive and widespread and enjoyed national and international attention as well as local scrutiny and some degree of apprehension and skepticism.

In Allister MacLeod's, *Birds Bring Forth the Sun*, a Celtic revival is described in the thoughts of a fictional character, the displaced miner, but they may reflect a realistic description of how some people feel about the Celtic revival experienced in Cape Breton.

> . . . the younger children are taught individual Gaelic words in the classroom for a few brief periods during each month. It is a revival that is different from our own and it seems, like so much else, to have little relevance for us and to largely have passed us by. Once it was true, we went up to sing our Gaelic songs at the various Celtic concerts which have become a part of the summer culture and we were billed by the bright young school teachers who would run such things as MacKinnon's Miners Chorus; but that too seemed as lonely and irrelevant as it was meaningless. It was as if we were parodies of ourselves, standing in rows . . . only then to mouth our songs to batteries of tape recorders and to people who did not understand them.[77]

Jim Watson, the strong proponent of Gaelic retention in Cape Breton for socioeconomic reasons and as one who had acquired the language using the classic immersion method, visiting the kitchens in rural Cape Breton, expressed concern at a 1987 heritage conference in Toronto about the manner in which efforts to maintain the language are promoted.

Most courses of instruction, with the best of intentions, are offered as recreation classes and often attended by students with nostalgic or romantic motivations. The result of such classes is frequently a student experience not directly applicable to the reality of the surrounding social community. Gaelic as a consequence becomes a less credible life force even for those who would foster it.[78]

Again, Silver Donald Cameron in his 1996 essay, "The World Which Is At Us,"[79] describes the seemingly paradoxical efforts which emerge when one attempts to retain the Gaelic language in Cape Breton. Through a series of interviews with several of the main players who today are actively advocating more Gaelic retention in Cape Breton, Cameron acknowledges the desperation in their endeavour to keep the language alive. Cameron suggests that the work of some may very well be in response to the interested parties outside Cape Breton who want to speak and read the Gaelic.[80]

The informants for Cameron's essay (including Frances MacEachern, from Mabou and Rosemary McCormack from Iona) recognize that the language is dying, and they say that as a community, Cape Breton must address the need to establish an effort to reverse the trend. Among the reasons they site for retaining the language is the interest in learning Gaelic "in all the big American cities." The Americans want materials translated, explains MacEachern, and she shares the story about the Celtic Buddhist monk who "calls here all the time to buy books and tapes." These stories highlight the international interest in learning the Gaelic and the potential for building a viable business in Gaelic recordings, books and other publications and general information about the Gaelic language, the history and the folklore.

Among the points MacEachern makes, according to Cameron, is that the economic asset in the Gaelic language should be among the prime reasons for retaining the language. She says the culture and language are dying despite the national and international attention to the Celtic music which is currently basking in awards and tours, a lucrative enterprise in themselves.

Ron Caplan's long-standing enterprise *Cape Breton's Magazine*, a successful publication devoted to the history, natural history and future of Cape Breton Island, offers a quote from Rosemary McCormack in the first issue of the magazine in 1972 concerning Gaelic language retention.

Gaelic is a very old language. It's had a long, hard struggle. Some people think we should let it die in peace. But I fervently believe in my heart that it is precisely *because* of this struggle that it should not die.[81]

Whatever rationale one may suggest for retaining the Gaelic language, in essence, the language is integral to a culture rich in tradition, values, and convention, and that culture is often expressed in the creative genius of musicians, dancers, and composers as well as those who speak the language. The Celtic music in Cape Breton has been sustained through generations by families and individuals, and a community of mentors and bards like Dan Joe and Mike MacLean and Neil R. MacIsaac and Joe Neil MacNeil.

Perhaps, the Celtic culture in Cape Breton today is one which aspires more to the music in defining those traditions, values, and conventions, and for that reason, the Celtic music of Cape Breton may be one of the most significant elements in celebrating and sustaining the culture of the Gael.

Notes

1. Charles Dunn, *The Highland Settler: A Portrait of the Scottish Gael in Nova Scotia* (Toronto: University of Toronto Press, 1953).
2. John Lorne Campbell, *Songs Remembered in Exile* (Scotland: University Press, 1990).
3. Elizabeth A. Doherty, "The Paradox of the Periphery, Evolution of the Cape Breton Fiddle Tradition 1928-1995," unpublished doctoral dissertation, Ireland: University of Limerick, 1996.
4. Ibid., p.91.
5. Kenneth MacKinnon, "Two Peoples or One? The Shared Culture of Cape Breton and the Western Isles," paper presented at the 7th Atlantic Canada Studies Converence, Edinburgh, Scotland, May 5-7, 1988.
6. Joe Neil MacNeil ed. Dr. John Shaw. *Tales Until Dawn.* (Montreal, Kingston: McGill - Queen's University Press, 1987).
7. John Lorne Campbell, 1990, p. 41.
8. Charles Dunn, 1953, p. 146.
9. This quote was taken from an article entitled "Fight for the Gaelic ... ," which was included in the information booklet for the "Options for the 1990's" conference, June 8-9, Sydney, Nova Scotia (Community Initiatives for Gaelic Language and Cultural Development in Nova Scotia).
10. Brian MacLeod, "For Gaelic's Sake: The Right Choice Needed," *The Clansman*, 4:2, 1990, p. 5.
11. Ibid., p. 5.
12. Ibid., p. 5.
13. See Note #6.
14. John Campbell, "Storyteller Joe Neil MacNeil Says Medal Belongs to People "Who Gave Me the Stories,"" *Cape Breton Post.*
15. "Doctorate Degree to Storyteller," *The Clansman*, 4:2, April, 1990.
16. The Sons of Skye wrote the song "Joe Neil" in 1981 to celebrate Joe's visit to Scotland in 1979. Joe toured with the group as we visited the islands. Joe was so well received and acquired near celebrity status especially in Barra. The song was recorded by the Sons of Skye in 1981.
17. See Note #2.
18. Margaret MacDonell, *The Immigrant Experience: Songs of Highland Immigrants of North America* (Toronto: University of Toronto Press, 1982).
19. Citation read at UCCB's 1996 graduation exercises, at which time Mae Campbell received a Doctor of Letters degree.
20. Ibid.

21. Ibid.

22. James B. Lamb, *The Celtic Crusader* (Hantsport, N.S.: Lancelot Press, 1992), pp. 9-10.

23. Ibid., p. 24.

24. David E. Whisnant, *All That is Native and Fine* (Chapel Hill and London: The University of North Carolina Press, 1983), p. 106.

25. Ibid.

26. Ibid., p. 107.

27. Ibid., p.108.

28. Ibid., p.128.

29. Royal Scottish Dance Society, *Fifty Scottish Dances*, Edinburgh, Scotland.

30. David E. Whisnant, 1983, p. 170.

31. Barry Shears. *The Cape Breton Collection of Bagpipe Music*. (Halifax: The House of Music, 1995).

32. James B. Lamb, 1982.

33. Ibid.

34. Ibid., p. 44.

35. Brendon Kennedy, "Island Musicians to Teach at Celtic Music School," *Cape Breton Post*, April 6, 1996, p. 9A.

36. "Gaelic Scholar Dies Suddenly," *Antigonish Casket*, Antigonish, Nova Scotia, June 23, 1977.

37. Kenneth MacKinnon, *Gaelic, A Past and Future Prospect* (Edinburgh, Scotland: Saltire Society, 1991), p. 75.

38. Ibid., p.77

39. Ibid., p.90

40. "Gaelic Scholar Dies Suddenly," 1977.

41. Minutes of a meeting which took place July 18, 1973 where members of the Gaelic Society met with UCCB representatives to discuss the possibility of setting up a centre of Celtic studies. The Gaelic Society (Comunn Gaidhlig Cheap Breatunn) prepared a formal proposal for the "New University" dated November 29, 1973.

42. College of Cape Breton Summer School Program, 1973.

43. "Universities Recognize Need for Community Involvement," *The Clansman*, December/January, 1991-92, p. 11.

44. "Gaelic Products from B.& R.," *Am Braighe*, Summer, 1995, p. 6.

45. See Note #9.

46. Brian McCormack, "Proposal for Assistance: Nova Scotia Highland Village Society," November 1988.

47. Julie Collins, "Gaelic Singer Triumphs at Ontario Mod," *Cape Breton Post*, June 12, 1989, p. 11.

48. Francene Gillis, "Lantern Burn - Here We Come," *The Inverness Oran*, May 4, 1994, p. 20.

49. Ibid., p. 20.

50. Ibid., p. 20.

51. Ibid., p. 20.

52. *The Clansman*, April/May 1990 reported that Donald A. Ferguson, Gaelic scholar and author, received the Award of Merit on Highland Village Day, August 5, 1989. Jim St.Clair introduced Professor Ferguson noting his "outstanding contribution to the preservation of the Highland Scottish culture through his documentation of the lives of the pioneer Scottish settlers . . ." (p. 12) [*Beyond the Hebrides* is one of his publications.]

53. Jim Watson, "Gaelic Will Writhe Its Last Without United Intervention," *The Manitoba Heritage Review*, Vol. 6, Autumn, 1990.

54. *Gaelic Songs from the Mira*, recorded by Laughie Gillis, CR1-8137, 1985.

55. Ibid.

56. Refer to Note #34, Chapter 5.

57. Resolution No. 563 on Gaelic language in Nova Scotia, presented by Hon. William Gillis to the House of Assembly, Halifax, N.S., May 19, 1987.

58. The National Mod 1985 Sub-Committee of the City of Sydney Bicentennial Committee, "This Proposal to Host The National Mod 1985 of An Comunn Gaidhealach," Sydney, Nova Scotia, 1982.

59. Barbara Carver, "National Mod Coordinators Satisfied Sydney Can Stage '85 Scottish Event," *Cape Breton Post*, February 4, 1983.

60. As reported by Brian Wilson, in the West Highland Free Press, 1982.

61. Editorial, Cape Breton Post, May 31, 1982.

62. The Bicentennial Office issued a letter in February 1984, cancelling the Mod.

63. TBA

64. Sheldon MacInnes, "Conclusions: International Conference for Gaelic Language and Culture," unpublished paper presented to the Gaelic Society's annual meeting, Sydney, N.S., November, 1987.

65. Cape Gael Associates Co-Op was formed to organize a series of projects involving research, concerts, publications, and the marketing of some audio-visual productions. Cape Gael published a series of booklets through the UCCB Press dealing with songs and stories about the Gaelic immigration ("Participaction," Inverness County, October 1987).

66. International Conference brochure, 1987.

67. John Campbell, "Grassroots Approach to Gaelic Language Needed, Former Chief Gives Warning," *Cape Breton Post*, Oct. 19, 1987, p. 3.

68. Sheldon MacInnes, Chair, Ad Hoc Committee. Letter to Dr. Ora McManus, Director, Continuing Education, UCCB, December 21, 1989.

69. John Campbell, "Gaelic Conference Winds Down, Plan of Action Agreed Upon," *Cape Breton Post*, October 19, 1987, p. 3.

70. Ibid., p. 3.

71. Silver Donald Cameron, "The World Which is At Us," in Carol Corbin and Judith A. Rolls, editors *The Centre of the World at the Edge of a Continent* (Sydney: UCCB Press, 1996), p. 220.

72. Community Initiatives for Gaelic Language and Cultural Development In Nova Scotia, "Options for the 1990's." Booklet circulated at conference, June 8-9, 1989, Holiday Inn, Sydney.

73. Ibid.

74. Scottish Societies Association of Nova Scotia, "Turning A Way of Life Into A Way of Living," draft concept document for Nova Scotia's Celtic Arts and Music Industry, October 18, 1983.

75. See Note #72. "HIDB Credited with Playing a Role in Turnaround of People's Attitudes" by John Campbell.

76. Weldon Bona, "Cape Breton Culture Industry, Strategy for Growth," report to ECBC and UCCB, Sydney, Nova Scotia, January 1995, p. 123.

77. Allistair MacLeod, *As Birds Bring Forth the Sun* (Toronto: McClelland and Stewart, 1986), p. 24.

78. Jim Watson's presentation to the Canadian Heritage Conference in 1987.

79. Silver Donald Cameron, 1996.

80. Silver Donald Cameron, 1996.

81. Rosemary McCormack, in the first *Cape Breton's Magazine*, 1972.

Special Tunes

My Brothers and Sisters

hornpipe

Jamie MacInnis

Dan Joe MacInnis' Jig

Sandy MacInnis
Mar. 15, 1975

John Willie MacInnis' Strathspey

Raymond Ellis
Oct. 21, 1987

Colleen MacInnis' Jig

jig

Mike MacLean

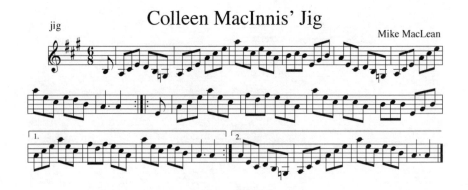

My Friend Dan Joe

Stanley MacKinnon

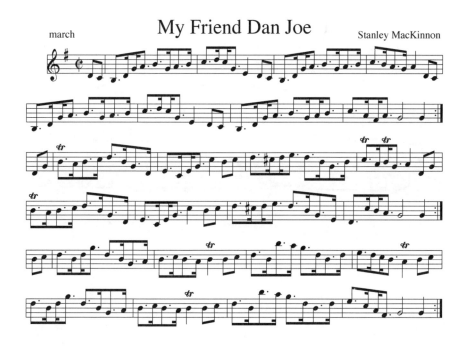

Big Pond Reel

pipe reel

Jimmy MacLellan

Elizabeth Ann's Welcome to Rosemount

march

Harry Slaunwhite
Xmas, 1982

Malcolm Deleskie

pipe march

Malcolm Campbell

Bibliography

A Brief History of St. Mary's Parish, East Bay 1838- 1988. A Time to Remember. Compilation under the direction of the Anniversary Committee and Parish Council.

"A Visit with Ray `Mac' MacDonald, In Honour of the 50th Year of CJFX Radio." Edited from conversations with Marjorie MacHattie. *"Cape Breton's Magazine,"* #64, pp. 75-92.

Ardenne, Michael, Head of Performing Arts, Nova Scotia Department of Culture, Recreation, and Fitness. (1982, February 17). Letter to Sons of Skye, Big Pond, N.S.

Arsenault, Tim. (1990, January 12). "Macphee Proves He's a Master." *The Chronicle Herald.*

Arsenault, Tim. (1992, November 2). "Hi How Are You Today?: Expands MacIsaac's genre hopping abilities." *The Chronicle Herald.*

Aulenbach, James, Cultural Affairs Music Officer, Nova Scotia Department of Culture, Recreation and Fitness. (1980, August 29). Letter to Sons of Skye, Big Pond, N.S.

Balmur Ltd. (1992, June 29). Rita's Special Big Pond Concert. Press Release.

"Barde Popular Group." (1978, March 9). *Cape Breton Post.*

Barr, James, Vice-President, Policyholder Relations, Cumis, Burlington, Ontario. (1981, September 28). Letter to Sons of Skye, Big Pond, N.S.

Baynes, John. (1970). *The Jacobite Rising of 1715.* London: Cassell and Company Ltd.

Beaton, Joey. (1989, December 13). "Cape Breton MacPhee Releases Album." *The Casket.*

Beaton, Virginia & Stephen Pedersen. (1983). *Maritime Music Greats.* Halifax: Nimbus.

Bennett, Margaret. (1989). *The Last Stronghold, Scottish Gaelic Traditions in Newfoundland.* St. John's: Breakwater Books.

Big Pond. (1989). Television documentary for CBC Quebec (Producer: Roger LeClerc).

Blackwood, Don, Executive Director, Cape Breton Tourist Association. (1986, May 1). Letter to Sheldon MacInnes, Big Pond Concert, N.S.

Bobyk, Valerie, Chair, Museum Committee, Cape Breton Centre for Heritage and Science. (1996, October 22). Letter to Sheldon MacInnes, University College of Cape Breton, Sydney, N.S.

Bona, Weldon. (1995, January). *Cape Breton Culture Industry, Strategy for Growth.* Report to ECBC and UCCB, Sydney, N.S.

British Broadcasting Corporation, Glasgow, Scotland. (1985, October 3 & 4). Itinerary for film crew's visit to Cape Breton to produce a television series on "The Celts" - prepared by Sheldon MacInnes.

Brown, Keith. (1994, August 12). *Strategic Economic Action Plan.* Cape Breton County Economic Development Authority, Sydney, N.S.

Brown, Richard. (1979). *A History of Cape Breton Island.* Belleville, Ontario: Mika.

Bruford, Alan, Archivist, University of Edinburgh, School of Scottish Studies, Scotland. (1983, September 13). Letter to Margaret Gillis, Sydney, N.S.

Burrows, Linda, Secretary to the Minister of Culture, Recreation and Fitness, Halifax, NS. (1980, March 10). Letter, on behalf of Honourable Bruce Cochran, to Sons of Skye, Big Pond, N.S.

By-Laws of Comhairle Na Gaidhlig, Alba Nuadh [Gaelic Council of Nova Scotia], approved in 1990.

Cameron, Charles W. (1975). *Curiosities of Old Edinburgh*. Edinburgh: Albyn.

Cameron, Eric. (1975). "College of Cape Breton Promotes Art of Fiddling." *Cape Breton Post*.

Cameron, Isabel. (1938). *Angus Our Precentor*. London: Lutterworth.

Cameron, Mae. (1996). Citation read at UCCB's 1996 graduation exercises, at which time Mae Campbell Cameron received an honourary Doctor of Letters.

Cameron, Silver Donald. (1996). "The World Which is At Us." In Carol Corbin and Judith A. Rolls (Eds.), *The Centre of the World at the Edge of a Continent*. Sydney: UCCB, pp. 213-220.

-   (1980, November). "John Allan Cameron, Entertainer." *Atlantic Insight*.

Cameron, W.M. (1951). *Highland Dances of Scotland Textbook*. Aberdeen, Scotland: Aberdeen Journals.

Campbell, Ann Marie. (1989, Spring). "Big Pond Homecoming." *Forerunner 3: Cape Breton's Community Magazine*, 2:1.

Campbell, John Lorne. (1990). *Songs Remembered in Exile*. Scotland: University Press.

-   (1983, October 21 and December 16). Folklorist, Isle of Canna, Scotland. Letters to Margaret Gillis, Sydney, N.S.

-   (1953, October). "Highland Links with Nova Scotia." *Scots Magazine*.

Campbell, John. (1996, November 2). "Cape Breton not only home for Scots in North America." *Cape Breton Post*.

-   (1990, August 18). "Fiddle Festival at Gaelic College Celebrates Our Musical Heritage." *Cape Breton Post*.

-   (1989, October 30). "MacKinnon still acclaimed by authors worldwide." *Cape Breton Post*.

-   (1989, October 19). "Tourism Minister Listens." *Cape Breton Post*.

-   (1989, October). "Storyteller Joe Neil MacNeil Says Medal Belongs to People 'Who Gave Me The Stories.'" *Cape Breton Post*.

-   (1988, August 30). "Cape Breton music, Carl's magic carpet." *Cape Breton Post*.

-   (1987, October 19). "Gaelic Conference Winds Down, Plan of Action Agreed Upon." *Cape Breton Post*.

-   (1987, October 19). "Grassroots Approach to Gaelic Language Needed, Former Chief Gives Warning." *Cape Breton Post*.

Campbell, Mary L. (1996, July 24). "Foreign Element Infringing and Infecting Our Music" (Letter to the editor). *The Inverness Oran*.

Campbell, Mary C., Chair of the Whycocomagh Summer Festival. (1978, April 25). Letter to Sons of Skye, Big Pond, N.S.

Bibliography

"Canadian Gaels a hit." (1979, November 8). *Oban Times*, Scotland.

"Canadian Gaels go on tour." (1979). *Weekend Scotsman*, Scotland.

"Canadians at the Mod." (1979). *Weekend Scotsman*, Scotland.

"Cape Breton Gaels in Portnalong." (1979, November 1). *Oban Times*, Scotland.

Cape Breton Post. (1982, May 31). Editorial.

Cape Breton Post. (1973, August 9). Editorial.

Capercaillie, Gaelic Songs and Traditional Music from Scotland. (1985, July). Program brochure of Cape Breton tour.

Carson, Ciaran. (1986). *Irish Traditional Music*. Belfast, Ireland: Appletree Press.

Carver, Barbara. (1983, February 4). "National Mod Coordinators Satisfied Sydney Can Stage '85 Scottish Event." *Cape Breton Post.*

- (1982, April 23). "Ambition A Simple One for Sons Of Skye." *Cape Breton Post.*

Castle Bay Parish Bulletin. (1979, October 14). Barra, Scotland.

"Ceilidh Na Bliadhn' Ura A Ceap Bhreatainn." (1979, January 19). *West Highland Free Press*, Scotland, No. 351.

"Ceilidh." (1973, January 3). Cover Page Photo in the Travel and Entertainment Guide, *The Dartmouth Free Press.*

"Celtic Forum on Air Tonight Over CBC Network." (1938, July 15). *Post Record.*

Chafe, Winnie. (1995). [Citation read at UCCB's 1995 graduation exercises, at which time Winnie Chafe received a Doctor of Letters.]

Chaffey, Ches, Manager, Chignic Lodge, Codroy Valley, NFLD. (1975, January 23). Letter to Sons of Skye, c/o Fred White, Big Pond, N.S.

"Coast to Coast." (1977, January 5). *Cape Breton Post.*

Collins, Julie. (1997, May 14). "Final season Gaelic workshop set for B & R Heritage Saturday." *Cape Breton Post.*

- (1989, June 12). "Gaelic singer triumphs at Ontario Mod." *Cape Breton Post.*

Cooke, Peter. (1986). *The Fiddle Tradition of the Shetland Isles*. Great Britain: Cambridge University Press.

Cooke, Stephen. (1996, July 7). "Graham Lets 'er Rip." *The Mail Star / Chronicle Herald.*

Cooper, Derek. (1977). *Skye*. Great Britain: Morrison & Gibb.

Cranford, Paul Stewart. (1996). *Lighthouse Collection of newly composed Fiddle Tunes*. Cape Breton Island: Cranford Publications.

Creighton, Helen & Calum MacLeod. (1964). *Gaelic Songs In Nova Scotia*. Ottawa: Queen's Printer.

"Dance Nova Scotia Activities - Ceilidh in the Schools." (1992, Summer). *The Octopus*, 5:3.

Dingwall, David C., Member of Parliament, Cape Breton-East Richmond. (1986, May 22). Letter to Sheldon MacInnes, Big Pond Concert, N.S.

"Discovering Our Gaelic Heritage." (1982, March 1). In newsletter issued by Mod Ontario.

"Doctorate Degree to Storyteller." (1990, April). *The Clansman*," 4:2.

Doherty, Elizabeth A. (1996). "The Paradox of the Periphery, Evolution of the Cape Breton Fiddle Tradition 1928-1995." Unpublished doctoral dissertation. Ireland: University of Limerick.
- (1994). *The Music of Cape Breton - An Irish Perspective.* Cork, Ireland: The Traditional Music Archive / The Irish Traditional Music Society, University College.
- (1993). Accompanying booklet for the C.D. entitled "Traditional Music from Cape Breton Island." UK and USA: Nimbus Records Ltd.
Donahoe, Terence, R.B., Q.C. (1991, July 12). Minister, Nova Scotia Department of Tourism and Culture. Letter to Sheldon MacInnes, Big Pond Summer Festival, Cape Breton, N.S.
- Minister, Nova Scotia Department of Tourism and Culture. (1991, April 5). Letter to Sheldon MacInnes, Big Pond Summer Festival, N.S.
Donaldson, Gordon. (1957). *Scots Overseas.* London: Robert Hale Company.
Donham, Parker Barss. (1996, August 28). "Out of Tune." *The Daily News.*
Donovan, Ken (ed.). (1990) *The Island: New Perspectives on Cape Breton's History."* Sydney, N.S.: UCCB Press.
Ducharme, Mary Anne. (1997, January/February). "Creignish Fiddlers, Interview with Frank MacInnis," in *Celebrate Our Music 1997-98,* a publication sponsored by Inverness County Recreation and Continuing Education, 18:1.
Dudley, Wendy. (1988, December 1). "Rita Has Audience Flying On its Own." *Calgary Herald.*
Dunlay, Kate & D.L. Reich. (1986). *Traditional Celtic Fiddle Music of Cape Breton.* East Alstead, NH: Fiddlecase Books.
Dunlay, Kate. (1996/97, Winter). "Review by Kate Dunlay." [of Winnie Chafe's "Legacy" recording]. *Am Braighe.*
- (1996). *Traditional Celtic Violin Music of Cape Breton.* Toronto, Ontario: DunGreen Music.
- (1989, Fall). "A Cape Breton Primer; Canada's Old World Music." *Sing Out!* 34:4.
Dunn, Charles W. (1953). *Highland Settler: A Portrait of the Scottish Gael in Nova Scotia.* Toronto: Univeristy of Toronto Press.
Dunn, Jacqueline A. (1991). "The Sound of Gaelic is in the Fiddler's Music." Senior essay, St. Francis Xavier University, Antigonish.
Eadie, Douglas, Co-producer, Pellicula Films Limited, Glasgow, Scotland. (1985, February 12). Letter to Sheldon MacInnes, Continuing Education, University College of Cape Breton, Sydney, N.S.
Emmerson, George S. (1971). *Rantin' Pipe and Tremblin' String: A History of Scottish Dance Music.* Montreal: McGill-Queen's University Press.
Fairlie, Margaret C., British Broadcasting Corporation, Glasgow, Scotland. (1979, February 15). Letter to Sons of Skye, Big Pond, N.S.
Ferguson, Donald A. (1977). *Beyond the Hebrides.* Halifax, N.S.: Lawson Graphics Atlantic.

"Fight for the Gaelic." (1989, June 8-9). Program for Options for the 1990's Conference, Sydney, N.S.

Finlay J. MacDonald & Friends, Scotland. (1985, July). Itinerary for Cape Breton tour - prepared by Sheldon MacInnes and Angus MacDonald.

Flett, J. & T. Flett. (1964). *Traditional Dancing in Scotland*. London: Routledge and Kegan Paul.

Fraser, Brien E., Co-ordinator, Major Attractions and Events, Nova Scotia Department of Tourism. (1980, July 11). Letter to Big Pond Concert Committee, N.S.

Frew, Chris. (1986, January 31). "Travels With a Fiddle." *West Highland Free Press*.

"Gaelic Products from B. & R." (1995, Summer). *Am Braighe*.

"Gaelic Scholar Dies Suddenly." (1977, June 23). *Antigonish Casket*, Antigonish, N.S.

Gaelic Society of Cape Breton. (1973, November 29). Submission regarding proposed Gaelic and Celtic programs at St. F.X. Sydney-NSEIT.

Garrison, Virginia. (1985). "Traditional and Non-traditional Teaching and Learning Practices in Folk Music: An Ethnographic Field Study of Cape Breton Fiddling." Unpublished doctoral dissertation. University of Wisconsin, Madison.

Gibson, John. (1994, August 10). "Pipers' styles in contrast at Broad Cove Concert." *The Oran.*
- (1991, October/November). "What Can Be Expected of the Highland Heart of Nova Scotia?" (Letter to the editor). *The Clansman.*
- (1982, April 26). "Sons of Skye solo concert part of CBC radio opening." *Scotia Sun.*
- (1972-73). Collection of articles on Scottish fiddlers Donald Angus Beaton (#12), John Donald Cameron (#21), Angus Allan Gillis (#11), John Mac-Dougall (#15), Dan Hughie MacEachern (#16), Sandy MacLean (#6), and Morgan MacQuarrie (#22). *The Scotia Sun.* [From Hughie "The Barber" MacEachen, Port Hawkesbury, N.S.].

Gilchrist, Anne G. (1910). "Notes on the Modal System of Gaelic Tunes." *Journal of the Folk Song Society*. Volume 4, pp. 150-53.

Gillis, Francene. (1994, May 4). "Lantern burn - Here we come." *The Inverness Oran.*
- (1992, August 26). "A Visit with Buddy MacMaster." *The Inverness Oran.*

"Glendale Man Tops in Gaelic." (1989, May 30). *Cape Breton Post.*

"Gordie Sampson Update." (1997, April). *The Big Pond Times*, IV:4. Big Pond, Cape Breton, N.S.: Big Pond Community Council.

Grant, I.F. (1961). *Highland Folkways*. London and New York: Routledge.

Greenberg, David. (1989, April). "Dialogue with David Greenberg." [Written material]

Guy, Greg. (1995, November 2). "The Devil In the Kitchen: Ashley fires up major label debut." *The Chronicle-Herald.*

Hamilton, Cicely. (1937). *Modern Scotland*. New York, New York: Dutton.

Hamilton, Derek. (1979, September). "Cape Breton Scottish Fiddle - Topic 12TS354 in Record Review." *Box and Fiddle*, Scotland.

Hanratty, John. (1988, Autumn). "Initiatives for Local Employment' Is Theme, Cautious Optimism Marks C.C.E.D. Meet." *Forerunner 2, Cape Breton's Community Magazine*, 1:2.

Harkin, Bosco, CHFX FM Radio, Halifax, N.S. (1982, October 11). Letter to Sons of Skye, Big Pond, N.S.

Harmer, Gordon, Chief Executive Officer, Tourism Industry of Nova Scotia. (1991, February 14). Letter to Sheldon MacInnes, Big Pond Summer Festival, N.S.

Hartman, David W. (1974). *Immigrants and Migrants*. Detroit: University Thought Publishing Company, USA.

Harvey, Daniel C. (1941). "Scottish Immigration to Cape Breton." *Dalhousie Review*, Vol. 22.

Headlam, Bruce. (1995, September). "The Devil Went Down to Cape Breton." *Saturday Night*.

Hunter, James. (1979). *The Fiddle Music of Scotland*. Edinburgh: Constable.

"International Gathering of the Clans Nova Scotia 1979." (1978, December 9). Executive Director's Report, unpublished.

International Gathering of the Clans. (1983, July). Official program prepared by Sheldon MacInnes for the Gaelic College, St. Ann's, N.S.

"Interview with Bishop MacDonald." (1980). *The Island Fiddler, 3*. Newsletter of the Prince Edward Island Fiddlers' Society.

"John Allan's Music." (1978, October 21). Editorial in *Cape Breton Post*.

Johnson, Stanley. (1913). *A History of Immigration From the United Kingdom of North America, 1763-1912*. London: Routledge.

Johnston, A.A. (Rev.). (1971). *A History of the Catholic Church in Eastern Nova Scotia Vol. 2 - 1827-1800*. Antigonish, Nova Scotia: St. Francis Xavier University Press.

- (1971). *A History of the Catholic Church in Eastern Nova Scotia Vol. 1 - 1611-1827*. Antigonish, Nova Scotia: St. Francis Xavier University Press.

"Joyous Courage." (1977, August 24). *Scotia Sun*.

Kennedy, Brendon. (1996, April 6). "Island musicians to teach at Celtic music school." *Cape Breton Post*.

Kerr, Greg. Minister, Nova Scotia Department of Tourism and Culture. (1992, June 19). Letter to Sheldon MacInnes, Big Pond Summer Festival, N.S.

Laidlaw, Alexander F. ed. (1971). *The Man from Margaree, Writings and Speeches of M.M. Coady*. Toronto/Montreal: McClelland and Stewart.

Lamb, James B. (1992). *The Celtic Crusader*. Hantsport, N.S.: Lancelot.

LaRue, Jan. (1970). *Guidelines for Style Analysis*. New York: Norton.

LeBlanc, Alfred. (1994, December 9). "The Reel Thing." *Equinox Magazine*.

LeBlanc, Barbara & L. Sadousky. (1986). "Inverness County Dance Project." Unpublished report to the Museum of Man, Ottawa.

MacAoidh, Caoimhin. (1994). *Between the Jigs and the Reels*. Ireland: Drumlin.

McCormack, Brian. (1988, November). Proposal for Assistance: Nova Scotia Highland Village Society.

McCormack, Rosemary. (1989, Autumn). "This playgroup looks the same but sounds different." *Forerunner 4, Cape Breton's Community Magazine*, 2:2.

MacDonald, Alexander. (1996, July 17). "Cape Breton Fiddle Music, Is It Unique? Yes! What Makes It So?" *The Inverness Oran*.

MacDonald, Allan, Senior Gaelic Producer, British Broadcasting Corporation, Inverness, Scotland. (1979, March 7). Letter to Sons of Skye, Big Pond, N.S.

- British Broadcasting Corporation, Inverness, Scotland. (1979, June 5). Letter to Christie MacInnis, Big Pond, N.S.

MacDonald, Angus. (1991 & 1992, December/January). "In Defence of Scotland's Piping Tradition - Dr. Angus Responds." *The Clansman*.

MacDonald, Dan Alex. (1986). *Songs from Framboise*. editors Kay MacDonald & Effie Rankin; collector Eunice Lively, Cape Breton, N.S.

Macdonald, Frank. (1996, July 24). "Willie Francis Fraser Brings Scotland 'Close to the Floor.'" *The Inverness Oran*.

- (1996, July 17). "Scottish Fiddler Finds Cape Breton Musical Landscapes a Lot Like Scotland." *Inverness Oran*.

- (1996, July 17). "Full House for Lecture on Cape Breton Fiddle Signatures." *The Inverness Oran*.

MacDonald, Jim. (1968, November). "Piping in Cape Breton." *Piping Times*," 21:2. In John Gibson. (1991, October/November). "Old and New World Piping - A Piper's Perspective in 1968." *The Clansman*.

MacDonald, M. Elizabeth. (1981). *To the Old and the New Scotland*. Sydney: City Printers.

MacDonald, Mary Janet, et. al. (1992, October). *No Less No More Just Four on the Floor: A Guide to Teaching Traditional Cape Breton Square Sets for Public Schools*. Halifax: Dance Nova Scotia.

MacDonald, Norman. (1992). *A Highland University, Some Lessons in the Politics and Planning of Higher Education in North and Northwest Scotland, 1829-1992*. Published paper available from Barail, the Centre for Highlands and Islands Policy Studies, Sabhal Mor Ostaig, Teangue, Sleat, Isle of Skye IV44 8RQ.

- (1979, April). "Jonathan G. MacKinnon Memorial Lecture, The Gaelic Language Today." Brochure prepared for circulation by the Beaton Institute, UCCB, Sydney, N.S.

- (1979, March 24). "Leading fiddler dies at 94." *Oban Times*, Scotland.

MacDonald, Rankin. (1996, October 30). "Scots Tour Cape Breton for Five-part BBC Radio Series." *The Inverness Oran*.

- (May 26, 1993). "Important instructional video on Cape Breton fiddling to be released Thursday." *The Oran*.

MacDonald, Steve. (1979, April). "College of Cape Breton heralds New Year with live Ceilidh broadcast to Scotland." *College Canada*, 4:4.

"MacDonald's Lament . . . Or, piping and the competition straitjacket." (1986, August 22). [Interview with piper Allan MacDonald]. *West Highland Free Press*, Scotland.

MacDonell, Margaret. (1982). *The Immigrant Experience: Songs of Highland Immigrants of North America*. Toronto, Ontario: University of Toronto Press.

MacDougall, John Lorne. (1972). *History of Inverness County, Nova Scotia*. Belleville, Ontario: Mika Publication.

MacEachen, Allan J. (1997). Citation read at UCCB's 1997 graduation exercises, at which time Allan J. MacEachen received an honourary Doctor of Letters.

MacEachen, Frances. (1995, Summer). "The MacIntyre Pipers of French Road." *Am Braighe*.

- (1991-1992, December/January). "A Traditional List with a Taste for Challenging Tunes." *The Clansman*.

- (1991, Oct./Nov.). "A Tribute to Dan Joe MacInnis: A Lifetime of Scottish music." *The Clansman*.

- (1991, October/November). "The Broad Cove Concert - The Best Gift of All." *The Clansman*.

- (1991, October/November). "Successful Christmas Island Feis Brings Gaelic Together." *The Clansman*.

MacEachern, Rev. John Hugh. (1973). "Scotland Tour, October 3-18, 1973." Journal by Rev. MacEachern, from Broad Cove, Inverness County.

MacGillivray, Allister. (1988). *A Cape Breton Ceilidh*. Sydney, Nova Scotia: Sea Cape Music Limited.

- (1981). *The Cape Breton Fiddler*. Sydney, N.S.: City Printers Ltd.

MacInnes, Dan. (1991-92). "Highland Settler - A Word Picture of What Was." *The Clansman*.

- (1991, October/November). "MacInnes Replies." *The Clansman*.

MacInnes, Sheldon. (1997, Winter). "Cape Breton Fiddler - A Symbol of Cape Breton Culture." Short article submitted to the Beaton Institute, UCCB, Sydney, N.S. for Heritage Canada.

- (1996, January). "Rural Cape Breton Festivals - A Research Project with Recommendations." Research report submitted to Enterprise Cape Breton, Sydney, Nova Scotia.

- (1995, Spring). Discussion paper. "A rationale for teaching square dancing in the Inverness County school curriculum - physical education program." Presented to Inverness County school teachers at a workshop sponsored by DANS, Mabou, Inverness Co., N.S.

- (1993, June 12). "Cape Breton Stepdance: An Irish or Scottish Tradition?" Paper presented at the International Symposium on Irish Culture, Louisbourg, Cape Breton, N.S. [Published as "Both Sides of the Water" in C. Corbin and J. Rolls. (1996). *The Centre of the World at the Edge of a Continent*. Sydney: UCCB Press.]

- (1991, April 12). "Cape Breton's Gaelic Culture." Discussion paper presented to the Nova Scotia Arts Advisory Committee, Halifax, N.S.

Bibliography

- (1989, December 21). Chair of Ad Hoc Committee. Letter to Dr. Ora McManus, Director, Continuing Education, UCCB.
- (1989, November 4). "Festivals in Rural Cape Breton: A Unique Event." Paper presented at a workshop hosted by the Scottish Societies Association of Nova Scotia, Iona, Cape Breton, N.S.
- (1987, November). "Conclusions: International Conference for Gaelic Language and Culture." Paper presented to the Gaelic Society's annual meeting, Sydney, N.S.
- (1987, October). Program summary for the International Gathering of the Clans, Sydney, NS.
- (1987, June 2). A Brief on the Canadian Broadcast Service. Paper presented to the Standing Committee on Communications and Culture, House of Commons, Halifax, N.S. In "Minutes of Proceedings and Evidence of the Standing Committee on Communications and Culture" (pp. 47:40-47:48). Ottawa, Ontario: House of Commons.
- (1987, June). "Glencoe Dances - The Real Stuff." Unpublished article submitted to Dance Nova Scotia, Halifax, N.S.
- (1981, July 13). "A Case for Scottish Strings." A brief presented to CJFX Radio Station, Port Hawkesbury, N.S.
- Leader, Sons of Skye, Big Pond, Cape Breton, N.S. (1979, April 11). Letter to Malcolm MacLeod, National Mod, Glasgow, Scotland.
- (1977). "Folk Society in An Urban Setting." M.A. Unpublished master's thesis, The Merrill-Palmer Institute (Wayne State University), Detroit, Michigan.

MacInnis, John William. (1991, August). Article published in the *Cape Breton Post.*

MacIntyre, Sandy. (1996, Summer). "Fiddling Cape Breton Style." *Fiddler Magazine,* 3:2, California, USA.

MacIsaac, Jack, Minister, Nova Scotia Dept. of Culture and Tourism. (1986, May 20). Letter to Sheldon MacInnes, Big Pond Concert, N.S.

MacIsaac, Lionel. (1996, October). "Michael MacLean 1932-1996." *The Big Pond Times,*" III:10, published by Big Pond Community Council.

MacIsaac, Mary. (1965, July 3). "Valley gives warm welcome to Scots pipers, fiddlers." *The Western Star,* Newfoundland.

MacIsaac, Merle. (1993, November/December). "Cape Breton Hit Parade." *Bluenose, First Anniversary Issue.*

MacKenzie, A.A. [Tony]. (1979). *The Irish in Cape Breton.* Antigonish, N.S.: Formac Publishing Co. Ltd.

MacKenzie, Archibald A. (1984). *The MacKenzie's History of Christmas Island Parish.*" Sudbury, Ontario: MacKenzie Rothe.

MacKinnon, Ian. (1989). "Fiddling to Fortune: the Role of Commercial Recordings Made by Cape Breton Fiddlers in the Fiddle Music Tradition of Cape Breton Island." Unpublished master's thesis, Department of Folklore, Memorial University, Newfoundland.

MacKinnon, J.G. (1973). *Old Sydney*. Belleville, Ontario: Mika.

MacKinnon, Kenneth. (1991). *Gaelic, A Past and Future Prospect*. Edinburgh, Scotland: Saltire Society.

- (1988, May 5-7). "Two Peoples Or One? The Shared Culture of Cape Breton and the Western Isles." Paper presented at the 7th Atlantic Canada Studies Conference, Edinburgh, Scotland.

- (1974). *The Lion's Tongue*. Inverness, Scotland: Club Leabhar.

MacLeish, Kenneth. (1970, May). "Scotland's Outer Hebrides." *National Geographic Magazine*.

MacLellan, Terry, Director of Corporate Affairs, Cape Breton Development Corporation, Sydney, N.S. (1980, March 11). Letter to Sons of Skye, Big Pond, N.S.

MacLeod, Allistair. (1986). *As Birds Bring Forth the Sun*. McClelland and Stewart: Toronto, Ontario.

MacLeod, Brian. (1990). "For Gaelic's Sake, The Right Choice Needed." *The Clansman*, 4:2.

MacLeod, Darryl. (1996, August 14). "Dunlay/Greenberg Lecture Was Informative, Interesting" (Letter to the editor). *The Inverness Oran*.

MacLeod, Ken. (1996, October 4). "Butler award to help aspiring musicians." *Cape Breton Post*.

- (1996, June). "Scottish museum to get taste of Cape Breton fiddle." *Cape Breton Post*.

- (1995, January 7). "ECMAs may be musicians' break." *Cape Breton Post*.

- (1994, July 23). "Rita comes home again." *Cape Breton Post*.

- (1991, June 25). "Rita Mac Neil Will Headline Big Pond Summer Festival." *Cape Breton Post*.

MacLeod, Rev. Roddy, Church of Scotland Manse, North Uist, Scotland. (1979, May 12). Letter to Sheldon MacInnes, Continuing Education, College of Cape Breton, Sydney, N.S.

MacNeil, Jack. (1996, November). "Joe Neil MacNeil 1908-1996." *The Big Pond Times*, 3:11.

- (1996, August). "The Coming of The Gaels." *The Big Pond Times*, 3:8.

- (1988, Fall). Letter to residents of the Big Pond community. [Regarding homecoming plans].

MacNeil, Joe Neil. (1987). *Tales Until Dawn*. Dr. John Shaw (ed.). Kingston, Montreal: McGill-Queen's Universtiy Press.

MacNeil, John. (1989, October 20). "Promote Cape Breton Festivals, Thornhill Told." *The Chronicle Herald*.

MacNeil, Kenzie. (1996, July). "A Champion Retires, An Interview with Allan J." *The Cape Bretoner*, 4:4.

MacNeil, Neil. (1948). *The Highland Heart In Nova Scotia*. New York: Scribner.

MacNeill, Seumas and Pearston, Thomas. (1953, June).

Tutor For the Highland Bagpipe Part 1. Glasgow, Scotland: The College of Piping, Kelvin House.

Macpherson, Duncan. (1955). *Macpherson's Pocket Guide to the Isle of Skye, Lochalsh and the Outer Hebrides.* Twenty-third edition. Kyle of Lochalsh: The Kyle Pharmacy.

Magill, Charles W. (1993, May). "Rita MacNeil: Flying High." *Reader's Digest.*

"Makes Recordings of 100 Gaelic Songs" [references John Lorne Campbell's visit to Cape Breton from Scotland]. (1937, November 10). *Post Record.*

"Margaret MacPhee Guest of Honor." (1980, September 5). *Cape Breton Post.*

Martin, Robert. (1996, May). "Sonic Boom. Nova Scotia Open to the World." *Atlantic Progress*, Halifax, Nova Scotia.

McCabe, Carol. (1995, October). "Cape Breton: Where the Music Never Ends." *Islands.*

McCrystal, Cal. (1996, December 15). "Celts reverse the tide of history." *Guardian Weekly.*

McNamara, Frank, Regional Representative, Cape Breton, Nova Scotia Department of Recreation. (1977, August 18). Letter to Sons of Skye, Big Pond, N.S.

Meisner, Glenn, Network Variety Producer, CBC Radio, Halifax, NS. (1983, March 10). Letter to Sons of Skye, Big Pond, N.S.

Memorandum of Association for Comunn Na Gaidhlig, Scotland. (1983).

Menzies, Gordon, Executive Producer, British Broadcasting Corporation, Glasgow, Scotland. (1985, September 11). Letter to Sheldon MacInnes, Continuing Education, University College of Cape Breton, Sydney, N.S.

Milligan, Dianne, Executive Director, Dance Nova Scotia, Halifax, N.S. (1991, March 22). Letter of invitation to speak to Nova Scotia Arts Advisory Committee, Halifax to Sheldon MacInnes, Extension and Community Affairs, UCCB, Sydney, N.S.

Mills, Steve. (1978, October 21). "Cape Breton's Singing Ambassador John Allan Cameron Returns Home." *Cape Breton Post.*

Minutes. (1989, November 18). Council on Gaelic Language - Iona Meeting, Cape Breton, N.S.

"Mod Nan Eilean." (1979). Program Booklet produced by An Comunn Gaidhealach, Scotland.

Monaghan, Alex. (1995, November/December). "Records, Television, Everything." *The Living Tradition.*

Napier, David. (1995, October). "Lovely Rita, Ratings Queen." *Saturday Night.*

"New Cape Breton Gaelic Program Is Highly Praised." (1938, July 18). *Post Record.*

Newton, Pamela and Ellison Robertson. (1984). *The Cape Breton Book of Days.* Sydney: UCCB Press.

"New Year's Eve Ceilidh." (1978, January 4). *Cape Breton Post.*

"No Lazy Days at C.B. College." (1981, August 11). *Cape Breton Post.*

Nova Scotia Department of Economic Development. (1993, January). "A Discussion Paper on Community Economic Development." A Working Document Prepared by the Planning and Policy Division, Halifax, Nova Scotia.

"Nova Scotia's Prime Minister [sic] Praises Radio Programme." (1982, January 9). *Stornoway Gazette*, Scotland.

Patterson, Elizabeth. (1994, July 23). "Ear to the Future; Winnie Chafe uses variety of teaching methods to preserve fiddling heritage." *Cape Breton Post*.

Patton, Wayne, VP of Business Affairs and Music Publishing, Holborne Distributing Company Ltd., Ontario. (1996, June 4). Letter to Sheldon MacInnes, Extension and Community Affairs, University College of Cape Breton, Sydney, N.S.

Pedersen, Steven. (1995, November 2). "Imaginations Set a Glow With Kid Paper's Release." *The Chronicle Herald*.

-    (1991, November 14). "Fiddlin' Around: Fiddlers on the Rise." *The Chronicle-Herald*.

Pelicula Films Limited, Glasgow, Scotland. (1985, May). Itinerary for film crew's visit to Cape Breton to produce *Down Home* documentary - prepared by Sheldon MacInnes.

"Pioneer Gaelic Singer Remembered on Album." (1985, August 22). *Cape Breton Post*.

Prebble, John. (1973). *Glencoe*. Great Britain: Penguin.

-    (1965, November). *The Highland Clearances*." London: Secker and Warburg.

Pryde, George S. (1962). *Scotland from 1603 to the present day - A New History of Scotland. Vol 11*. Edinburgh, Scotland: Thomas Nelson and Sons Ltd.

Quigley, Colin. (1985). *Close to the Floor: Folk Dance in Newfoundland*. St. John's, Newfoundland: Memorial University.

Rambeau, Leonard. President, Balmur Limited. (1992, June 27). Letter to Sheldon MacInnes, Big Pond Summer Festival, N.S.

Redfield, Robert. (1947, January). "The Folk Society" in *The American Journal of Sociology*, Vol. L11, No. 4. Chicago: The University of Chicago Press.

Reesor, Sandie, Canadian Parks/Recreation Association, Halifax, NS. (1980, August 22). Letter to Sons of Skye, Big Pond, N.S.

Resolution No. 563. (1987, May 19). [On Gaelic language in Nova Scotia]. Presented by Hon. William Gillis to the House of Assembly, Halifax, N.S.

Review of Cape Breton Scottish fiddle recordings, "The Music of Cape Breton Volume 2: Cape Breton Scottish Fiddle" and "Cape Breton Fancy" (1984, November/December). *Scottish Merchant*, United Kingdom.

"Review of Carl MacKenzie's CD, `Cape Breton Fiddle Medleys.'" (1997, January). *The Loch Michigan Fiddler*, the monthly newsletter of the Great Lakes Scottish Fiddle Club (Chicago), 3:4.

Rhodes, Frank. (1964). "Dancing in Cape Breton Island," Nova Scotia. In J.P. Flett & T.M. Flett, *Traditional Dancing in Scotland*, pp. 267-285. London: Routledge and Kegan Paul.

Riddell, George. (1927). "Scott Skinner, A Friend's Estate." In James Scott Skinner, *My Life and Adventures*." (1994). City of Aberdeen in Association with Wallace Music. (Reprinted from *Aberdeen Journal*, 27:4).

Bibliography

Roberts, Warren E. (1988). *Viewpoints On Folklife*. Ann Arbor, London: Research Press.

Robinson, Paul. (1988, October). "A Future for the Gaelic Language." A report prepared for the Croileagan A'Chaolais, The Iona District Playgroup, Iona, Cape Breton, N.S.

Rodeo and International Music. (1995). Holborne Catalogue, Ontario.

Rogers, Jerry, Public Relations Manager, Atlantic Lottery Corporation, Moncton, N.B. (1979, September 28). Letter to Sons of Skye, Big Pond, N.S.

Rolls, Judith A. & Michelle Strenkowski. (1993, October 28). "Report on the Canada Room Project, Balnain House, Inverness, Scotland." University College of Cape Breton, N.S.

Rooyakkers, Donalda. (1997, May 9). "Gaelic order of the day at Mabou school today." *Cape Breton Post*.

Sabhal Mor Ostaig. (1994). *Short Courses Calendar*, An Teanga, Isle of Skye, Scotland.

"Scottish Entertainment at the Gaelic College." (1984, July and August). Official program of activities prepared by Sheldon MacInnes for the Gaelic College, St. Ann's, N.S.

Scottish Societies Association of Nova Scotia. (1983, October 18). "Turning A Way of Life Into A Way of Living." Draft Concept Document for Nova Scotia's Celtic Arts and Music Industry.

Senchuk, Barbara. (1983, January 8). "Sons of Skye Debut on ATV." *Chronicle Herald*.

Shaw, John. (1978). Booklet accompanying Topic LP 12TS354, *Cape Breton Scottish Violin*. London: Topic.

Short Course and Staff Development Seminar. (1981, July 6-15). Brochure prepared by Continuing Education Staff, College of Cape Breton.

"Show 'Total Success.'" (1979, January 8). *Cape Breton Post*.

Sinclair, D. MacLean. (1939, July 29). *Gaelic Lessons for Beginners*. Sydney, N.S.: Post.

Society of Inter-Celtic Arts and Culture. (1985). Newsletter, Boston, Massachusetts.

"Sons of Skye in Scotland." (1980, January). *Cape Breton Post*.

"Special Cultural Life Award Presented to Louis Stephen." (1993, Spring). *The Octopus* [published by the Cultural Federations of Nova Scotia], 6:2.

Stang, Ron. (1989, June 5). "Culture department should review priorities for funding Cape Breton festivals." *Cape Breton Post*.

"St. Mary's Parish, East Bay, Cape Breton Souvenir Booklet." (1995). [In recognition of pastor Rev. Francis J. Abbass' years of service in the priesthood.] East Bay, N.S.: C.W.L.

"Stornoway Group Wins Folk Contest." (1979, October 13). *Stornoway Gazette and West Coast Advertiser*, Mod Nan Eilean Souvenir Edition.

Sydney's 175th Anniversary Week. (1960, July 24 to 30). Official Program.

Taylor, Wilkie. (1986, April 22). "Scottish culture focus of new tourism campaign." *Chronicle Herald*.

"Thank You!" (1997, April). *The Big Pond Times*, 14:4. Big Pond, Cape Breton, N.S.: Big Pond Community Council.

"Thanks to CBC." (1977, January 5). Letter to the editor. *Cape Breton Post.*

"The Bagpipe in Cape Breton, From a Conversation with Barry Shears, Piper." *Cape Breton's Magazine*, #52.

The Green Linnet Records Catalogue. (1996). Danbury, CT06810, USA, p. 9.

"The Guggenheim Concerts, 65th Season." (1982, June 20). Program detail for 5th concert, Damrosch Park, New York, USA.

The Blood is Strong. A three-part documentary filmed in Scotland, the United States, and Canada by Grampion Television, Scotland for Channel 4 Britain (Producer: Ted Brocklebank), 1987.

The Rita MacNeil Homecoming. Filmed at Big Pond in 1989 and produced for television by CTV, Toronto (Producer: Gordon James).

"The trouble with Glasgow Gaels." (1979, November 9). *West Highland Free Press*, Scotland.

Tobin, Harry, Public Relations, CBC Radio, Sydney, N.S. (1980, January 25). Letter to Sons of Skye, Big Pond, Cape Breton, N.S.

Tomkins, George. "Canadian Education and the Development of a National Consciousness: Historical and Contemporary Perspectives," article contained in a study guide and compilation of readings for Dr. Redomond Curtis' course, July 1989, Education 511: Teaching Canadian Culture, UCCB.

"Universities Recognize Need for Community Involvement." (1991-1992, December/January). *The Clansman.*

"Visit to Canada for Uist Minister." (1979, March 13). *Aberdeen Press and Journal*, Scotland.

Wallace, Robert. (1987, February 27). "'Ceilidh piping' the way to reach a wider audience." *West Highland Free Press.*

Watson, James. (1990, Autumn). "Gaelic will writhe its last without united intervention." *The Manitoba Heritage Review*, Vol. 6, published by the Manitoba Association for the Promotion of Ancestoral Languages.

Westhaver, Marie. (1979, February 20). "Transatlantic Ceilidh Focal Point." *The Coastal Courier.*

"Westray, day to day story since deadly explosion." (1992, May 16). *Cape Breton Post.*

What's goin on. (1996, February). Sydney, N.S. [publication editor Dave Mahalik].

Where the Heart is Highland. (1987). ATV television documentary on the Nova Scotia Gathering of the Clans (Producer: Dick Pratt).

Whisnant, David E. (1983). *All That Is Native and Fine.* Chapel Hill and London: University of North Carolina Press.

Wilson, Brian. (1987, October 30). "Great oaks from the little acorns of the Sir John Maxwell Gaelic Unit." *West Highland Free Press*, Scotland.

Wood, Wendy. (1955). *People of the Glen.* Edinburgh: Serif Biiks.

Woodham-Smith, Cecil. (1962). *The Great Hunger.* New York and Evanston: Harper and Row.

Writer Seeks Songs of Barra. [references John Lorne Campbell's visit to Cape Breton from Scotland]. (1937, October 22). *Post Record.*

Discography

Dan Joe MacInnis

The following list comprises original commercial recordings.

MacInnis, Dan Joe. (1962). "The Cape Breton Fiddle of . . ." Banff/Rodeo 1066.
MacInnis, Dan Joe. (1963). "The Scottish Canadian Fiddle of . . ." Celtic CX 14.
MacInnis, Dan Joe. (1964). "Dan Joe MacInnis." Banff/Rodeo RBS 1247.
MacInnis, Dan Joe et. al. (1978). "The Music of Cape Breton, Volume 1, Gaelic Tradition in Cape Breton." Topic 12TS353.
MacInnis, Dan Joe, et. al. (1978). "Cape Breton Scottish Fiddle, Volume 2." Topic 12TS354.
MacInnis, Dan Joe, Donald MacLellan & David MacIsaac. (1984). "Celtic Music of Cape Breton." UCCB Press 1007.

The following collections include re-issues of Dan Joe's original recordings (as cited above).

MacInnis, Dan Joe, et. al. (N.D.). "Cape Breton Fiddlers on Early LP's." Breton Books and Music (no ref. number).
MacInnis, Dan Joe, et. al. (N.D.). "Collector's Item — The Fiddlers of Cape Breton." Celtic SCX57.
MacInnis, Dan Joe, et. al. (N.D.). "16 Great Fiddle Tunes by 16 Great Fiddlers." Banff SBS5-5123.
MacInnis, Dan Joe, et. al. (1967). *"24 Cape Breton Fiddle Medleys."* Celtic SCX53.
MacInnis, Dan Joe, Paddy LeBlanc., et. al. (N.D.). "This is Sydney." Celtic CX51.

Special Collection

Bain, Aly. (1984). "Aly Bain." Whirlie 001.
Barra MacNeils. (1994). "The Traditional Album." Polygram 314523251-4.
Battlefield Band. (1982). "there's a buzz." Temple TP010.
Beaton, Donald Angus. (1985). "A Musical Legacy." DAB4-1985.
Beaton, Kinnon. (N.D.). "Cape Breton Fiddle I." CDAB-3 26-1.
Beatons of Mabou. (1977). "The Beatons of Mabou." Rounder 7011.
Boys of the Lough. (1980). "Regrouped." Flying Fish 225.
Briand, Elmer. (1975). "Elmer Briand and His Cape Breton Fiddle." Celtic SCX58.
Cameron, John Allan. (1972). "Lord of the Dance." Columbia ELS-383.
Cameron, John Allan. (1969). "Here Comes John Allan Cameron." Apex AL71645.
Campbell, Dan J., Angus Chisholm, and Angus Allan Gillis, et. al. (N.D.). "Cape Breton Violins." Celtic CX1.

Campbell, John. (1976). "Cape Breton Violin Music." Rounder 7003.

Campbell, John. (N.D.). "Heritage Remembered." JC123.

Cape Breton Gaelic Choir. (1988). "Oranaiche Cheap Breatuinn." World WRC15863.

Cape Breton Symphony. (N.D.). "Fiddle Volume I." Brownrigg. BRGGMI001.

Capercaillie. (1984). "Cascade." Etive SRT4KL178.

Chafe, Winnie. (N.D.). "The Bonnie Lass of Headlake." Inter-Media Services Ltd. IMS-WRC1-1546.

Chieftains, The. (1975). "The Chieftains." Island ILPS9334.

Comhaltas. (N.D.). "Comhaltas on Tour." Green Studio CL26.

Cormier, Joseph. (1974). "Joseph Cormier." Rounder 7001.

Cremo, Lee. (N.D.). "The Cape Breton Fiddle of Lee Cremo and His Band." AUDAT 4779032.

Dares, Tracy. (N.D.). "Crooked Lake." CBC Maritimes GSR 077.

Draught Porridge. (1984). "A Celtic Band." McMac Music (no ref.#).

Dunn, Jackie. (1995). "Dunn to a T." JAD-1.

Fitzgerald, Winston Scotty. (N.D.). "The Inimitable Winston 'Scotty' Fitzgerald." Celtic CX44.

Five MacDonald Fiddlers. (N.D.). "Scottish Reels, Jigs, and Strathspeys." Celtic CX.30.

Gillies, Anne Lorne. (1982). "Anne Lorne Gillies Sings . . . The Songs of the Gael." Lochshore LOCLP1014.

Gillis, Laughie. (1985). "Gaelic Songs from the Mira." CR1-8137.

Graham, Glenn. (1996). "Let 'er Rip." GGCAS1-4.

Greenberg, David/Puirt a Baroque. (1996). "Bach Meets Cape Breton." Marquis ERA 181.

Holland, Jerry. (1982). "Master Cape Breton Fiddler." Boot BOS7231.

Kennedy, Calum. (N.D.). "Islands of Scotland." Ace of Clubs ACL 7726.

Kennedy, Calum. (N.D.). "Ye Highlands and Ye Lowlands." Beltona SBE135.

LeBlanc, Donny. (N.D.). "Traditional Cape Breton Music Vol. I." World WRC4-5741.

LeBlanc, Paddy. "The Best Damn Fiddling in the World." Rodeo BDFM 5-7009.

MacDonald, Dan R. (N.D.). "Dan R. MacDonald." Celtic CX47.

MacDonald Howie. (1993). "The Ceilidh Trail." Atlantic 0193.

MacDonald, Howie. (1997). "the dance last night." HMD123.

MacDonald, Howie. (N.D.). "Howie MacDonald and His Cape Breton Fiddle." World WRC4-4344.

MacDonald, Howie. (N.D.). "Live and Lively." 02 77657 50231 25.

MacDonald, John A. (N.D.). "Scottish Fiddling." Celtic CX11.

MacDonald, Little Jack. (N.D.). "The Bard of Scottish Fiddling." Celtic CX.23.

MacDonald, Rodney. (1995). "Dancer's Delight." RMD-CAS1.

MacDougall, Mike. (N.D.). "Tape for Fr. Hector." Breton Books and Music ACC-49236.

MacInnis, George. (1994). "The Gift of Music." ACC-49394.

MacInnis, Jamie in Natalie MacMaster's "Fit as a Fiddle." (1993). CBC Maritimes NMAS 1972.

MacIntyre, Sandy. (1980). "Cape Breton . . . My Land in Music." SLMC-1001.

MacIsaac, Ashley. (1996). "fine thank you very much." Ancient Music 79602 2002-2.

MacIsaac, Dave. (1995). "Nimble Fingers." Pickin Productions 045399.

MacIsaac, Wendy. (1994, May). "The `Reel' Thing." World WMR004.

MacKenzie, Carl. (1977). "Welcome To Your Feet Again." Rounder RO 7005.

MacKenzie, Carl. (1981). ". . . and his sound is Cape Breton." World Records WRC11548.

MacKenzie, Carl. (1996, June). "Highland Fiddle & Dance." Compiled and produced by Paul MacDonald and Carl MacKenzie. CLM9.

MacLean, Joe. (1967). "Joe MacLean and His Old Time Scottish Fiddle." Banff RBS 1246.

MacLean, Joe. (N.D.). "Joe MacLean and His Old Time Scottish Fiddle." Banff RBS 1248.

MacLellan, Theresa, Donald MacLellan, and Marie MacLellan. (N.D.). "The MacLellan Trio of Cape Breton." Breton Books and Music BBM5-003.

MacMaster, Buddy. (1991). "Glencoe Hall." Buddy MacMaster BM91.

MacMaster, Natalie. (1996). "No Boundaries." WEA.

MacMaster, Natalie. (N.D.). "4 on the Floor." Astro ACC-4979.

MacNeil, Rita. "Part of the Mystery." Big Pond Publishing and Productions Ltd.

MacNeil, Rita. "I'm Not What I Seem." UCCB Press 1006.

MacPhee, Doug. (1977). "Cape Breton Piano." Rounder 7009.

MacPhee, Doug. (1985). "The Reel of Tulloch." MacPhee DMP6-27-2.

Moore, Hamish. (1994). "Stepping on the Bridge." Greentrax CTRAX073.

Morrison, Peter. (N.D.). "Piper Peter Morrison Plays Dance Tunes with Introduction and March Off." Banff RBS5-1108.

Munroe, Deanie. (N.D.). "Scottish Dances." Celtic CX9.

North Shore Gaelic Singers. (N.D.). "A Tribute to the North Shore Gaelic Singers, Songs from Cape Breton Island." Solor WRC1-4705.

Octet. (1985). "Songs of the Cape." UCCB Press 1008.

Ossian. (1981). "Seal Song." Iona IR002.

Primrose, Christine. (1981). "Aite Mo Ghail." Temple TP006.

Rankin Family. (N.D.). "Fare Thee Well Love." RF9001.

RunRig. (1979). "The Highland Connection." Ridge RR001.

Skinner, J. Scott. (1975). "J. Scott Skinner: The Strathspey Ring." Topic 12T280.

Sons of Skye. (1981). "Both Sides of the Water." Inter-Media Services Ltd. IMS-WRC1-1522.

Stubbert, Brenda. (N.D.). "In Jig Time." Celestial Entertainment CECS001.

Various Artists. (1955). "Songs from Cape Breton Island." Folkways Records and Service Corporation P450.

Various Artists. (1967). "Souvenir Album. Gaelic Mod, St. Ann's, Cape Breton, Nova Scotia." Celtic CX15.

Various Artists. (1971). "Scottish Tradition 2: Music from the Western Isles." Tangent TNGM110.

Various Artists. (1973). "Festival of Scottish Fiddling 1973." World WRC160.

Wills, Stephanie. (N.D.) "Traditions Continued." STEPH1-94.

Wilmot, Johnny. (N.D.). "Another Side of Cape Breton." Breton Books and Music BBM002.

Wolfstone. (1994). "Unleashed." Green Linnet CSIF3093.

Featured Interviews

The following "non-commercial" recordings feature conversation, interviews, tributes, and stories to which I refer in "A Journey in Celtic Music — Cape Breton Style."

Buddy MacMaster Testimonial. (1982, November). University College of Cape Breton, Sydney, N.S. Tapes 1, 2, & 3. (Located in Beaton Institute Holdings/Restricted).

Interview by Cher Radio, Sydney, N.S. (1973, March 25). Reference to Malcolm H. Gillis, Margaree, Cape Breton, NS.

MacDougall, Kate, Ben Eoin, Cape Breton, N.S. (1960's). Conversation about the people and the community of Ben Eoin.

MacInnes, Johnny Hughie, Woodbine, Cape Breton, N.S. (1973). Conversation with Dan Joe MacInnis and Cyril MacInnis concerning MacInnes genealogy. [Dan Joe and Cyril were preparing for a 1973 visit to Scotland.]

MacInnes, Sheldon. (1981). Interviewed by Hal Higgins, CBC Radio, Sydney, N.S. as a tribute to fiddler, the late Mike MacDougall, Ingonish, Cape Breton, N.S.

MacPhee, Danny and Fr. M. MacEachern, Windsor, Ontario. (1976). Interviewed by Sheldon MacInnes as part of research for master's thesis, "Folk Society in an Urban Setting.

Index